Reluctant Meister

Reluctant Meister

How Germany's Past is Shaping its European Future

Stephen Green

First published in Great Britain in 2014 by
Haus Publishing Ltd
70 Cadogan Place
London SW1X 9AH
www.hauspublishing.com

A CIP catalogue record for this book is available from the British Library

Print ISBN 978-1-908323-68-2
Ebook ISBN 978-1-908323-69-9

Typeset in Minion by MacGuru Ltd
info@macguru.org.uk

Printed and bound by CPI Group (UK) Ltd, Croydon, CR0 4YY

Contents

For Jay and our daughters Suzannah and Ruth

And for our grandchildren: Heather, James, William,
Andrew, Samuel, Hannah and Phoebe

Preface

SINCE MY SCHOOLDAYS I have been fascinated by all things German. To start with, it was the German language – a language which seemed to me such a robust kindred spirit of English. All those Anglo-Saxon words that earth the English language – they had cousins you could recognise in German. And German also had all those wonderful multi-syllable mouthfuls built up from the basic words. You could construct things in German, as if it were a Lego language.

The classic example, which was guaranteed to produce hilarity in the classroom, was the legendary *Donaudampfschifffahrtsgesellschaftskapitän* – the Danube steamship company captain. And it was easy to make up words that were still longer. But even without going to such lengths, German compound words are often so expressive – or hard to translate – that English, that great borrower from all languages, has simply taken them on board as they are: Apfelstrudel, Bildungsroman, Blitzkrieg, Dachshund, Delikatessen, Doppelgänger, Edelweiss, Einsatzgruppe, Glühwein, Götterdämmerung, Kristallnacht, Lebensraum, Leitmotiv, Poltergeist, Realpolitik, Schadenfreude, Singspiel, Übermensch, Untermensch, Volkswagen, Wanderlust, Weltanschauung, Wirtschaftswunder, Zeitgeist. And many others. I was enthralled by the mixture of the good, the profound, the innocuous and the sinister in the language that English borrowed from Germany. I always felt it revealed much about the culture from which those words came.

Then there is the literature that the language unveils if you grapple with it. Above all *Faust*, which I studied (not nearly thoroughly enough) at university. And the philosophy (ditto). And the music – yes, the music. My first serious brush with classical music was at school. It was the autumnal tones of Brahms: first, the Variations on a Theme by Joseph Haydn, played – I can remember it now – by the Concertgebouw Orchestra under Eugene Ormandy. Especially the seventh variation that soared into a heaven which was entirely new to me. Then the Third Symphony, on an LP with a cover photograph of woodland trees with their colours turning. So Brahms became my first real musical love. Now I listen to him on my iPad as I write this preface.

Over the years my love of classical music has broadened and deepened: later – in some cases, much later – I came to know something of the intricate geometry of Bach and the huge panoramas of Wagner, not to mention the agility of Mozart, the passion of Beethoven, the exquisite tunefulness of Schubert, the sumptuousness of Richard Strauss. And so on. Other musical traditions have transported me too: Italians and Russians in particular. But my first love remains the breadth, depth and intensity of German music, which has never been surpassed.

My first visit to Germany was to a family who lived in Bavaria. It was the school holidays: I was meant to improve my German. I don't think I made much progress over the three weeks. But I was introduced to what the mother described firmly as 'richtige Bergwanderungen' – real mountain hikes. Another love that has remained with me ever since.

I have been to Germany many times over the years – as a student, then later on business and on holiday. In fact, I have probably seen more of the country than many Germans have. One experience out of many stands out: the day I crossed the Wall at Checkpoint Charlie. We were two young management consultants visiting a client in West Berlin. We had some spare time in the late afternoon and decided to head east. It was just before Christmas, cold with a bright sun shining on the snow that had fallen the previous day. The snow had turned to a muddy slush on the streets: but on the death strip it was pure, untouched white. We found ourselves talking to the East German border guard – who was around our age – about some European football match that was about to take place. The ordinary amidst the extraordinary.

We don't know nearly enough about this country, with its extraordinary culture and history. Go into a bookshop and look at the history section: you will be confronted with shelves of books on the Third Reich and the Holocaust, as well as a few items on the Second Reich and maybe Frederick the Great. This year there is also a flood of books on the First World War. But all too rarely can you find anything on the deeper history of the German lands, or on the new Germany and its role in the new Europe of today. It is as if nothing much in Germany is interesting outside of the 12 years from 1933 to 1945.

Yet this will not do. There is no culture on the planet greater than that of Germany. No country has contributed more to the history of human ideas and creativity. No country has been deeper into the abyss. And no country has seen a more remarkable redemption and renewal. It is all this that makes the story of Germany so compelling and which gives it profound and universal human significance. It is why I have continued – long after those schooldays spent trying to master German compound words – to love the place, its ways, its literature, its music.

There is also a more practical point. No country is more central to Europe's destiny today. The British may have a fractured relationship with the European Union: but if there is any lesson we learn from the events of one hundred years ago, it is surely that we cannot turn our backs on Europe. We are inevitably involved, and at so many levels, whether we like it or not. So no country is more important to Britain today than Germany. We need to know it better. We need to learn from it. We need a much deeper relationship with it.

There is nothing like writing to develop and crystallise thought. Although the result – for better or worse – is all my responsibility (this is a very personal take on the German phenomenon), I have had the enormous benefit of very kind and indulgent input from others. In particular, I have been able to tap the wisdom of Helen Watanabe O'Kelly, Professor of German Literature at Oxford University and Emeritus Fellow of my alma mater, Exeter College; Georg Boomgarden, former German ambassador in London; Sir Michael Arthur, former British ambassador in Berlin; Neil MacGregor, Director of the British Museum; Martin Roth, Director of the Victoria and Albert Museum (and formerly Director General of the Dresden State Art Collections); Baroness Ruth Henig, formerly Dean of the Faculty of Arts and Humanities at Lancaster University; Alan Sharp, Professor Emeritus (International History and Diplomacy) at the University of Ulster; and Hans Kundnani, Director of Research at the European Council on Foreign Relations. At Haus Publishing, Barbara Schwepcke, the Principal, and Isabel Wagner have both provided enthusiastic, knowledgeable guidance, both overall and in detail. All this help has ensured that writing this book has itself been enormously rewarding – and enjoyable – for me.

And finally, my heartfelt thanks to Jay, who continues to put up with me ...

1

Springtime in Berlin

BERLIN, EASTER. Rich impressions of life in an evolving world city.

The famously aggressive sparrows which will attack the piece of cake you are eating as you hold it in your hand at a table outside one of the countless street cafes.

The new green of the Tiergarten – that 200 hectare stretch of woodland in the heart of the city which was originally a hunting preserve of the royal family (hence its name: the garden of animals), which then became the place where the bourgeois went to stroll on a Sunday afternoon and to see and be seen in the seemingly confident years before the First World War; and where Berliners foraged for firewood in the cold winters after the Second World War. A place where you can now wander amid trees and along canals, where you can forget you are in the midst of Europe's third largest city.

The sun glints on the graceful TV tower on the Alexanderplatz (one of the few attractive monuments of the old East Germany); the spherical silver grey structure which contains the observation deck just below the TV mast, high above the city, catches the light in the form of a glistening cross – a source of wry comment in the days of the old atheists who ran the German Democratic Republic a quarter of a century ago.

And on the other side of the meandering Spree from the Alexanderplatz, there is the space in the centre of the city where there was once the Berlin Schloss, the palace of the Hohenzollern dynasty, the rulers of Brandenburg-Prussia and the Emperors of the Second Reich from its unification in 1871 until its collapse in 1918. The old Schloss was imposing rather than beautiful. It dominates the old photographs of pre-war Berlin. Damaged by bombing in the War, it was blown up by the new East German government in 1950 in a symbolic gesture of ideology: the past had been destroyed. The future was the glass and concrete people's palace of the East which replaced it – until it too was torn down after reunification. Shoddily built and riddled with asbestos – or was it also a hideous and embarrassing reminder of the 40 year period of division and pain, brutally enforced by a government which was the cat's paw of the Soviet Union?

In any event, the site is now busy again: the new version of the old Schloss is rising one more time, as the Humboldt Forum takes shape – a close replica which will once again dominate the central Berlin landscape and help reinforce the already striking impression of continuity between the old and the new at this end of Unter den Linden. If you stand on the nearby Bebelplatz (where they burned books in 1933), with the Catholic cathedral behind you, the opera house on one side and buildings of the Humboldt university on the other side and opposite you, nothing seems to have changed: everything you can see was there before the war.

Nearby is the solid brick neo-gothic Friedrichswerder church – now a museum (to Karl Friedrich Schinkel who built it and so much of the splendour nearby) but still with old memorial tablets on its walls to long-forgotten worthies of the 19th century. And with its old war memorial too, to those fallen in the 1914–18 fight 'against a world of enemies'. Those words cry out. After the First World War – after the trauma of unexpected defeat, of the collapse of the Reich and of virtual civil war in the city – the sense that the world was against the country was as vivid as ever.

All in all, the new, the old and the incomplete jostling up against one another.

Because it is Easter, its sounds are everywhere: the huge church bell of the Protestant cathedral solemnly tolling (it has no peal of bells and so cannot avoid sounding ponderous even at Eastertime); and the music of Bach's *St Matthew Passion* and of Brahms's *German Requiem*. Crowds of tourists swarm up and down Unter den Linden. You can hear several European (and several Asian) languages.

New life mingles with ghosts. In a quiet corner of the city centre, not far from the cathedral, is the Sophienkirche. This is the only church in central Berlin to have survived the war undamaged by bombing. Near it is an old Jewish cemetery, which attracts a few visitors; it includes the gravestone of Moses Mendelssohn, grandfather of Felix Mendelssohn and one of the most brilliant intellectuals of the 18th-century German Enlightenment. Also nearby is the synagogue on Oranienburger Straße, which survived the anti-Jewish riots and burnings of Kristallnacht because a sympathetic and courageous local police chief gave it protection – only to succumb to Allied bombing later on. Now beautifully restored, it is the centrepiece of a street which has become a magnet for nightlife since reunification – nightlife which also draws prostitutes to their patches, dressed in what amounts to a distinctive uniform of shoulder-length black or fake blonde hair and white boots. The continuities with 1920s Berlin can seem all too obvious.

There are jagged discontinuities too in the midst of all the continuities and all the renewal which is everywhere to be seen. At the heart of Berlin, close to the Brandenburg Gate, are the irregular monoliths of the Holocaust memorial. It seems both empty and at the same time to go deeper and deeper downwards into the soul. It draws you into its darkness. In the warmth of a spring day, it is not so obviously sinister. Children happily play amongst the dark granite slabs; Asian tourists take photographs of each other posing on them. But at night, this is a forbidding place, as it should be.

There are other painful memories too. At the centre of what was West Berlin sits the Kaiser Wilhelm I Memorial Church – a striking combination of the broken tower from the bombed pre-war church together with a hexagonal new building, completed in 1962 (the same year as Coventry Cathedral and, like it, one of the most remarkable pieces of post-war architecture). To go into the church is to escape from the glitz of the Kurfürstendamm into an ethereal calm, quiet and lit by a deep translucent blue light from thousands of panes of stained glass.

There you can also see the Stalingrad Madonna: a piece of white cloth on which Kurt Reuber, a medical orderly in a field hospital in Stalingrad, drew a Madonna and Child as Christmas comfort for his wounded patients in December 1942. The child is at peace, the mother serene. Around the edge of the picture are the words '*Licht, Leben, Liebe*' – light, life, love. As he wrote these words he must have known there was very little hope of a good outcome for any of them. When the German Sixth Army surrendered just a few weeks later, Reuber went into captivity. A year later, he drew another Madonna and Child (though this one is in the possession of his family and is not on public display). This time the expression on the mother's face is very different. Her face is contorted in a way which is almost an echo of Edvard Munch's *Scream*. But the words are the same: light, life, love. Reuber died shortly afterwards. Very few of his companions ever made it home.

Coming out of the church, you are surrounded by a street market, by glass towers, by traffic, by people from everywhere, sauntering, bustling. When the British journalist Richard Dimbleby came here in 1945, he didn't think that it was possible for anyone to live in Berlin ever again, as the ruins and rubble stretched as far as he could see. That seems a long time ago now.

Just being in Berlin poses questions: everywhere there are signs of a great and living culture; signs of vibrant new life, of sharp-edged new art and architecture; signs, too, of a tragic past; places of beauty, as well as of emptiness, ugliness, desolation. So questions about history, culture and identity – questions that are relevant to all human beings at all times and in all places – are posed starkly here. Looking backwards: where did the national inferiority complex – which looked so much like a national superiority complex and which led to such untold destruction – come from? Looking forward, in a new century, what is the national identity in this increasingly busy crossroads of the world? The search for answers is relevant – not just to Germans, not just to Europeans, but to human beings universally. This is a journey which scales heights and plumbs depths, which are glimpsed by us all.

2

Tears for my Country

IN 1636 THE POET AND PLAYWRIGHT Andreas Gryphius
wrote a sonnet which seems to sum up the appalling experience of the German lands in Europe's worst war – its worst
man-made disaster – until the 20th century. 'Thränen des
Vaterlandes' (Tears of the Fatherland) he called it, a vivid and,
to this day, moving lament on the Thirty Years War, which
so traumatised Germany that the memory of its horrors has
remained deeply rooted in the folk memory ever since:

Wir sind doch nunmehr ganz, ja mehr denn ganz verheeret!
Der frechen Völker Schar, die rasende Posaun,
Das vom Blut fette Schwert, die donnernde Karthaun
Hat aller Schweiß und Fleiß und Vorrat aufgezehret.

Die Türme stehn in Glut, die Kirch ist umgekehret,
Das Rathaus liegt im Graus, die Starken sind zerhaun,
Die Jungfraun sind geschänd't, und wo wir hin nur schaun,
Ist Feuer, Pest und Tod, der Herz und Geist durchfähret
[…]

(Now our devastation is complete – indeed, more than complete! The brazen hordes of foreigners, the blaring bugles

6

of war, the blood-slaked sword, the thundering siege gun –
they have consumed everything we worked so hard for. The
towers are burning, the church is ransacked, the town hall
lies in ruins, the strong men have been hacked down, our
girls have been raped; and everywhere we look there is fire,
pestilence and death, enough to pierce heart and spirit…)

Yet the war, however terrible, was only one chapter in a
story covering many centuries which nurtured what became
by the 19th century a strong sense of victimhood – which is in
turn part of the cause of the catastrophe in the 20th century.

The victim lashes out; the abused turns abuser. In individual human beings, we see this pattern time and time again.
We know enough about the development of children to be
able to detect a 'normal' path of moral and social development – from a first stage of learning to see good and bad in
terms of direct rewards and punishments, through a second
stage where we come to see them in terms of the expectations of family, and finally to making adult judgements about
the common good and setting values in that context. We also
know how many individuals never make it beyond the second
stage (with the family often being widened to – or replaced
by – some larger community of belonging). Some never even
make it past the first stage. All too often early abuse leads to
distorted or even arrested development. To acknowledge this
is not to subscribe to a determinism which explains everything and removes culpability. Yet we do know how often
these patterns repeat themselves.

At the level of peoples, we can see the patterns of distortion too. It would be wrong to see the development of societies in any simplistic way as parallel to that of human beings

individually. But there are parallels nonetheless. Again, this is not to subscribe to a determinism which explains away guilt. *Tout comprendre, c'est tout pardonner?* No: we will never fully understand the mystery of human behaviour. And we do not forgive easily; in any case it is not ours to forgive, unless we ourselves are the victims. To seek to understand is, rather, to recognise the common humanity that unites us all, on the basis of which we know – in ourselves – what we as human beings are capable of. So to understand is to be open to a common humility (there but for the grace of God go we...), and to shared learning.

Germany is the starkest example of all this. But by no means the only one. Which is why it is a tragedy of universal significance. And as always with human tragedies, the background – the history – matters.

Peoples who lived in the German lands first make their presence felt on the European stage when Arminius (or Hermann, to give him his German name) and his tribesmen slaughtered three Roman legions in the Teutoburg Forest in AD 9, thereby effectively limiting the Roman Empire's expansion northwards and eastwards. Archaeologists and historians have debated exactly where the terrible battle took place, but in the 19th century a huge statue – the highest in Europe at the time – was built on one supposed site, to commemorate this figure who came to have something of the same mystique for the Germans of the 19th century as did Vercingetorix for the French and Boadicea (or Boudicca) for the English – although with a crucial and revealing difference, as we shall see later.

In the event, Arminius could not build on his success (any more than Vercingetorix or Boudicca could). The battle was a disaster for the Roman army – as bad as those it had suffered at the hands of Hannibal. But there was no chance of following it up. As they did so often, the Romans regrouped and twice in the next ten years Arminius was defeated by new Roman armies. He was soon afterwards murdered by fellow tribesmen for whom he was growing too powerful. But his main achievement stood: most of what became the German lands, with their impenetrable forests, did remain outside Roman control – unlike Gaul and unlike Britain.

Later on, as the Roman empire weakened under the impact of tribal movements and invasions from Central Europe and Asia, peoples from the German lands spread over much of Western Europe (including England). At the same time Germanic tribesmen became the backbone of a Roman army which was becoming more and more dependent on recruits from the regions of the empire. At the turn of the 5th century, during the final agonies of Roman Italy, people of Germanic stock were amongst those who defended as well as those who threatened the empire.

A vacuum followed in which various Germanic kingdoms formed and reformed in Western Europe. The most successful was the Frankish kingdom, which expanded to cover much of what later became France, the Low Countries, western and southern Germany, and northern Italy. On Christmas Day, AD 800, Charlemagne was crowned emperor in Rome by the Pope. The Roman Empire had been reborn. The centre of Charlemagne's empire was his stronghold at Aachen. The cathedral at Aachen, whose central basilica was built under Charlemagne, still stands today as a monument to his extraordinary achievement. Built to rival the splendours of the Eastern empire of Byzantium, the basilica is in the style of San Vitale at Ravenna – though without the mosaics – and was for 200 years the tallest building north of the Alps.

But the empire was too vast to control: after Charlemagne's death it fragmented, initially into three: a western kingdom including much of what is now France, the middle (largely what is now the Netherlands, Burgundy and northern Italy) and an eastern kingdom, which was all that was left in Carolingian hands and which covered most of what is now western Germany.

The first of these kingdoms evolved over the next five centuries into the nation of France. The rest was pulled together by a succession of strong Saxon kings into the Holy Roman Empire of medieval times, with the German lands at its core. They extended their control south towards Rome, and in 962 a Saxon king (Otto I) was crowned Emperor there by the Pope. This marked the beginning of an empire which, though it had lost much of its western territory (Burgundy was eventually absorbed by France) and though its position in Italy was never very secure, lasted in the German lands until Napoleon finally killed it off in 1806.

But coronation by popes was to prove a mixed blessing. It made for an uneasy relationship between ecclesiastical authority and secular power. It also meant that German rulers had to involve themselves in Italian power politics, often to the detriment of their ability to control their own lands. One result of this involvement was the beginning of a love affair with Italy, which is one of the most striking features of German cultural history – of which more in later chapters. But politically it contributed to a weakening of central power in the home lands, with profound long-term consequences for German history.

France grew gradually stronger and developed an ever clearer national identity, forged particularly through the Hundred Years War with England (the war had the same effect on England too). Germany evolved differently. It is not that there was no sense of a German identity: from the mid-15th century the empire began to be referred to as the Holy Roman Empire of the German Nation.[1] But the role of the empire repeatedly dragged German rulers into long campaigns in Italy, whose fruits were too often transient. And the contest with the popes for moral authority – manifest elsewhere in Europe, including England under Henry II, where the result was the infamous murder of Thomas Beckett – was at its most acute in the Empire.

This contest reached a climax (at least in German folk memory) in 1077 when the German emperor, Heinrich IV, submitted to one of the strongest of the medieval popes, the Germanic Lombard Hildebrand (Gregory VII), at Canossa – an event as imprinted on the German consciousness as is the Battle of Hastings on the English. Every German knows what is supposed to have happened there (or used to – it is not clear how much resonance Canossa continues to have in the minds of young Germans of the 21st century). The story is the stuff of which legends are made – and indeed historians have shown that it is largely a travesty of what actually occurred.[2] But the impact on the German consciousness over the centuries depended on the legend, not on what actually happened.

The story is dramatic and vivid. The background was a struggle for control of the church: who appointed bishops and other leading ecclesiastics? The Emperor or the Pope? Heinrich insisted on his right to this important lever of power. Gregory VII retaliated with a weapon whose psychological and political effectiveness is hard for us now to appreciate – he excommunicated Heinrich. And after some posturing, Heinrich makes his pilgrimage to the mountain retreat of the Pope at Canossa (now just a few ruins on a hilltop in Emiglia Romana), at dead of winter. And he waits outside, bareheaded in the snow, until the Pope grants him admission and accepts his penitence. The climb-down is complete, and gravely weakens Heinrich, triggering rebellion back at home in Germany.

Later on, Heinrich, who eventually got the better of his opponents, had his revenge and expelled Gregory from Rome. But the image of humiliation of the German Emperor at the hands of the Pope became embedded in German folk memory later on: it resonated especially strongly in a 19th century yearning for national identity. Otto von Bismarck referred to it in justifying his astonishingly aggressive attack on the Catholic Church in the newly formed and insecure Second Reich: 'nach Canossa gehen wir nicht, weder körperlich noch geistig' (neither in body nor in spirit will we go to Canossa). Adolf Hitler also used the phrase to describe his effort to get the Bavarian minister president to reverse a ban on the Nazi party after his failed Munich putsch and imprisonment. By his day, the 'Canossagang' – the walk to Canossa – had become a byword for an act of self-humiliation. Somehow, with that image, a tone was set.

The high Middle Ages produced only two figures on the German scene of European stature. The first is the Hohenstaufen Emperor Friedrich Barbarossa. He was a rough contemporary of England's Henry II. All accounts imply that he was strongly charismatic, with a physically imposing figure and his famous red beard. His military prowess in repeated campaigns against the Lombards of northern Italy made him feared and respected throughout Europe. Like other European rulers of his time he was seduced into crusading; and he died, perhaps by drowning, in a river in what is now Turkey on the way to the Holy Land. But he lived on as legend – he has not died, it was said, but sleeps in a cave in the Harz Mountains deep in Germany, ready to wake in the country's hour of need. And perhaps that legend highlights the slow-moving tragedy of Germany which was beginning to get under way. Not for almost seven centuries would there again be any strong, unifying rule in the German lands.

The Emperor Friedrich II, Barbarossa's grandson and the other great medieval emperor, is famous for his clashes with successive Popes and his energetic crusading. But his domination of Italian and Mediterranean power politics came at the price of tenuous control over Germany. By any standards, he must have been remarkable. This was a man who spoke six languages, including Arabic. His court became renowned around the European world – and beyond – for its cosmopolitan sophistication and for its interest in science and in culture. He was known as the 'stupor mundi': the wonder of the world. But his court was at Palermo – far from Germany, both literally and in atmosphere. He had no appetite for the bleak and arduous life north of the Alps. Viewed from his affluent base in Palermo with its ease of communication all around the Mediterranean world, which was still then Europe's centre of gravity, this would indeed have seemed a grim alternative. He rarely went there, and the centrifugal forces went increasingly unchecked.

But he sponsored one initiative which was to have profound long-term significance for his homeland. It was during his reign that the Teutonic Knights began to lead a German expansion far away to the north, along the Baltic coast – part missionary, part colonising, part commercial. The Teutonic Knights had originally been founded as a religious military order – similar to the Knights of Saint John or the Templars – to provide support for German warriors in the crusades. As the Christian states in the Holy Land weakened towards collapse, the leadership sought new areas for activity and, after some intervening excursions in Central Europe, found themselves taking on the mission of subduing the bleak, inhospitable and dangerous north-eastern forest areas around the Baltic. In 1226 Friedrich II signed the Golden Bull of Rimini, which launched this new and different crusade. It was to be a great deal more successful than anything that had been achieved in the Holy Land.

The first target was the Prussians. The original Prussian tribes were pagans, worshipping wood gods long after most of the rest of Europe as well as Russia had been Christianised. They and their language have disappeared into history, leaving very little trace apart from the name of the region in which they lived, which eventually became the name of Germany's most powerful state. But that was far in the future. For the knights, a much more powerful foe than the Prussians was represented by the Lithuanian tribes whose centre of gravity was further east, and who were, like the Prussians, pagan.

The geography was difficult and the climate brutal. Spheres of influence and areas of strength constantly shifted. Eastward expansion by the Knights was checked by the famous encounter with a Russian force under Alexander Nevsky – classically memorialised in the film by Sergei Eisenstein with its electrifying Prokofiev score – on the frozen Lake Peipus (now on the border between Russia and Estonia) in 1246. And in 1410 the Knights went down to catastrophic defeat at the hands of the Poles in the battle at Tannenberg (or, as the Poles know it, Grunwald). These two battles are part of the folklore of Russia and of Poland respectively. In the German mind, Tannenberg was the more searing. The defeat was never forgotten – certainly not five centuries later, when another battle was fought there in the opening weeks of the First World War – this time between Germany and Russia (Poland having vanished from the map for the time being). This time victory was all the more sweet for the memory of that ancient disaster.

Not that Tannenberg meant the end of the Knights. But it broke their expansionary power. They were never again a major threat to others in the region, although they effectively consolidated their hold on much of what they had. The knights' bruising encounters with the Lithuanians, the Russians and the Poles gradually defined the outlines of a German East Prussia which would, in centuries to come, have a baleful influence on German self-understanding out of all proportion to its demographic weight or economic significance.

Whilst the pattern of German influence in the east was congealing in this way, fundamental change was under way in the German heartland. The various principalities were becoming more defined, the power of their rulers more entrenched and institutionalised. They became the power bases of great dynasties who were to dominate German history over several centuries – the Habsburgs of Austria, the Hohenzollerns of Brandenburg, the Wittelsbachs of Bavaria and the Wettins of Saxony. At the same time, the cities were becoming more important as crossroads of commerce and finance. And universities were being founded: the German lands started later than either France or England, but then progressed much more rapidly (14 universities were founded over the 150 years up to the start of the 16th century). And around 1450, Gutenberg began working his printing press in Mainz. It was by far the most important technological development for a thousand years – in comparative terms, at least as significant as the digital revolution of our times.

All in all, an intellectual ferment was being unleashed in Germany which was part of a wider current of Renaissance humanism strongly influenced by Italian thinkers, and which the printing presses helped to spread throughout northern Europe. The challenges this posed for the church and its assumed monopoly of intellectual life were many-faceted. An institution which had become at many levels spiritually ossified, politically compromised and corrupt found it difficult to respond. There had already been harbingers of trouble, in such different places as England in the 14th century (the Lollards) and Bohemia in the 15th (Jan Hus). But resentment, particularly at Rome's demands for money to finance ambitious papal building programmes, and disgust at the way the money was raised by preying on people's superstitious gullibility, was growing. It was felt nowhere more deeply than in Germany. There the tinder was as dry as anywhere. When the fire was lit, the conflagration spread fast.

It was the larger-than-life figure of Martin Luther who lit the fire. He may not actually have nailed his famous 95 theses to the door of the castle church at Wittenberg in 1517, but they certainly became known throughout Germany very rapidly (and in 1520 he did publicly burn the papal bull which threatened him with excommunication unless he recanted). What began as an attack on corruption in the Church unleashed a reformation which spread with unprecedented speed by means of the newly available printed pamphlets – fast to write and fast to produce. What Luther had started became rapidly not just a campaign for reform, but a movement of revolutionary schism.

We probably know more about Luther than almost any other figure before modern times. He stands before us in the round, flesh and blood, warts and all, revealed in his pamphlets, his sermons, his hymns, his table talk. He was intelligent, passionate, impulsive, explosive, courageous and eloquent. When he was summoned to appear before the Imperial Diet at Worms in 1521, he knew he was risking his life. The new young Emperor, the Habsburg Charles V, had many things to worry about in his huge domains (which included Spain and the New World as well as the Empire). In particular, the Turkish menace was growing in south-east Europe. Wittenberg must have seemed an irrelevant backwater, and Luther a troublesome distraction. It must have been tempting to eliminate him, as Jan Hus had been burnt to death a century before. And Luther must have known that. But he refused to recant his attacks on the Church. His defence echoes down history – even if it is mostly a paraphrase of what he actually said: 'Here I stand; I can do no other. So help me God, Amen.'

He had an instinctive power to express himself in a language that spoke to ordinary people. His translation of the Bible – he completed the New Testament in 1522 whilst imprisoned for his own safety in the Wartburg castle by the Elector of Saxony – standardised and stabilised the German language. His impact on German self-understanding and thought is incalculable, not limited only to Lutherans, and has lasted down to the present day. His theology made the

individual responsible before God for his or her own life decisions. You believe alone, he said, just as you die alone. You
live in two realms – the realm of your relationship with God;
and the realm of this world and its tasks and obligations. As
we shall see, the social and cultural impact of all this was to
be profound.

Luther did not intend a social revolution in any modern
sense. Notoriously, he encouraged the princes and nobility as
they brutally suppressed the peasant rebellion of 1525 (whose
leader Thomas Münzer was promoted to hero and martyr by
the East German Communist government after the Second
World War). Equally notoriously, Luther wrote some unpleasant diatribes against the Jews, notably his emotive 1543 treatise
Von den Jüden und iren Lügen – On the Jews and Their Lies.
Historians debate how much impact this had on the slowly
improving legal position of Jews in the Empire; but evil minds
eagerly seized on his words in later centuries.

Luther failed to achieve reform – or at least, the kind of
reform he wanted – in the Church. Instead, there was schism,
virulent argument about doctrinal points (some of which
now seem unbelievably abstruse), the emergence of separate
Lutheran churches, and then civil war as the Emperor tried
to re-establish religious uniformity. The outcome was a stale-
mate reflected at another Imperial Diet at Augsburg in 1555,
which left each prince to determine whether his territory
was Catholic or Lutheran – the so-called principle of *cujus
regio ejus religio*. Apart from its religious significance, this
settlement underscored more clearly than ever the power of
regional rulers and the relative weakness of the Empire. The
Empire was a long way from becoming irrelevant in German
politics: but there was by now little or no likelihood that it

could be turned – let alone evolve spontaneously – into a centralised state in the way that England and France had done by
this time.

It was also during this period that Lutheranism began to be
deeply embedded in the culture of what would later become
Germany's most powerful state. Duke Albrecht of Prussia,
who as the last Grand Master of the Teutonic Knights had
converted to Lutheranism, became the first European ruler
to make Protestantism the official religion of his lands in
1525. But East Prussia was never part of the Empire: and the
deep significance of this Prussian inheritance for the whole of
German development would become clear only much later.

The settlement kept the peace for some 60 years. But it was
not stable. For one thing, it made no legal provision for other
Protestant churches – in particular for Calvinism, which was
becoming a force in several regions and which represented
itself as a more thoroughgoing implementation of Luther's
Protestant vision. Could they have coalesced? There were
moments when it seemed possible. But despite some efforts at
bridge-building, the outcome was in fact a three-way fracture
in the religious landscape of Germany, reflecting the different
decisions of the rulers (and their varying degrees of success in
imposing their convictions on their populations). This status
quo has largely persisted to this day, uniquely amongst the
major nations of Europe. It is easy to underestimate the effect
of this on German social psychology even today. In the 19th
century it was to make the journey towards eventual unification much more fraught.

Worse – much worse – was to come. The precarious balance
of power between Catholics and Protestants in the Empire
was foolishly disturbed by some confessional manoeuvring

in 1617/18. A contest between a new, militantly Catholic ruler in Bohemia and his Protestant nobles led to the famous defenestration of Prague – and to an invitation to the Calvinist Elector from the Palatinate on the Rhine, Friedrich (son-in-law of James I of England), to take the throne in Prague. He lasted there for a winter before the Protestants were crushed in battle by imperial forces – a victory which they followed up by invading the Palatinate. Like the later follies and misjudgements of 1914, this unleashed a war that lasted for 30 years – far more prolonged, devastating and far-reaching in its consequences than anyone envisaged.

More and more of the German lands got swept up in the vortex; more and more of Europe became involved – especially the Swedes and the French. As if in some huge Shakespearian tragedy played out on a vast stage, its main actors show almost every conceivable human emotion, ambition, folly, wickedness – from the pathetic figure of the winter king Friedrich wandering the western parts of the empire after his ejection from Bohemia, through the hubris of Albrecht von Wallenstein (whose fate is the subject of Friedrich Schiller's great trilogy *Wallenstein*), to the charisma of the young Swedish king Gustavus Adolphus who loses his life on the battlefield of a strategically important victory, to so many other calculating, manoeuvring, vacillating rulers and generals – all struggling to control or take advantage of events which took on a bewildering momentum of their own.

And mostly unknown, but occasionally finding a voice, were the millions of ordinary folk caught up in it all – the soldiers (often mercenaries from all over Europe); the townsfolk of devastated cities which had earlier been leading European centres of trade and intellectual exchange; and, as ever, the hapless peasants. The sack of Magdeburg by imperial troops in 1631 is the iconic horror; its burning and the slaughter were etched into the consciousness of Germany (especially Protestant Germany) as sharply as is the sack of Drogheda by Cromwell in the memory of Ireland. The word 'magdeburgisieren' – meaning to raze to the ground, to comprehensively and savagely destroy – entered the German vocabulary. It was Magdeburg's first death by firestorm (the second, and still more terrible, would come in 1945).

The individual stories are of course almost all untold. But one remarkable author brings some to life: Hans Jakob Christoph von Grimmelshausen's picaresque story of Simplicissimus shows how war came and went in and out of people's lives, and is in some ways a rumbustious corrective to the air of melancholy which inevitably surrounds the Thirty Years War, as well as being a vehicle for moral and religious reflection on human experience and the need (and possibility) of redemption. He also wrote a much bleaker tale from the same setting of the war: Courasche (Courage) is a cross-dressed soldier, a camp follower and prostitute, whose daily battle with life is unremitting. The story is without resolution or redemption; she survives because she is an allegory for the temptations of the world. On the eve of another war, 300 years later, Bertolt Brecht makes Mother Courage the protagonist of another tragedy about the bleakness of war and the strategies for survival, and the apparent pointlessness of the effort, showing how it is the cupidity of the 'little people' which ultimately keeps wars going.

The Treaty of Westphalia in 1648 broadly reaffirmed the approach to religious settlement of almost a century before, except that this time there was explicit provision for the

Calvinist Reformed presence. But by now dynastic and international power politics were becoming more important than confessional motives for conflict. Within the Empire, power had effectively moved largely to the territorial rulers and away from the centre. The Habsburgs might hold the title of Emperor, but they acted mainly in the interests of their Austrian (and other) domains. Saxony and Bavaria had both been strengthened by the settlement too. And the Hohenzollerns were on their way to welding their possessions in Prussia, Brandenburg and a few western territories into an effective state which would eventually, two centuries later, dominate a united Germany.

Other changes were afoot too. The economic dynamism of Europe was shifting away from its geographic centre – the German lands – to its Atlantic coasts. So Germany's cities were no longer as strong a social power as they had been a century before. The hereditary rulers – both large and small – were the beneficiaries. Because they did not adopt primogeniture to determine succession, however, their territories were in most cases divided into ever smaller units. So this became the time of *Kleinstaaterei* – the proliferation of small ducal and other territories, a patchwork that interspersed itself amongst the large centres of power all over the map of Germany.

It was to be the age of a cultured absolutism. Courtly culture flourished all over the place. In Vienna, in Dresden and in Munich, as well as in such second-tier centres as episcopal Würzburg, rulers built and built – churches, palaces and other cultural monuments. And not just rulers, but also city governments and the church; in general this was a new and remarkable outpouring of a cultural energy strongly influenced by Italy and impacting both Catholic and Protestant centres. The results are with us today (in some cases after careful restoration following terrible destruction in the 20th century): the Zwinger, the Hofkirche and the Frauenkirche in Dresden, the Theatinerkirche in Munich, Schloss Charlottenburg in Berlin, the Residence in Würzburg, to name but a few.

None of this meant that at this stage there was any widespread consciousness of a German national identity ready to assert itself on the European stage. Austria was preoccupied with the Ottoman threat – which saw the Turks at the gates of Vienna in 1683 (their defeat by a combined European force led by the Polish king was one of the great turning points of European history). Prussia's time would come, but not for another century. Meanwhile, Sweden gained somewhat from the settlement at Westphalia, although it could not sustain its holdings along the Baltic coast for long against the rapidly growing power of Prussia. It was France – the only nation to have gained significantly from the Thirty Years War – which emerged as the dominant European power.

Under Louis XIV France turned into Europe's most bellicose state, becoming involved in war with almost all its neighbours in a series of complicated struggles, part dynastic and part national aggrandisement. In particular, France soon began to throw its weight eastwards as it crystallised an ambition to control power in the Rhineland. At one level, France saw this as a defensive objective. But it could hardly seem that way to the Emperor in Vienna or to the local German rulers. Already in 1680 France had seized the historic imperial city of Strassburg. Soon thereafter it became embroiled in a war in the Rhineland that lasted nine years. And in what may have been the first planned scorched earth campaign in European history, French armies in 1689 razed a whole series of German

Rhineland cities to the ground. War dragged on over several years as Louis XIV's brutal strategy failed to achieve definitive success; imperial and local German forces began to organise themselves in effective defence and France's campaign slowly exhausted itself. But not before another totemic event: the sack of Heidelberg by French troops in 1693. To this day you can see the burnt-out ruins of the Schloss above this beautiful university town. The seeds of a sense of victimhood – of a resentment with a specifically anti-French twist – were being sown.

Eventually, this seed would produce some very poisonous fruit. Indeed, by a stroke of historical irony a unified but insecure Germany would in the early 20th century come to see its own need to go on the offensive for what it also considered to be defensive reasons – as we shall see. But not during the 18th century. And indeed, for much of the century French culture had enormous influence in German intellectual and courtly circles. Gottfried Wilhelm Leibnitz wrote many of his most influential works in French. The absolutist rulers of the German lands – famously including Frederick the Great – were often strong admirers of French culture. Frederick himself spoke and wrote French better than – and in preference to – German. His friendships were with Francophiles and (albeit more successfully by correspondence than face to face) with the great French *philosophe* Voltaire.

Not that this cultural affinity had any impact on power relationships. French armies fought Prussian and other German armies – typically alongside other Germans – more than once in the 18th century interlude between the decline of confessional conflict and the French Revolution. Later on, a resentful sense of victimhood come to warp the German identity

– when deep memories from the Thirty Years War and from the French depredations in the Rhineland would prey on German minds yearning for national unity and recognition. Even Frederick, for example, who was no natural champion of a German identity, understood what the 'deadly imprint' of the Thirty Years War had done to his own lands of Brandenburg. But in the 18th century the German political stage is – with one important exception which we will come to – more a story of changing power balances amongst the German states (albeit often with foreign involvement) rather than of external entanglements or aggression. The century was to see the rise of Prussia at the expense of other German powers.

Prussia was becoming Europe's most modern and organised state, and a major force to be reckoned with. The cultured Frederick the Great – he who played the flute and composed sonatas – turned out to be the most aggressive leader of the century.[3] His seizure of Silesia from Austria, with its rich mineral wealth, in the very first year of his reign, transformed the economic power balance. But an appetite for aggressive adventure is not easily slaked. Within a few years, Frederick had overreached himself. An out-of-the-blue attack on neutral Saxony (which included the bombardment of Dresden in which numerous cultural treasures were lost) provoked savage retaliation. Prussia was nearly brought to its knees when Austria orchestrated a coalition with Russia, and the ever-ready French joined forces to deal with the upstart.

But this was still the era of the whims of individual dynastic leaders: the Empress Elizabeth of Russia died at a crucial moment and was succeeded by her son, the Prussophile Peter III, who took Russia out of the conflict. Frederick was lucky. Peter III was soon overthrown on behalf of his wife, the German whom history knows as Catherine the Great: she took Russia back into the war on Austria's side. But it was too late. Austria too was exhausted. Frederick escaped catastrophe, and Prussia kept Silesia (losing it finally to Poland in the post Second World War settlement).

Austria was a long way from being out for the count, but it would never again be the dominant force in the core German lands. In any event, it was increasingly focused on its interests in Central and South-eastern Europe. By now, Germans were in a minority in the Habsburg domains. Austria had started on a journey which would end with its finding itself outside a unified Germany and – finally, after the Second World War some 200 years later – with an effectively separate, non-German identity.

Another loser in the German balance of power was Saxony, which never fully recovered from its savaging by Prussia. One of the Empire's electorates, it could look back on earlier times of greatness – not least when the Elector of Saxony gave Martin Luther protection and thus played a vital role at a crucial moment of German history. Much earlier, it was Saxon kings who had led Germany after the break-up of Charlemagne's empire. And earlier still, it was Saxons who – alongside the Angles and the Jutes – settled in England, leaving their imprint on the names of counties and towns to this day. By the 18th century, the rulers of Saxony ran a highly cultured court, and Dresden was becoming one of the most beautiful cities of Europe. But they would never dominate German politics again.

Saxony regained the independence Frederick had wanted to crush. And there was one momentary ray of hope for something new: the Elector Friedrich Christian came to power deeply imbued with the principles of the new Enlightenment thinking. A highly cultured man, musically gifted – like Frederick – he was also clear in his views of the obligations of princes, who, he wrote in his diary, 'exist for their subjects, not their subjects for them'. But Friedrich Christian died after a reign of just 40 days: he remains a poignantly intriguing might-have-been. Thereafter, Saxon rulers showed neither wisdom nor strength. They supported the French in the coming Napoleonic Wars and paid the price for this at the Congress of Vienna in 1815 by losing most of their territory to Prussia. The rump kingdom of Saxony was later swept up by Bismarck into the new Reich (although it remained a separate kingdom within the Reich until 1919).

Meanwhile, Bavaria had become the centre of a determined counter-reformation Catholicism. It had brought the Jesuits to Germany and fought with vigour against the Protestants in the Thirty Years War. It had gained both territory and influence in the process: but it suffered too from the vagaries of its ruling Wittelsbach dynasty. One of them, Maximilian III Joseph, made serious efforts to stabilise finances and promote economic development in the 1760/70s. But for the rest, Bavaria seemed to distinguish itself mainly by getting on the wrong side of almost every conflict going. Its rulers repeatedly played power politics with quite remarkable ineptitude, at one point pushing Austria for a deal to take over its dominions in the Netherlands (present day Belgium) in return for handing Bavaria itself over to Austria. This was a scheme which would clearly have shifted the centre of gravity in Germany back to Austria. Frederick the Great wasted no time in organising a coalition of other German rulers (including the British king George III in his capacity as Elector of Hanover) to prevent it. Come the Napoleonic Wars, however, the Bavarian leadership would play its cards more cleverly and more opportunistically than the Saxons. And absorbing Bavaria into the Reich would prove a much greater challenge for Bismarck. To this day, Bavaria retains a more distinct identity in Germany than any other region.

It was the sparring between Prussia and Austria which was now central to Germany's political future. But they were not above acting together with Russia in the partition of a defenceless and politically weak Poland. This was the critical exception to the rule about the lack of external entanglement by the German states in the 18th century. In three separate carve-ups, its three neighbours took what they wanted, bringing Polish independence finally to an end in 1796. Not for 200 years would the Poles again know a stable and enduring independence. The partitions were lucrative, especially for Prussia. The sense of victimhood which would soon develop into an important element in German self-understanding did not extend to a recognition of the victimhood of this other great nation. The omens were sinister: a century and a half later Hitler and Stalin would again dismember Poland – with the same cynicism but this time with unbelievable brutality.

Culturally, in Germany as elsewhere, the 18th century was a time of intellectual and spiritual ferment. This was not new: change had been in the air since the middle of the previous century. Leibnitz, who formulated the differential calculus contemporaneously with Isaac Newton, was also a scientist, engineer and philosopher. He was the first of what was to be a line of major figures who would ensure that German culture was unsurpassed in its contribution to human thought and creativity in the modern era. Above all, Immanuel Kant bestrides the thought world of the 18th century. More than any other philosopher, this man who never married and never travelled, spending all his life in the East Prussian city of Königsberg, set the terms of most subsequent debate in the philosophy of knowledge, ethics, aesthetics and religion. His direct and indirect influence, recognised or unrecognised, on so much human intellectual discourse globally is indisputable. And in particular his influence on the self-understanding of the German intellectual elite from the 19th century to the present day is as profound as that of Luther.

The new vibrancy in intellectual life took many forms: the age of Enlightenment was also an age of interest in the mystical, in freemasonry and – amongst many – the search for authentic religious experience. This saw the spread of Pietism in Protestant Germany, whose significance for the Romantic movement we will come back to in a later chapter. More generally in Germany, as elsewhere, this was a time of blossoming culture: of philosophy, literature, architecture, science, music, geographical exploration and a new fascination for history. Not coincidentally, it was also the time when German intellectuals began to write in German – rather than in Latin or in French – and to ask what meaning a German identity could have, what were its origins and how it could and should be realised on the European stage.

Few foresaw the events of 1789; no one understood just what an earthquake the French Revolution would be. In Germany, the hopes raised were as dramatic as was the subsequent disillusion. It is hard for us now, over 200 years later and after so many experiences of new dawns, to put ourselves in the minds of those who were so excited about the sudden new possibilities. *Liberté, fraternité, égalité*: the phrase is now a cliché. Then it was a vibrant new hope. This was the time when the calendar was reset to zero. It was the first great revolution of the modern, urban world. The old regime with its old power structures and prejudices was being swept away. It was the age when reason would finally triumph. For Germany, so some hoped, it could mean nothing less than the realisation of a new, free identity.

The disillusion was to be bitter. The new French republic declared war on Austria in 1792 and demonstrated an astonishing degree of military effectiveness as it first fought off Austrian and Prussian armies and then took the fight into the Netherlands and the Rhineland. The Marseillaise – surely one of the most bloodthirsty of national anthems – was first used at that time, when it was known as the *War Song of the Army of the Rhine* (*le Chant de Guerre de l'Armée du Rhin*). A vicious struggle over the soul of the revolution produced terror and chaos in France, but eventually saw the emergence of Napoleon as dictator, and then as self-crowned Emperor. His expansionism, his military brilliance, his reforming zeal and his sheer irrepressibility were to impact the whole of Europe and change Germany irrevocably.

Over the first few years of the 19th century, wave after wave of French armies surged eastwards across Europe, giving Germans a bitter taste of defeat and humiliation. Austria was brought to its knees at the battle of Austerlitz in 1805, Prussia the following year at Jena and Auerstädt. Napoleon reorganised a series of German principalities as client states in a Confederation of the Rhine. In 1806, the Holy Roman Empire was formally dissolved, bringing an end to over 800 years of an intricate continuity, which had by the end become threadbare and entirely inadequate to the challenge of the

Napoleonic upheaval. That challenge was to the very identity of Germany. Twenty years of French control changed the
Rhineland (by reorganising governance, administration and
the legal system) irreversibly.

More fundamentally still, the challenge crystallised an
existential question: who were the Germans? In every one of
Napoleon's eastward campaigns, there were German troops
fighting on the French side. Large numbers of Germans were
in the Grande Armée which invaded Russia in 1812. The following year, the weakened French were confronted with a new
coalition of Russia, Prussia, Austria and Sweden. Even then
the French had German troops on their side: Saxony, unlike
Bavaria, had not had the sense to change sides. The French
forces were decisively defeated at the battle of Leipzig in 1813
(known to the Germans as the Völkerschlacht – the battle of
the Nations). But the question was posed starkly: how could
it be that Germans were fighting Germans, on German soil,
in the interests of foreigners? The question of the German
identity had been brought into focus by Napoleon, and would
become more and more insistent.

Within a year, the coalition led by Russia occupied Paris,
and it was all over – except for one last, and potentially very
dangerous, hurrah. Famously, it was Prussian troops who
saved the day for Wellington at Waterloo. But by then the
world had changed. New yearnings were now stirring in the
German spirit, nourished by a rich – and uniquely German –
cocktail: a romanticism which took new pride in Germany's
ancient imperial glory and in its beautiful lands; an industrial
revolution which was slower to start than Britain's, but which
now began rapidly to gain ground; a sense of destiny in the
east (born of the legacy of the Teutonic Knights, upheld by

Lutheran heirs to their austere sense of duty, and nurtured by rulers who encouraged new settlers to cultivate and make the land their own); and resentment of foreigners – especially the French for the repeated humiliations and for the theft of lands west of the Rhine. A yearning for denied national identity was taking root, alongside the sense of past victimhood.

The Congress of Vienna in 1815 resulted in the establishment of a new German Confederation, with roughly the borders of the old Holy Roman Empire. But neither of its two dominant members – Austria and Prussia (both of which also had substantial territories outside these borders) – had any intention of sponsoring radical political reform, or of allowing the Confederation to evolve into a real, unified German polity. The leadership of the old order – quintessentially embodied in the arch-conservative Austrian minister Metternich – moved quickly to suppress nationalist student movements which had begun to proliferate at various universities, as well as removing those who he considered to be unreliable university professors from their posts, and tightening up censorship.

The yearnings could be suppressed for a time; and even after 1848, when another French revolution sparked more upheaval in Germany, they were denied again. There was a moment when it seemed possible that a new, unified German state might be born. In the ancient imperial free city of Frankfurt, a group of representatives from the various German lands hammered out a constitution for an empire with a hereditary Kaiser and an elected legislature. But this was never going to succeed unless actively supported by the two main German powers – Prussia and Austria. This was not to be forthcoming. A tragicomedy of muddle and mistakes resulted in revolutions not quite succeeding in both Vienna and Berlin (as well as in many smaller states). And there was no way either the Austrian emperor or the Prussian king would countenance real authority over their domains by the Frankfurt parliament. In the case of Austria, moreover, there was a further, insuperable difficulty: the Habsburg domains included a majority of non-Germans. Inclusion of all their territories in a German polity would be plainly artificial (and probably unsustainable, given the aspirations of the Hungarians and the Czechs in particular for their own political identity); it was clear that the Austrian emperor would never agree to divide his realm. The Frankfurt assembly lost momentum and gradually crumbled away. The would-be representatives of the new German empire went home. This failed experiment was followed by a return – if not to the status quo ante, then to a stasis which allowed economic development but little or no political change.

Yet this did nothing to extinguish the yearning for a national identity and unity. And meanwhile, the modernising forces of the industrial revolution were rapidly gathering pace: they would inevitably drive economic integration, as well as creating a new bourgeoisie that would demand greater political recognition. In 1834 Prussia led the construction of a new Customs Union, to which eventually all members of the Confederation – with the hugely significant exception of Austria – adhered. The Customs Union, it would soon become clear, had set the pattern for eventual political union. Railway expansion drove urbanisation and industrialisation in Germany (to a greater extent than in Britain the railways created demand for output rather than responding to it) as well as connecting up the German regions and opening up military possibilities which would be better understood by German tacticians than by anyone else. Although the term 'military-industrial complex' has its origins in post-war US political discourse, it is certainly an apt term too for the dovetailed industrial and military ambitions of the Prussian elite in the second half of the 19th century.

If the 18th century saw extraordinary intellectual ferment, the 19th century was a time of unprecedented social change driven by the urbanisation which came with the industrial revolution. The growing influence of a new bourgeoisie was felt, not so much in the political domain where the repeated failure of revolution denied it anything other than a muted voice, but in the world of culture. This was the time of Biedermeier taste – an appetite for an ordered, pious domesticity with a focus on the inner life and self-development – reflected in much of the literature, art, architecture, design and to some extent in the musical developments of the period. It was also the time of a new interest in Germany's history, its legends and its folklore – popularised and celebrated in a profusion of Romantic art, as we shall see in a later chapter. This interest both fed, and was fed by, that growing search for national identity which was so entirely natural a part of a much broader European stream of consciousness (echoed in various particular ways amongst peoples as different as Italians, Hungarians and Poles, as well as being paralleled by the strong surge of patriotic pride stimulated in Britain by the Napoleonic Wars).

All this cultural creativity was underpinned by an apparently self-satisfied bourgeois prosperity based on the fruits of the industrial revolution. It was also paralleled by – and threatened by – the growing numbers of rural and urban poor, as in Britain. The revolt of the Silesian weavers in 1844 – in which property and machinery were destroyed and lives lost – was suppressed harshly. But it shocked the political leadership and the bourgeoisie and became a recurring motif in German literature and art – in Heinrich Heine, in Gerhart Hauptmann and in Käthe Kollwitz, to name but three. In Germany as elsewhere, urbanisation and industrialisation were rapidly creating a new working class consciousness, which would find a voice – or rather, voices – in several figures who emerged on the German public scene in the aftermath of 1848: Karl Marx and Friedrich Engels above all, of course, became world famous as exponents of a new communist cause – but they did their most important work in London. They were less immediately influential on the German domestic scene than Ferdinand Lassalle, August Bebel and others, whose political activism – and sometimes furious debates and disagreements – were fundamental to the emergence of Germany's social democratic movement during the second half of the 19th century.

A noisy pluralism was emerging in Germany, just as it did elsewhere in urbanising societies of the age. But all these figures stood in the shadow of the man who came to bestride the German – and European – stage in the second half of the century, and who master-minded the eventual unification of Germany: Otto von Bismarck.

Other European leaders faced the challenge of adjusting politics to massive social change, increasingly vocal media and ever more articulate demands especially by the urban classes. On top of this, in the case of the Germans, there was the complex question of identity and unity. Bismarck's achievement in dealing with all these challenges is nothing short of astonishing. On the domestic scene, he was a social conservative whose vision was of a nation in which political leadership would remain in the hands of a landed and military elite, in which the economic drive would come from bourgeois capitalists and traders, and in which working class aspirations and concerns would be met by government provision of appropriate education as well as the world's first welfare system covering health, accident and old age insurance. It was a remarkable and deft achievement which allowed Germany to emerge rapidly as the strongest economy in Europe in the decades leading up to 1914.

But Bismarck's historic significance lies even more in what he achieved on the European stage. For in a remarkably short period of nine years from 1862, when he was first appointed to lead the Prussian government, Bismarck played the international game like a chess grandmaster. If Germany was to be unified, he was determined that it would be under Prussian leadership (and indeed domination). On the way to this goal, he had to resolve three questions about the extent of this new German nation: the northern border with Denmark; whether the new entity would include or exclude Austria; and the relationship with the old enemy of the Germans – France. Bismarck dealt decisively with all three.

He manipulated the famously obscure Schleswig-Holstein question to defeat the Danes and settle the first issue in favour of a joint administration by Prussia and Austria. Conveniently for him, the resulting friction with the Austrians gave him an ideal excuse for war with them next. The battle of Königgrätz in 1866 saw the Austrians go down to a crushing defeat. It was the last time Germans would fight Germans on a battlefield. The outcome of the Austro-Prussian War definitively removed Austria from the German political scene: unification of Germany would proceed on Prussian terms – i.e. without Austria. The next move in the game was to take over those north German states that had made the mistake of siding with

Austria – notably Hanover, with its large secret royal trea-
sury. Bismarck later used this quietly to pay King Ludwig II
of Bavaria for his support of the nomination of the Prussian
king Wilhelm I as Kaiser of a new German Reich. (The secret
payments to Ludwig continued for the next 16 years until he
died, helping to finance the strange, melancholy romanticism
which produced the fairytale castle of Neuschwanstein as
well as his support for Richard Wagner's ambitious plans in
Bayreuth – of which more in a later chapter.)

To deal with the third issue, Bismarck teed up the Franco-
Prussian war with consummate skill, exploiting old-fashioned
dynastic manoeuvrings in Spain to encourage the foolish French
emperor Napoleon III as he declared a war which – although it
was no blitzkrieg – resulted in a decisive French defeat. Bismarck
was also lucky: Napoleon III was overthrown and a new republic proclaimed in Paris; no other European power was likely
to come to their rescue. The 'national patriotic war' was thus a
complete success for the new Germany. Bismarck used the settlement to seize back Alsace and much of Lorraine, as well as to
extract a huge reparation payment from France (calculated as
the exact equivalent per head of population of the levy imposed
by Napoleon on Prussia in 1807). Ancient scores had thus been
settled. France reaped a whirlwind sowed by Louis XIV and by
Napoleon Bonaparte. Equally certainly, seeds of resentment
had now been sown again – this time by the Germans. Few in
Germany, for example, recognised how strong republican sentiment was in German-speaking Alsace. France would never
forgive or forget. The consequences for Germany in 1918 would
be very bitter. Vengeance breeds vengeance.

The long-standing question of German identity had finally
found a solution. Ever since the Holy Roman Empire had

begun to weaken six hundred years before, the question had called for an answer – more and more stridently from the 18th century onwards. Germany was not alone in this at all. There were stirrings in the various domains of the Habsburgs. Polish yearnings were given voice by Adam Mickiewicz from his exile in Paris. Most dramatically, the Italian Risorgimento was creating huge excitement around Europe, finding its own marvellous – if coded – voice in Giuseppe Verdi's 'Va pensiero'. Somehow this was different, though. It had the makings of tragedy in it, this German solution. It did not feel so much like the realisation of a German dream; it was more the result of a calculated series of manoeuvres designed to ensure the supremacy of Prussia and of Prussian values. The ethos of the new Reich was a long way from the Italian sunshine of the Risorgimento: it was that of Prussia east of the Elbe – austere, rigorous, military, Lutheran in its sense of order and duty.

Moreover, the settlement was not a comfortable or a stable one. When the modern German state was finally born as the Second Reich, after decades of frustration and disappointment, it was something of a bastard child – part democratic and part autocratic, unified but not including the Germans of Austria, fathered with less than total enthusiasm by a collection of German kings and rulers under the domination of Bismarck – and proclaimed on French soil, at the Palace of Versailles, in the wake of a stunning military victory. What this said about the German mood at the time was not reassuring: bellicose, at one level triumphalist, at another level divided and insecure. A nervous Europe looked on.

Under the right conditions, the governance of the Second Reich would probably have evolved in the direction of either a British-style elected parliamentary government or of an American-style separately elected executive and legislature. But Bismarck's new Germany was neither: the government had to get budgetary authorisations through a Reichstag which was directly elected under universal male suffrage, but the Chancellor was appointed by and accountable to the Kaiser alone. So was the military: they answered to nobody but the Kaiser – not to his ministers, let alone to the Reichstag. This limited the significance of the universal male suffrage (as did the fact that the electoral system in Prussia itself – the geographic and political core of the Reich – was heavily weighted towards conservative and military interests). The separation of military and civilian authority had been one of the 'defining flaws'[4] of the Prussian constitution, and this flaw was retained in the constitution of the Second Reich. Wrangling over military expenditure became a chronic feature of its politics. Failure to control or call the military to account in the colonies, or even in the much more politically sensitive circumstances of Alsace, was an important contributor to Germany's growing reputation as a bully on the European stage in the decades preceding the First World War.

The effectiveness of the Second Reich depended – given the way it was constructed by Bismarck – on one key relationship: that between Kaiser and Chancellor. Strength and wisdom in at least one of them could ensure an efficient state internally and sound relationships on the European stage. The relationship between a dominant Bismarck and an elderly Kaiser Wilhelm I lasted for the first 17 years until Wilhelm died at the age of 90. It delivered that efficacy. But Wilhelm's successor, Friedrich III, husband of Queen Victoria's eldest daughter Vicky, was already dying of cancer when he took the throne. He lasted just 99 days. So it was his bombastic, immature, impulsive, insecure son who became the new figurehead of the Reich and remained in that position until its collapse in 1918. Bismarck was summarily dismissed in 1890, after almost 30 years of virtually unchallenged supremacy. No one after him had either the stature or the wisdom to balance the Kaiser or the military leaders whom he championed (and was increasingly dominated by).

Hence it was a small group of men (yes, all men in this society with its very assertive male psychology) who took all the major decisions that impacted foreign and military affairs: Kaiser Wilhelm II, a series of Chancellors with varying degrees of influence and a coterie of military figures. They saw themselves as the representatives of a society which they wanted to be conservative and harmonious. Yet in varying degrees they were aware of – and afraid of – the growing tensions in a society which was in fact changing fast.

On the surface, the mood in Germany might have been triumphalist and technocratic; within, it was a dangerous cocktail of dissatisfaction, romantic yearnings and resentment. As we shall see later, the voice of an aggressive nationalism – a belief that this was Germany's time in history – spoke with a growing virulence (and often with a strongly anti-Semitic tone). Meanwhile, perhaps Bismarck's most important mistake had been to launch a very aggressive attack on the Roman Catholic Church – his so-called *Kulturkampf* or cultural struggle – which was socially and regionally divisive, and which in the end ran out of steam, but not before leaving a legacy of resentment and mistrust in Germany's large Catholic communities. It also left on the statute book – until after the Second World War – a law making it a criminal offence for clerics to use the pulpit for political comments that might endanger the peace. (This law was later to be used against Catholic clergy by the Nazis.)

This was just one of the fissures in what the ruling elite saw as the national identity. Overlaying religious and regional divisions was a class structure which came under increasing stress. The threat did not come from the educated bourgeoisie. They may have found access to the levers of political power barred by the constitutional set-up of the Second Reich. But the state delivered them a secure legal environment for their businesses; they owned the capital that drove the industrial revolution; infrastructure and military spending meant growth; and in any event their formal and informal political power at local level was enormous. They dominated local communities not just economically but through their control of local community associations. In a society riddled with voluntary associations – professional, charitable, musical, sporting – their influence was pervasive and intrusive, more than in any other European country. Yet overall, they were not as content or as self-confident as their strong social position might suggest. Their social dominance was in relative decline, as other voices became more clamorous. This seemed to translate itself into a form of cultural pessimism (notable for instance in Oswald Spengler's *Untergang des Abendlands* – The Downfall of the West) which was not unique to Germany at the time, but which was all the more ironic given the barnstorming success of Germany's industrialisation, the economic and social success of the bourgeoisie and the triumphalism of the Reich's public persona.

But such inner self-doubt certainly did not translate into a demand for more political power for the great bourgeois interests. No, the threat to Germany's conservative settlement came from three other groups which were making their present felt (as they were elsewhere in Europe at the time) in a rapidly modernising society: the peasantry, the petit bourgeoisie and the working class. Peasant discontent with falling incomes, rising debt and perceived exploitation by the Junkers and by the urban elites was welling up in direct relationship to the pace of urbanisation. Meanwhile, the petit bourgeoisie had been savagely mauled by the huge economic convulsions that had racked the whole of Europe during the first few years of the Second Reich's existence – in what was to be the first of a series of global financial and economic crises which have continued to bedevil the capitalist system up to the present day.

Gravest of all these threats, in the minds of the establishment, was the working class, which was flexing its muscles in Germany as everywhere else in the industrial world at the time. Bismarck had bound them in through his insurance system (as well as through the ploy of universal male suffrage for the Reichstag). But this did not allow the conservative establishment to relax: worker representation in the Reichstag increased over time, and the programme of the Socialist Party was becoming more clearly impregnated with Marxist thought. Moreover, industrial action was becoming more frequent and often violent; and an urban subculture was evolving – graphically captured in the irreverent cartoons and drawings of Heinrich Zille, for example – which seemed not to belong and to know nothing of received values. In the 1912 elections the *Sozialdemokratische Partei Deutschlands* (SPD) – the Social Democratic Party of Germany – became the largest party in the Reichstag. There was no parallel to this in any other major country. No one knew where the loyalties of these representatives of the working class really lay or how they would vote when the hour of crisis came.

Yet in the end the conservative leadership need not have worried, on this score at least. For now, in a new century which seemed to be their age, there were many Germans in all walks of life for whom there was a powerful sense of belonging in the new Germany. There was an underlying sense (often not fully recognised even by themselves) of quiet pride or of yearning fulfilled, which transcended – even if it in no way negated – the tensions and differences that arose from their specific economic circumstances, religious backgrounds or political agendas. This was, moreover, true not just for the conservative establishment or for rabid nationalists – of whom there were certainly plenty – but also for many of the cultivated and cosmopolitan intellectual elite.

Not all nationalist sentiment was of this sophisticated kind, of course. In the noisy public domain of the late Wilhelmine age there were also those who argued that it was Germany's right and duty to crush the Slavs – and these same voices were typically virulently anti-Semitic as well. The *Alldeutscher Verband* – the Pan German League – was the most influential such grouping. Founded in 1891, it included amongst its 20,000 or so members none other than Max Weber, although he later left the Verband and became increasingly opposed to its aggressive nationalism and expansionism. In 1912 a pamphlet by one of its noisier members called for the conquest, depopulation and Germanisation of Slav lands to the east. This was a straw in the wind.

By 1914 the new international balance of power had become precarious – even if the tension seemed to have abated somewhat compared to the previous year. The bombast of this period was by no means unique to Germany. But Germany had behaved in the two previous decades like the adolescent who feels bullied as a child, is now conscious of his new strength, and senses that the world is against him even as he seeks to assert his identity. Indeed, Britain, France and Russia – unlikely bedfellows – did find themselves aligned against Germany. This adolescent felt encircled. But it was also an adolescent who felt his ties of kinship deeply. Germany became the faithful backer of Austria – *Nibelungentreue* it was called, or the loyalty unto death, which was celebrated in Germany's ancient myth of the Nibelungs (of which more later). The conditions were set for tragedy to unfold. All it needed was a trigger, which was pulled in Sarajevo on 28 June 1914.

Germany in the summer of 1914 is a paradox. Its economy was strong, its trade networks extensive, its cultural life was remarkably vibrant and, likewise, extensively connected to wider European currents of creativity. It was also new and assertive – with a new identity which was the answer to a century or more of yearning. But it was also a society in the throes of rapid change and many saw in this a grave threat to the cohesion of this newly united nation. Competing class interests and religious fractures seemed to make it impossible to find common cause on almost any policy issue. For some, there was a strange sense of impending doom. Inevitably, there were those conservatives who blamed all this on the noisy democracy of Reichstag politics. Such people saw the great German community, or *Gemeinschaft*, being vitiated by the vulgar, self-seeking materialism of the modern transactional society (or *Gesellschaft*, to borrow the terminology of one of Germany's most prominent sociologists, Ferdinand Tönnies, who first drew the distinction before the First World

War). Some, at least, had a growing sense that a violent thunderstorm would sooner or later break over them – especially Helmuth von Moltke, Chief of the General Staff, who was obsessed by the rising economic and military power of Russia, and was convinced of the need for a showdown sooner rather than later.

When the storm finally broke, there was a strange mixture of responses: part relief that the heavy atmosphere was about to be cleansed by the purity of elemental strife; and part deep, deep fear of what this would do to Germany's newly won identity. The SPD promised on 28 July that it would support action to defend Germany against Russian attack, and the party famously voted for the war credits: even Karl Liebknecht, who was to go on to be one of the founders of the German Communist Party, voted (after much agonised debate) in support. This was partly because they saw Russia as a medieval anachronism that needed to be confronted, however ambivalent they might be about conflict with France (where the popular and charismatic socialist Jean Jaurés was an internationally respected champion of peace). But partly because they were, for all their Marxist dogma, Germans.

To say this is not at all to argue that they were crass nationalists; but it is to argue that they partook of that newly won sense of identity which was pervasive in the German consciousness of the time, and which it is all too easy from the vantage point of a hundred years later to caricature, to patronise or even to ignore altogether. It is this which unlocks the puzzle of support for the Second Reich as it went to war in 1914 not only by leaders of the SPD but also by figures of huge intellectual importance and international stature such as Max Weber and Thomas Mann. A century on, it seems like an embarrassing lapse on their part. Seen in the context of German history up to the 20th century, it is not so strange. (In the present age there are obvious parallels – notably in the modern China.)

August 1914. German military planning was based on the principle that the best form of defence is attack – though the whole lesson of the subsequent war on the Western Front was that given the state of technology, defence was stronger than attack. But the psychology of encirclement – and the instinct to hit out first – was deep seated. The violation of Belgian neutrality (and brutality there by German troops); the huge economic damage done to north-eastern France; followed by unrestricted submarine warfare – the hatred generated by all this led the Allies at Versailles after the war to treat Germany with a humiliating severity which set the scene for the next and final act in the great tragedy. To this day, you can see the commemorative plaque in the salon in the Hotel Trianon where the victors presented the terms to the delegation of the new German republic. The very way it is worded, with its long list of victor powers followed by the single name of Germany, underlines the humiliation.

Many have argued that John Maynard Keynes's famous attack on the economic consequences of the peace settlement was wrong and that the terms were not unreasonable or unaffordable.[5] But that is to miss the point. At home, the politicians who had agreed to an armistice (not a surrender) had, Hitler would argue, stabbed the army in the back. The new rump country of Austria – or German Austria, as the new republic there styled itself – was not allowed to merge with the new Germany. The French occupied the Rhineland and took back Alsace-Lorraine. Once again, the demons of resentment had been stirred. Vengeance bred vengeance again. The abused turns abuser again and sees his punishment as victimisation. The pattern recurs. This time the results would be truly terrible.

The Weimar years leave a sense of weary sadness. Almost nothing goes right. The republic was born in the midst of collapse and civil war. From the start, neither the militaristic and aristocratic right nor the communists on the left showed any loyalty to the new republic. Hyperinflation bankrupted the middle classes and impoverished the working classes, spreading fear and insecurity throughout society. The French in the Rhineland behaved like the famous Bourbons who have learnt nothing and forgotten nothing. For a period from the signing of the US-sponsored Dawes Plan in 1924 – which helped loosen Germany's financial straitjacket – the economy began to improve. Given more favourable international economic circumstances, the recovery might have continued, jobs might have been there for the many who had been economically or psychologically dispossessed by all the traumas and upheaval, and the threats might have slowly receded. But from 1930 onwards German economic recovery was torpedoed by the Great Depression. Unemployment began rising fast. By late 1932 one in four adult males was unemployed and the Nazis were the largest party in the Reichstag. The Communists refused to make common cause with the Socialists to keep them out of power. In January 1933 the Faustian pact was signed.

The rest is a countdown to zero hour – *Stunde Null* – in May 1945. The story still has the power to enthral and dismay. There were some early triumphs both domestically (a rebounding economy) and internationally (the reversal of one after another of the provisions of Versailles). War was not popular, but produced some easy victories including – surprisingly but gratifying to a large majority of Germans – over France. The plans for dealing with undesirables – above all the Jews – became ever darker. Then comes the fatal error – the over-extended campaign in the Soviet Union, where early successes were soon followed by vicious winters and unspeakably savage fighting which sapped the energy and morale of the Third Reich. Meanwhile, Allied bombing of more and more cities brought the war and its terror to German civilians even before the Red Army arrived. From the failure of the July 1944 plot against Hitler, everything moved towards a Wagnerian total immolation: the extermination of the Jews continued; the bombing of cities continued to within days of the end of the war (in March 1945 Magdeburg died its second death); and savage street-by-street fighting in one city after another marked the retreat towards Berlin.

Then came the end: a military, physical and moral collapse so utter that this did indeed feel to many like Stunde Null. The German philosopher Jürgen Habermas argued that Auschwitz was the great caesura of German history, and hence that the future would have to be built on entirely new foundations. And in the public mind outside Germany it seemed as if German history ended there – as if the moral and physical rubble that was Germany in 1945 meant the end of all those centuries of the German *Kultur*. Stunde Null. Whatever the future was to be, there was nothing in the past to build on. All that was left was collapse and total disorientation.

And yet, of course, it was not Stunde Null. It was not true that Germany's history ended there or that there was nothing to build on. In fact, its story is precisely one which, uniquely, invites us to face the complexities of human nature – the peaks it can scale, the depths it can plumb, and the mysterious possibilities for redemption and reconciliation which always exist, even at the darkest moment of failure.

For that is the story of the modern Germany which can now be seen to be taking the leading role destined for it in the evolving Europe of the new millennium. A hundred years after the beginning of the denouement which reached its climax in May 1945, we can see how a new German self-understanding has emerged, at peace with its neighbours and reconciled with itself for the first time in a thousand years – slowly but nonetheless clearly over the two generations born after Stunde Null. The victim turned aggressor and abuser has found redemption and atonement (in its original meaning) despite the terrible deeds that were done, and has become the reluctant leader in a new era for Europe. There are lessons in this for others in our irreversibly global world – as will become clear at the end of this story. But first we have to follow the German journey.

3

That Cursed Duty

THAT THERE COULD ever be such a future for Germany was not remotely evident in 1945.

It seemed as if, from Arminius onwards, Germany could find a secure identity only in aggression. And yet, of course, an identity that seeks security through aggression is fundamentally insecure. Aggression is one step away from self-doubt – one manifestation of a sense of, or fear of, inferiority gnawing away at the self. And in the end, the aggression reached an intensity, a ferocity, a totality which could barely be believed. Both at the popular level and in academic circles in the aftermath of the Second World War – both in Germany and amongst the victorious allies – the question was asked insistently: how was this dreadful result possible? What was it in German political developments, or in German culture, or in the German people that had allowed the Third Reich to come to power and to lead the nation into this abyss?

The British historian AJP Taylor, for instance, writing his classic polemic *The Course of German History* in the closing months of the war, opens with the provocative assertion that 'the history of the Germans is a history of extremes. It contains everything except moderation, and in the course of a thousand years the Germans have experienced everything except normality'. He goes on:

... they have produced the most transcendental philosophers, the most spiritual musicians, and the most ruthless
and unscrupulous politicians. 'German' has meant at one
moment a being so sentimental, so trusting, so pious, as to
be too good for this world; and at another a being so brutal,
so unprincipled, so degraded, as to be not fit to live. Both
descriptions are true: both types of German have existed
not only at the same epoch, but in the same person. Only
the normal person, not particularly good, not particularly
bad, healthy, sane, moderate – he has never set his stamp
on German history.

Taylor argues that in the West, Germans had seen themselves as victims of French aggression, but that in Eastern
Europe 'no other people has pursued extermination as a
permanent policy from generation to generation for a thousand years; and it is foolish to suppose that they have done
so without adding something permanent to their national
tradition.'

If nothing else this diatribe, which seems – from the vantage-
point of 70 years later, in a new millennium – so one-sided
and prejudiced as to be little more than a caricature, reminds
us of the depth of hatred towards Germany that was by then
widespread throughout Europe. But in the decades after the
war, many more sober judges than Taylor have focused on the
so-called 'Special Path' – or *Sonderweg* – which Germany is
said to have followed in becoming a nation, starting at the
political level with the wrong turns taken in the 19th century:
the failure of the 1848 revolutions and the Bismarckian settlement under which (a) too much social and political power
were retained by the conservative Prussian Junker aristocracy

and (b) Chancellor and government were too dependent for their legitimacy on the whim of the Kaiser.

Ironically, the Sonderweg had originally been the proud claim of that same Second Reich establishment: the new Germany was to pursue its own strong way into the future, not that of the effete democracies of Britain and France or of the backward autocracy of Russia; it had demonstrated the fore-sight to provide broad-based education and social security, and it had developed the most successful economy in Europe. (Uncomfortably, too, this cannot help reminding us of some contemporary Asian claims to be following a special Asian path which avoids the decadent indecisiveness of Western democracies and which invests in the long term development of a harmonious society.)

But after 1945 the Sonderweg became a hypothesis about the causes of the disaster, not a celebration of success; and it was about so much more than just the constitution of the Second Reich. Thus, for example, Taylor's conclusion that 'the Nazi regime represented the deepest wishes of the German people' – or William L Shirer's argument in his hugely suc-cessful *The Rise and Fall of the Third Reich*, first published in 1960, that there was a clear continuity from Luther to Hitler which made 'blind obedience to temporal rulers the highest virtue of Germanic man and put a premium on servility'. He and many others of the time argued that a deep-seated aggression, combined with the sense of duty, discipline and obedience which lay at the heart of the cultural journey from Luther onwards, made it too easy for the Nazis to win hearts and even minds for their brutal programmes.

When Taylor wrote *The Course of German History*, he was flying in the face of an 'official' view amongst the Allies (both in the West and in the Soviet Union) which held that the Third Reich was a disastrous aberration imposed on the German people by the Nazi leadership. But in fact opinion polls in Germany from 1945 until well into the 1960s showed that a significant share of the population thought there had been beneficial aspects of the Third Reich even if it had failed because of its excesses, rather than that it had been wrong or evil in principle – suggesting that Taylor and others were on to something after all. Notoriously, the German historian Friedrich Meinecke, writing in 1946, described the Third Reich as a *Betriebsunfall* – an industrial accident – of history.

In the decades that followed, as the German intelligentsia sought to deal more honestly with the past, Taylor's thesis came to have greater resonance in Germany as well as elsewhere. A whole series of writers have explored the broad involvement of so many German institutions and so much of ordinary society in Nazi crimes: this was not just an affair of fanatics and thugs egged on by an evil elite. In particular, the image of the good soldier and his commander carrying out their duties in accordance with the highest military standards did not stand close inspection. Nor did the notion that ordinary citizens had no idea what was going on. The complicity of the Wehrmacht itself – not just of the SS – in war crimes in the east, and the passivity and complicity of so many ordinary citizens in deportations of Jews from in their midst, have been remorselessly exposed.

The historical background of Nazi ideology, particularly in the 19th century but also earlier, and – yes – all the way back to Luther, has been closely examined for anything that seemed to foreshadow or explain what happened. Perhaps there really was a deeper sense in which Germany had followed a special path – and had been doing so for a very long time? In the emotive decades of what the Germans came to know (in one of those wonderfully complex German compound words) as *Vergangenheitsbewältigung* – dealing with, or coming to terms with, the past – such arguments could seem in a strange way comforting, in that they provided the basis for a sense of being crushed by their inheritance. But also to others: Britons who had lived through the experience of one or both wars, for example, wanted to be able to feel that 'all this could never have happened in Britain'. So they wondered out loud: was there something about the German identity that made it innately disposed to the evil that had occurred?

Historians more recently have largely ceased to find the notion of a German special path a helpful concept in understanding what happened.[6] For one thing, it is striking that no less than four of the great cultures of Europe at the beginning of the 20th century – German, Russian, Spanish and Italian – were subverted by anti-democratic or totalitarian forces within four decades, all of them in varying degrees brutal. Germany's experience was in the end unspeakable, and indeed unique. But the veil has still not been fully lifted on the awfulness of the Stalinist purges. And whilst the fascism of Italy and Spain were not in the same league as either the Third Reich or the Soviet Union, both had sins enough to answer for. Both were following their own particular paths: Italy was on its own journey to discover and create its identity, Spain on a long journey of decline from great power to weak European state trying to cope with the technological and ideological challenges of the 20th century. The Soviet Union, needless to say, made no bones about its own special path from benighted Tsarism to the Marxist-Leninist new world.

But in that case, how useful is the concept of a special path for Germany? Don't all societies follow special paths as they cope with the kind of change that was accelerating and spreading from the time of Renaissance, of Reformation and of the printing press? Germany's long struggle with the question of its identity certainly took a particular direction in the 19th century. But equally certainly such a struggle for identity is not necessary to explain what happened later. For if it were, then what about Japan – whose eruption onto the world stage at around the same time was also ferocious in the extreme? Yet Japan never had to struggle with the question of identity or of unity: on the contrary, its geographical and political identity has been clearly defined for centuries, and it remains to this day one of the most profoundly cohesive societies – with one of the most strongly corporate social psychologies – anywhere in the world.

In any event, the whole idea of some special German path can easily seem deterministic, as if a momentum whose origins lay far back in history made the outcome inevitable – like a tsunami whose causes lie deep in the ocean and a long way from the beaches it overwhelms. But this is to duck questions about what was going on amongst the various groups in the rapidly changing German society of the Second Reich: the role, or roles, of the bourgeois capitalist groups, of officialdom, of the Junker aristocracy, of the military; and of those who were not the elite but whose voices were becoming more insistent in an age of at least partial democracy and of vociferous media – the petit bourgeoisie, the peasantry and the urban working classes.

It also risks blinding us to the inconvenient role of chance in human affairs. The 'what ifs' of history matter. By their nature, the questions cannot be answered satisfactorily. But asking them reminds us about happenstance and should make us wary of any determinism that takes away from the openness of the present and our responsibility for it. In this case: what, for example, if Salic Law had not prevailed in the Kingdom of Hanover? This law, whose origins lie deeply buried in the history of the Holy Roman Empire, prevented a woman from ascending the throne. So when Queen Victoria took the British crown, she could not become Queen of Hanover, even though the electorate – and then the kingdom – of Hanover had been in the hands of British monarchs ever since the then elector became George I of England in 1714. Instead, it was her uncle – a son of George III – who became King of Hanover.

How different things might have been. It is hard to imagine that Hanover would have sided with Catholic Austria against Protestant Prussia in the run-up to Königgrätz, if Queen Victoria had been on its throne. Even if it had, it is certainly hard to imagine that Bismarckian Prussia would have swallowed it up in the ruthless way it did, given that this would have meant provoking war with Britain. Either way, how would this have affected Germany's path towards unification? At the very least, Bismarck would have had to entice and woo, rather than bully and bribe, his way to unification. He might well have got to the same end. But the unified Reich would surely have had a different temper, a different ethos, a different mood.

Or what if Kaiser Wilhelm I had died ten years earlier, at the venerable age of 80 instead of 90, and if Kaiser Friedrich III had lived ten years longer instead of dying of cancer at the age of 57, after just 99 days on the throne? This would have given this intelligent and liberalising monarch 20 years to change the course of German history. (He might well have dropped Bismarck too, just as his son did, but with very different results.) We could go on: what if the Communist Party had joined with the Socialist Party in 1932/33 to keep the Nazis out of power? Together they had more votes in the Reichstag and could have formed a government. In practice this was never remotely likely: their relationship was characterised by deep mutual suspicion and bitterness. In any case, the Communists were marching to Stalin's tune and playing a very different and dangerous game dictated by the perceived interests of the Soviet Union, which at that time involved non-cooperation with socialist parties. Or, later still, what if the Valkyrie plot against Hitler on 20 July 1944 had succeeded – if Stauffenberg had used both bomb parcels, or had placed his briefcase at a different point under the table, so that Hitler had indeed been killed?

And so on. There was nothing inevitable about what happened. Yet when human beings do terrible things, we inevitably ask about the psychological baggage they carry from the past. Sometimes there seems to be nothing that explains or points to what they later became and did. But more often there is. We can ask the same questions about peoples. In the case of Germany, what were the formative influences on this child as he (yes, this was definitely an aggressive male) grew up? What, for example, about the popular culture of the late 19th century, one strand of which celebrated a very masculine, physical, aggressive heroism? What about the belligerent militarism of the Second Reich? And where did the virulent anti-Semitism of the Nazis come from?

But in asking such questions, we need to avoid seeing the 19th century – let alone earlier centuries – through a 20th century prism. Take, for example, the anti-Semitism of Wilhelmine Germany. Nothing that happened in the Second Reich is in the same league as the Dreyfus affair in France – or as the widespread anti-Semitism of Russia which was given decisive expression in government laws in 1882. If a genius like Wagner could be anti-Semitic, so was Dostoyevsky. As we shall see, there was indeed a dark undercurrent of anti-Semitism in the popular culture of Wilhelmine Germany which certainly provided grist to the Nazi mill: there were writers in Germany who stood comparison with Charles Maurras (he who attacked the French Third Republic as the *'république juive'*) or with Edouard Drumont, who wrote a highly successful two volume rant called *La France Juive*. But it would be hard to argue that Germany stood out in the 19th century if you knew nothing about what happened in the 20th.

So does this mean that we are left with nothing that is distinctive about the evolution of German self-consciousness during the 19th and 20th century? No: there are indeed specific characteristics of the German thought-world in that period leading up to the tragic climax which are clearly distinctive. Did they make the tragedy inevitable? – No. But they did make it more possible and, when it occurred, more total and therefore more terrible.

Above all, we need to come face to face with two characteristics of German culture and self-awareness particularly as it was developing in the 19th century, in addition to that sense of victimhood that, as we have already seen in the last chapter, had taken root and was growing strongly at the same time. The first is the famous and very deep-rooted sense of duty; the second is the growing sense of national destiny, the sense that

Germany's time – indeed, Germany's age – had come. The sense of destiny was given specific, expansive form and a strident voice by the Nazis and thus became a sinister focus for the sense of duty. The latter gave the former a terrifying power – its effectiveness to begin with and then its utter destructiveness. We need to look closely at both.

The German obsession with duty and with the following of orders has taken on legendary dimensions. It can all too easily be the butt of jokes – even amongst Germans. But the real burden of it on the German consciousness over the generations is reflected in a telling phrase, used self-deprecatingly by Germans of the generations which grew up in the Second and Third Reichs when being thanked for doing something burdensome: *'Das ist meine verdammte Pflicht und Schuldigkeit'* – which translates as something like 'It is my cursed duty and obligation'. But its full resonance is almost impossible to convey naturally in English. The English phrase 'my bounden duty' has a stiffness about it: the more natural equivalent in actual usage would be something like: 'that's the least I could do'. But that doesn't do justice to the formality of the German – or to the adjective which is so revealing. It was a cursed duty – *eine verdammte Pflicht*. It tells its own tale of a deep-seated reflex, partly conscious, partly learnt so early in childhood and so consistently reinforced as to be almost automatic: verdammt – because of the weight of tradition and expectation which was part of what it meant to be German.

Its impact on behaviour has survived even into the 21st century, albeit in more trivial ways by this time. Even now you can see people waiting for the pedestrian light at a crossing (the famous *Ampelmann*) to go green before crossing a road, even if there is no car (or policeman) in sight. Even now *Pünktlichkeit* – punctuality – is venerated more than anywhere else in Europe. But in the mid 20th century, more serious issues were at stake: it is when the Berlin police chief hears Hitler's voice on the telephone after the Valkyrie bomb plot that he moves to arrest Stauffenberg. Until then it was not clear to him where his duty lay. Once he knows Hitler is alive, there can be no question for him. It is only when hearing that Hitler is dead that many of the generals begin to surrender in May 1945, even though they knew it was all over well before that.

So where does this cursed duty come from? No answer to this question can avoid going back to Luther. By the time of the Second Reich, Germany had lived for 300 years under the long shadow cast by Luther's world view, particularly his doctrine of the two kingdoms – the two realms of the individual's being, the inner relationship with God and the external relationship with the world. The impact of this on German culture has been profound and complex. It was not just that it derived from a radically new approach to the existential and theological questions of grace and salvation. It had clear implications for the responsibilities of rulers and ruled in society.

Luther saw the Christian as living in two realms – that of his/her spiritual experience of grace and salvation and that of interaction with others: the interior world and the exterior world. The interior world – this was Luther's great innovation – is an individual, personal one. It is here, not in the world of the community or even of the organised church, that we make our life decisions. For him, those decisions were of eternal significance. We are justified – eternally saved – by our own faith, through God's grace, not by the operation of any external authority. No institutional church can dispense forgiveness or guarantee our path to heaven. Churches could teach (although only on the basis of the truths established in the Bible, in accordance with Luther's famous watchword *sola scriptura* – by scripture alone). But the decision of faith – the central decision, of both existential and eternal significance – was for the individual alone.

Meanwhile, the exterior world of our social (including our church) relationships is one where the role of the civil authorities (the princes and the nobility of Luther's day) is to maintain peace and the social order, whilst the duty of the subject is to show obedience to the civil authorities. Luther was no democrat in any modern sense. He believed that if the world were full of true Christians – people who had made that life decision of faith – there would be no need of the civil authorities or the law. But he knew perfectly well that such people were few and far between, and just as Saint Paul had argued 1500 years before, he saw the role of the civil authorities as essential in a wicked world. The prince who kept order – by force as necessary – was doing the work of God's kingdom. Without the prince, the world would descend into unavoidable chaos.

There were others who held more radical ideas. If all Christians were an equal 'priesthood of believers' – the phrase from one of the letters of Peter in the New Testament which Luther made a cornerstone of his new Reformation theology – then why could the prince not be challenged by or held to account by the people? Almost instinctively, Luther knew this would lead either to revolutionary upheaval and chaos or to theocracy (which in practice meant not the rule of God but the rule of an ecclesiastical leadership). In the context of his age, he was probably right. The radical reformer Thomas Münzer led a huge peasants' rebellion within a few years of Luther's appearance at the Diet of Worms. And Calvin established his socially intrusive theocracy in Geneva. Neither offered the likelihood of utopia.

Luther's position was set out in what became one of the basic texts of the Lutheran settlement. It was to have enormous influence in Germany, where a century of violence and social disruption was to reveal all too clearly the importance of effective civil authority. Entitled *Von weltlicher Obrigkeit, wie weit man ihr Gehorsam schuldig sei* – On Secular Authority and How Far One Should Be Obedient To It – he wrote it (in German to ensure a wide readership) primarily to ward off any attempt by princes to interfere with the liberty of conscience of the ordinary believer in matters of faith. But he also laid out what he saw as the legitimate role of the ruler – the maintenance of the peace and the social order. It was the duty of the true Christian to serve the secular government in its effort to carry out that role.

This was not new. Traditional medieval scholarship took the same position. Nor was Luther a naive absolutist: it was clear to him that the prince who did not rule wisely – and therefore justly – risked the wrath of the people, and might have to take the consequences. What is more, he regularly railed at the iniquities of rulers, both in general and in particular. He was not above direct personal criticism of those who were his own secular rulers in Wittenberg. He more than once counselled disobedience if the prince commanded the Christian to go against the gospel. So while he was never prepared to put himself – or allow others to put him – at the head of any kind of socially revolutionary religious movement or theocracy, neither was he simply advocating an unquestioning obedience in any and all circumstances. There were those in later centuries, as we shall see, who were ready to risk their lives in a disobedience which they saw as being true to their faith.

Nevertheless, Luther faced one dilemma which was the necessary consequence of his overall settlement. If there was to be no more papal authority in the land, and if there was to be no Geneva-style theocracy, then the only way of providing structure, order and continuity in the community religious life was for the prince to act as, in effect, the successor to the Catholic bishop in governing the church. So the ironic result of Luther's reformation – which had stressed so much the inner life of the believer – was a high degree of official control over church life. The pulpit became more and more a means of reinforcing the responsibility of the Christian to support the social order, and less and less a means to present the existential challenge of the Christian gospel as Luther himself had so vividly experienced it.

Over the succeeding generations, the external social life of the Christian became ever more clearly subject to that insistent demand for order – which became deeply internalised in the German psyche as a sense of duty. The terrors of the religious and social wars in the 16th century surely contributed to this, and the unspeakable horrors of the Thirty Years War can only have reinforced the yearning for order and peace. And certainly Prussia's ruler at the start of the 18th century, the deeply religious King Friedrich Wilhelm, father of Frederick the Great, was obsessive, relentless and organised in his pursuit of this goal, building up an increasingly professional bureaucracy and a well trained standing army, and promulgating detailed lists of obligations for both.

So ask a reflective German where the 20th century obsession

with duty comes from, and Luther will often get much of the blame – more, perhaps, than his fair share. But not only Luther: sometimes the philosopher Kant – whose elevation of duty to the central principle of morality was a key part of his immense influence on German self-understanding – gets a share too. At one level it is clear why. Kant's view of morality derived from his whole understanding of reality. His was the age of the Enlightenment; gone was any easy certainty that there exists an established and known cosmic order of the kind that Luther (and virtually all his contemporaries) took for granted. And therefore gone too was any certainty that our goals can be deduced from that order.

On the face of it, Kant has travelled a long way from Luther. Moral purpose cannot be derived from any divine command. But he was equally clear that it cannot be derived from the empirical world either. Kant was a relentless opponent of any kind of materialist determinism just as much as he dismissed any form of divine order. The meaning of life cannot be deduced from the facts of life. The individual – the subject (or, to use Luther's terminology, the soul) – was an autonomous being who could and should make rational decisions about the good. Yet we cannot rely on our feelings to determine those decisions; human desires and perceptions can be misleading and they are not a reliable basis for, or source of, any obligation or duty. The true worth of an action can therefore be assessed only by its inner motivation, not by reference to its perceived outcome. Hence the central importance of dutiful action – action performed out of a sense of moral obligation, simply because the rational subject recognises it as such, without reference to its perceived consequences. Only such an action is unambiguously good.

Thus far, it is certainly possible to see danger in this, in the context of a Lutheran view of the social order. A sense of duty could become a slavish subjection to a system of duties determined by the culture of society – which was precisely the tendency of the Prussian state and then of the Second Reich. But Kant himself is a thousand miles from such a position. For him, it was the mind of the autonomous, free being which recognised duty as an imperative. This was his cornerstone. On a memorial plaque in Königsberg (now Kaliningrad and part of Russia) is his famous saying:

'Zwei Dinge erfüllen das Gemüth mit immer neuer und zunehmender Bewunderung und Ehrfurcht, je öfter und anhaltender sich das Nachdenken damit beschäftigt: der bestirnte Himmel über mir und das moralische Gesetz in mir.'

(Two things fill the mind with ever new and increasing amazement and reverence, the more often and the more persistly I reflect on them: the starry heavens above me and the moral law within me.)

This sums up his search for an all-embracing view of the nature of being. The moral law within me – within the autonomous individual – is what Kant called the 'categorical imperative': my duty as a rational being to act so that 'I could will my maxim to become a universal law': or, as he put it in an important alternative formulation, 'so act that you use humanity, whether in your own person or in the person of any other, always at the same time as an end, never merely as a means.'

This is of fundamental importance. It is not a specific commandment, imposed from outside on the autonomous subject. Kant does indeed articulate specific duties that follow generally from this imperative, in terms of (i) obligations and rights which can properly be enforced by the state, and (ii) those 'duties of virtue' which are not enforceable by the state, but which can be considered as duties of respect and love arising from our own recognition of the moral law. All such duties follow, however, from the basic imperative which is within us as rational beings.

All this is a long way from the more pragmatic and utilitarian view of ethics typically espoused by British thinkers of Kant's time. But it is easy to discern the similarity of outlook to that of another great Enlightenment figure: Jean-Jacques Rousseau – whom Kant greatly admired (and whose portrait was the only one he kept in his study). Rousseau too saw the inner voice of reason, or conscience, as the source of all obligation. Like Rousseau, and in keeping with the spirit of the European Enlightenment generally, Kant saw the egalitarian implications for society. For him, a republic based on a social contract was the ideal form of society; in such a society the individual had the right – and duty – to press for reform through the legislature (although not to rebel). And he argued that in the absolutist state of his time, the ruler had a duty in effect to rule as if such a republic was already in being.

But if the affinity to Rousseau is clear, there is a deeper continuity here too – with Luther. Kant was a long way from Luther's world of divine dispensation. But he was not so far at all from that inner world of Luther's where the individual made his or her life decisions free from any earthly authority. Kant insists that we make our moral judgments within the inescapable limits of our knowledge, either about metaphysics or about the world of our experience, on our own as autonomous beings. This is the language of Luther, transposed into the thought-world of the Enlightenment. When Kant erects dutiful action as the only sure test of good will uncontaminated by any selfish ends, he is nurturing what was already an ingrained cultural impulse whose origin is Luther himself.

It is easy therefore to detect the impact of Luther on Kant – to see how the paradigm of the two kingdoms left its trace on Kant's autonomous individual who acts in accordance with the categorical imperative and with the obligations of a citizen of the state. As we have seen, Luther's true Christians did not need social coercion: but they were rare, so that the power of the state was essential to prevent social chaos. Kant's republic of equal, free human beings was likewise a long way from reality. So in practice Lutheran society had become a culture of duty (and duties), and Kant's influence was going to do nothing other than reinforce this. The imprint of this culture is detectable in so many ways in German public life. All over the north of Germany, for example, gravestones from the time of the Second Reich celebrated the selfless devotion to duty of loved ones – in terms such as the following from the grave of one Emma Kessmann, buried in 1908 in a cemetery in the Prenzlauer Berg district, Berlin:

Stets einfach war Dein Leben,
Du dachtest nie an Dich.
Nur für die Deinen streben
Hieltst Du für Glück und Pflicht.

(Your life was always simple; you never thought of yourself.

To strive for your loved ones was all your happiness and
duty.)

Somehow the combination of Glück und Pflicht – happiness
and duty – is telling. They would not fit together so naturally on
an English tombstone. But this was not just a Lutheran preoccupation: reflecting on his life experience in 1962, the Catholic
Rhinelander Konrad Adenauer said: 'Das Glück besteht nicht
in großen Erfolgen oder in der Sicherung des einmal Erreich-
ten. Das Glück besteht allein in der Pflichterfüllung, und darin,
dass man zu dem steht, was man für richtig hält, auch wenn
man dabei unterliegt.' – 'Happiness is not to be found through
great success or in securing what you have achieved. Happiness lies only in fulfilling your duty, and in holding to what you
think is right even if it means losing.'[7] From the architect of the
new post-war West Germany – Catholic and no sympathiser
for anything that had been Prussian – comes that same sense
that duty is the source of happiness. This may have begun as
Lutheran doctrine and grown into a Prussian obsession; but it
became deeply embedded in the German psyche more broadly
and lived on through and beyond Stunde Null.

There was the risk that this sense of duty could be hijacked
by a state whose purposes were seen as transcending the purposes of the individual. In Germany, moreover, this risk was
all the bigger because the state could so readily play on deep-
seated fears of social chaos too, born of folk memories of the
Thirty Years War and much else besides. Maybe the inner
freedom of Luther's Christian or Kant's autonomous being
was sacrosanct; but the widely diffused sense of duty could all
too easily be degraded into supine obedience to the state, for
fear of the alternative.

Well before the ambitious state of the Second Reich came into existence, it was already clear that the fear of social chaos and the demand for obedience would leave their mark on the German consciousness. This is reflected in some of the greatest German literature of the age. Friedrich Schiller's *Die Räuber* – The Robbers (or bandits) – and Heinrich von Kleist's *Michael Kohlhaas* are brilliant treatments of the violence triggered by rejection and/or injustice, and of the complex issues of loyalty and obedience which could be exposed by social breakdown.

In Schiller's phenomenally successful first play from 1780, an elder son, popular and idealistic, is cheated of his inheritance by a calculating younger son who successfully manipulates his weak father. The elder son is banished and then becomes an ambiguous Robin Hood-like brigand who is dragged into a moral morass in which his oath of loyalty to his fellow outlaws prevents him from returning to the woman he really loves. In the end, the younger son kills himself in terror at the prospect of being captured by his brother's band; the elder son, distraught by the complex dilemmas of his violent career, is begged by his despairing lover to put an end to her life. He does so, before turning himself in to the authorities.

Kohlhaas, based loosely on a real figure from Luther's time, suffers extortion at the hands of a Junker's official. He is unable to get redress and goes on a rampage in pursuit of revenge; in Kleist's 1811 novella, Kohlhaas is finally given justice against the Junker, but is also condemned to death for his banditry. Whilst on the scaffold, he gets even with authority by refusing to reveal a prophecy he has been given by a gypsy as to the fate of the ruling dynasty; he submits willingly to execution, taking his secret with him.

At one level, for both Schiller and for Kleist, the circle is squared: both the inner compulsion for justice and also the social need to restore order are satisfied. But the resolution is deeply ambiguous. In reality, the story ends, in both cases, with an uncomfortable question, not with an answer. Both reflect the underlying fear that chaos lies just beneath the ordered surface. The tension is unresolved because of this perpetual possibility. What has happened before can happen again and cannot be forgotten. Order is precious and German history had looked the alternative in the face. Therefore duty is an existential imperative.

If *Die Räuber* and *Michael Kohlhaas* explore what happens when the disorder below the surface is laid bare, then Kleist's remarkable, provocative and controversial play *Der Prinz von Homburg* (written in 1810 but not performed until 1821, well after Kleist's death by suicide) explores just how far the demands of duty must go to preserve order. The play is centred on the battle of Fehrbellin in 1675, where the Prussians destroyed a Swedish army and brought their invasion and occupation of Brandenburg to an end. The play tests to the limit the demands of military obedience – even when disobedience achieves victory – and the price of disobedience. Does the duty of obedience unto death mean that disobedience – even in victory – must be punished by death? Once again, the answer is deeply ambiguous: the prince escapes execution – in an excruciating scene which is the reverse of the famous execution in Puccini's *Tosca* – because the king succumbs to the pleas of others to save the hero. Has the social order been strengthened or put at risk? Has duty triumphed or been sacrificed?

It is hard to imagine this play emerging from any other European culture. The unsettling questions – what is duty? what is loyalty? – would trouble the German soul with its deep fear of disorder until well into the 20th century. This sense of ingrained duty could produce remarkable and sacrificial heroism. Individuals – as true heirs of Luther or as true disciples of Kant – could see themselves as called to live out the full implications of their faith, to follow the full implications of that inner 'categorical imperative', and so were ready to risk the painful ambiguity of disobedience. We can see it in the heroism celebrated in Florestan's beautiful aria in Beethoven's *Fidelio*:

Wahrheit wagt' ich kühn zu sagen,
Und die Ketten sind mein Lohn.
Willig, duld' ich alle Schmerzen,
Ende schmählich meine Bahn,
Süßer Trost in meinem Herzen:
Meine Pflicht hab' ich getan!

(Boldly I dared to speak the truth, and my reward is these chains. Willingly I bear all the pain as I end my life in this disgrace. But sweet is the consolation in my heart: I have done my duty.)

This was the inner duty, a duty which called for defiance and was the exact reverse of slavish obedience. We can see it in such real life examples from the Third Reich as Dietrich Bonhoeffer or the Valkyrie conspirators or the Scholl family (all of whom we shall come back to later). But the culturally ingrained sense of duty could also produce the supine loyalty of very senior military leaders such as Keitel and Jodl, whose deference to Hitler even in the last days could seem almost comic, even at the time.

What neither Luther nor Kant envisaged was a state that could – so to speak – take on a life of its own. For both the state exists to keep order and maintain the peace. For Luther, as for any leader of his time, it also had a responsibility to maintain the true religion. He was clear as to the civil duty of obedience. Kant elaborates other duties, for example in connexion with the right to property and political rights and responsibilities. But that the state should develop ambitions or become a cultural entity with its own purposes over and beyond those of its members was alien to both. Yet that was the direction in which the 18th century was moving.

The change was subtle and gradual: it was paralleled by the decline of confessional and (more slowly) of dynastic politics, and was bound up with the growth of national consciousness throughout much of Europe. The interaction between dynastic ambitions of rulers and national identity was complex, and it would be easy to over-simplify the story. Louis XIV was the archetypal absolute ruler – even if there is no evidence that he ever actually said *'L'état, c'est moi'*. Yet even this monarch who subdued his aristocracy and built the resplendent palace of Versailles to ensure that all understood what absolute rule meant – even he knew that he was the embodiment of the grandeur of France and not just the Sun King.

As for Frederick the Great, half a century later and well into the age of the Enlightenment, he famously described himself as the first servant of the state. Frederick was of course an absolute ruler. But his description of himself reveals that there had been a subtle shift in the understanding of what 'absolute' meant. This is evidenced by his pithy summary of the responsibility of the citizen in his political testament of 1752: 'the first duty of the citizen is to serve the fatherland'. The duty was to the state – to the fatherland – not to the ruler per se (although of course for Frederick that duty to the state certainly entailed obedience to the ruler).

Whilst it may not have been obvious to Frederick, or to most other rulers of the time, we can see from a later vantage point how this could only be a transitional stage. It was not a durable settlement, for two reasons: firstly, absolutism would in the end be confronted with the intrinsically democratic claims of the Enlightenment. And secondly, no existing German state was coterminous with any definition of German cultural identity, so that none of them – not Prussia, not Austria, not Bavaria or Saxony, and certainly not any of the smaller principalities and dukedoms that dotted the face of the German map – was meaningfully a fatherland. As Europe as a whole was moving into the era of 19th century nationalism, this mattered more and more. Germany was, as we have seen, on a journey towards unification built around a national cultural identity for the first time in centuries. The journey was one which would end in the creation of a – or *the* – true German Vaterland (and even then would leave significant numbers of Germans, especially those of Austria-Hungary, outside it). Moreover, because there was an insecurity – a fragility – about this new Vaterland based on an old cultural identity, it would be proclaimed all the more aggressively and the demand for loyalty would be all the more assertive.

This change would give the sense of duty a whole new focus. The duty to the state was no longer just a recognition of its right and responsibility to uphold the social order and keep the peace. If the state was a cultural identity, then the individual became a part of that identity. The state was (or claimed to be) in a sense not just a Gesellschaft but a Gemeinschaft.

In that case, its citizens owed a duty to it which arose because their identity was part of its identity and its identity was part of theirs.

Thus the duty of obedience was now rooted not just in the fear of chaos but in identity. This was a much higher claim. It was as if – to use Kant's terminology – the duty to the state no longer consisted only of coercible duties of justice (Recht), but was now becoming what he would call a duty of virtue – a duty of love – to the state as an identity. It was as if the state could now compete for the faith, for the love and the loyalty of the inner Lutheran soul. It was as if the state itself could be the 'other' of Kant's 'categorical imperative', which had to be treated – like a person, a rational being – as an end and not just as a means. Where this could lead, we shall see in the next three chapters. But we already know about the journey's end, in the Berlin bunker.

But before continuing with that journey, it is worth noting something else about that sense of duty which is so distinctively German, with all its strength and its brittleness. Because perhaps it does not just begin with a seed sown by Luther. It may be that there is an even deeper root to this tree. The Teutonic Knights, whose realm morphed into East Prussia, took a solemn oath of obedience to God and to their Grand Master in the following terms:

Ich gelobe und verspreche Keuschheit des Leibes, ohne Eigentum zu leben und Gehorsam Gott und Sankt Marien sowie dem Meister des Ordens vom deutschen Haus und seinen Nachfolgern nach der Regel und der Gewohnheit des Ordens des deutschen Hauses, und dass ich gehorsam sein will bis in den Tod.

(I promise to be chaste in my body, to live without possessions and to be obedient to God, Holy Mary and to the Master of the Teutonic Order and his successors according to the rules and practices of the Order; and that I will be obedient unto death.)

When Duke Albrecht brought the Order to an end in 1525, many such Knights settled down permanently in Prussia and their families will have gradually evolved as Lutheranised Junkers. And perhaps something of the ethos of the Order lived on in a new way in this class which dominated the political life of the Prussian state and increasingly therefore in 19th century Germany as well, in addition to providing so much of the military leadership of both the Second and Third Reichs. A little over 400 years later, the Defence Minister of the Nazi Government, General von Blomberg, a Junker straight out of the mould, arranged for the entire Wehrmacht to take an oath of personal loyalty to Hitler whose terms clearly echo that ancient oath of the Teutonic Knights:

Ich schwöre bei Gott diesen heiligen Eid, daß ich dem Führer des deutschen Reiches und Volkes, Adolf Hitler, dem Oberbefehlshaber der Wehrmacht, unbedingten Gehorsam leisten und als tapferer Soldat bereit sein will, jederzeit mein Leben einzusetzen.

(I swear before God this sacred oath of unconditional obedience to the leader of the German Reich and people, Adolf Hitler, commander in chief of the Wehrmacht, and that I will be ready as a brave soldier at any time to give my life.)

The power of this oath came from its roots deep in the German psyche. Its hold over too many would become apparent as the Third Reich headed towards the abyss. So yes, it was a specifically German journey, and on this journey that widespread sense of duty provided the stamina which made it possible to keep going all the way to the end. *Die verdammte Pflicht und Schuldigkeit …*

But the compulsion of duty does not explain the direction of the journey: for that we have to look to that other striking characteristic of the German identity as it was emerging in the 19th century: the sense of destiny which drove and was nurtured by unification, and which was articulated, in different ways, by a series of thinkers, poets and other influential figures in the 19th century. The sense of destiny became a vivid inspiration within the Second Reich as it asserted itself on the European stage. It gave that ingrained sense of duty a new and fateful focus. And in the next chapter we turn to this vision which came to excite so many, but which in the end became a nightmare.

4

The Awakening of Germania

WE HAVE LOOKED that cursed duty in the face. Next we have to look at the sense of destiny which so marked the mood of Wilhelmine Germany. Not that it was unique. The British had a strong sense of imperial destiny at the same time; Russian nationalists were entranced by pan-Slav dreams; and the new United States had been imbued with a belief in their Manifest Destiny to absorb the whole of the North American continent; while in the first half of the 20th century, Japan was driven by its determination to create and dominate a co-prosperity sphere in East Asia. So the sense of destiny in the newly unified and superficially confident Germany was neither unique nor out of keeping with the temper of the age. And if the Second Reich felt that it was being denied its place on the world stage by the existing incumbents – and resented this deeply – so did Japan. So, much more recently, has China. So, perhaps, does post-Soviet Russia. The resentful assertiveness of Germany before the First World War is neither unique nor incomprehensible.

And yet this was different. It was distinctive, and dangerous, for two reasons. First, there was a fragility to Germany's identity which was quite unlike that of any of the other major powers then or since. This is not to say that others did not have identity crises: but it is to say that German insecurity about its identity was different in kind. Others were torn apart by civil war at different times in their histories: England in the 17th century, the United States in the 19th, Russia and China in the 20th. France spent the 19th century see-sawing between different forms of government punctuated by bloody uprisings, in the wake of the trauma of Revolution and the rise and fall of Napoleon. Both Britain and France have had what might be called colonial identity crises – Britain in Ireland and France in Algeria (and of course both, as well as Russia, have had to come to terms with the loss of empire more generally). Yet none of these countries has had a history which posed questions about its very identity in the way that the centuries of history had done for Germany.

Austria-Hungary did have an identity problem of course: but its problem was straightforward – it simply was a collection of nationalities and cultures with no natural identity or coherence. A closer parallel to that inner German vulnerability was perhaps that of Italy, and it is no coincidence that Italy's experience in the period up to the Second World War was in so many ways an inefficient mirror of Germany's. Italy too had been denied unity by the facts of history; and it had suffered too from the depredations of foreigners (including Germans of course). Even Italy, however, had not suffered from the religious and cultural fractures caused by the upheavals of the 16th and 17th centuries (albeit the relationship with the papacy and the Papal States posed specifically Italian issues).

This distinctive fragility of the German identity was not relieved by unification; indeed, the extraordinary way in which unification came about simply revealed how much self-doubt there was beneath the bombastic surface. If in the case of Italy weakness of identity and the resultant inferiority complex was to prove problematic and dangerous enough, how much more would it prove to be so in the case of a much larger, better run and more militarised Second Reich.

The second reason why the German sense of destiny was different is entwined with the first: part of the reason for that fragility was that it was underpinned by the strong sense of victimhood which we have already noted. Britain had no victim psychology: indeed, to its rivals in Europe and to the nationalists in its empire it seemed to be self-assured to the point of overweening. France had no victim psychology either, at least before 1871. Even after that, there was plenty of agonised dispute about what sort of state the modern France should be, as well as fear of what the new Germany might do next and a yearning for revenge for the loss of Alsace-Lorraine; but this was a long way from the sense of victimhood which became so deeply rooted in the German folk memory.

How real was this? It would of course be anachronistic to imagine any widespread yearning for national identity before the time of Luther. Yet even by his time the Empire had already become known as the Holy Roman Empire of the German Nation. By then it was already clear that the German lands had a shared sense of grievance against an increasingly worldly and corrupt Church of Rome. This was expressed in a highly influential document entitled *Gravamina Nationis Germanicae* – Grievances of the German Nation. Adopted by the Reichstag in 1458, it asserted amongst other things that the Curia in Rome was run by Frenchmen, Spaniards and Italians, whilst Germany was paying through the nose to fund all the decadence. Later, when Luther had become convinced that a break with the papacy was inevitable, he issued one of his most important pamphlets in 1521 under the title: *An den Christlichen Adel Deutscher Nation* – To the Christian Nobility of the German Nation.

Neither the *Gravamina* nor Luther's pamphlet should be taken as showing that a German nation already existed in the 19th century sense of the term. Even after Luther we should be careful about reading later attitudes into the thought world of the time. During the Thirty Years War, for example, how widespread was any sense of German identity? And how widespread at the time was any sense of resentment that the German lands were at the mercy of foreigners? The fact is that the identity of German lands and culture remained precarious; in the 18th century the Vaterland could just as easily have been Prussia or Saxony rather than Germany.

Yet, as we have already seen, we have the evidence of Gryphius's moving poem 'Thränen des Vaterlandes', written in the midst of the Thirty Years War, and in which the Vaterland is indeed Germany as a whole. And the sense of victimhood is clear. In the sonnet, Gryphius's anger at the 'frecher Völker Schar' – the brazen hordes of foreigners – who despoil and destroy in the German lands, is almost palpable. A century later, far from gradually fading, this outrage at what had happened was if anything growing in intensity. By the end of the 18th century, Schiller was explicit on the depredations of foreigners in his essay on the war which he published in 1792. A long paragraph on the devastation inflicted on the German countryside, the incineration of towns and the endless sufferings of ordinary people, all luridly and powerfully described, reaches its climax in the telling comment that:

Alle diese Wunden schmerzten umsomehr, wenn man sich erinnerte, daß es *fremde* Mächte waren, welche Deutschland ihre Habsucht aufopferten und die Drangsale des Krieges vorsätzlich verlängerten, um ihre eigennützigen Zwecke zu erreichen.

(All these wounds were all the more painful when one recalled that it was *foreign* powers that sacrificed Germany to their greed and deliberately prolonged war in all its harshness for their own purposes.)[8]

By the 19th century the message was clear: a host of writers graphically elaborated on the havoc caused by the war, typically echoing the perspective of the Protestants of the time (rather than of the Empire) not least because it dovetailed with a Prussian – so-called *'kleindeutsch'* or little German (because it excluded Catholic Austria) – approach to unification.

So the Germany that became the Second Reich, although increasingly powerful economically and militarily, had a fragility and an insecure resentfulness about it. As tragedy loomed, the cultural life of Germany was partly feeding this beast and partly seeking to escape from it along paths which took it deep into the German soul. This journey needs exploring because of its universal significance. For Germany, despite the trauma of its history and the extraordinary moral and physical collapse of 1945, is also the inheritor of one of the greatest, most prolific and creative human cultures the world has ever known. It is as much this as anything else that makes its self-destruction not just horrific but profoundly and enduringly mysterious.

None of us can ever escape our pasts. We know this is true of individuals: 'the child is father of the man' – to use

Wordsworth's famous line – whether we like it or not. But it is true of countries (or cultures) too: we cannot uproot the tree from its soil – whether in bursts of revolutionary zeal (France in 1789, Russia in 1917, China in 1949) or because collapse seems so total that there is nothing left worth saving (Germany in 1945 – far more so than Japan in 1945). As time goes by, some continuities become more and more obvious, for all the radical changes wrought by such terrible upheavals. This is as true for Germany's *Kultur* as for any other. It is fundamentally important to recognise that the German word Kultur is much more comprehensive than the English concept of culture. Kultur embraces not only the products of human creativity – the arts and architecture, the literature, the philosophy, the music – but also the roots of that creativity; the inner spiritual instincts, the view of the world, the approach to education, the corporate social psychology. In this deep sense, the Kultur has defined German self-awareness in the absence – for so much of its history – of a political or geographic identity.[9]

Much of German culture in medieval times was influenced by French sources of inspiration. In particular, the *Minnesänger* – the composers and singers of courtly love poetry of the high Middle Ages – traced their themes back to the troubadours of Provence. There was, however, one major literary creation of the period which was to have a marked impact on German self-understanding in the 19th and 20th centuries, and which had more deeply German roots: the *Nibelungenlied*, which dates from the early 13th century. The saga disappeared from the collective memory during the course of the upheavals of the 16th century, but it was rediscovered in the 18th, when it was trumpeted as the

German *Iliad*. It was, as we shall see, to become the source of a myth of loyalty and treachery that would be drawn on repeatedly in the Second and Third Reichs as Germany followed what the leadership defined as its destiny. And, after much reworking by Richard Wagner, it became – in the form of his magnificent and unique opera cycle *Der Ring des Nibelungen* – part of the patrimony of humanity in the modern world. We shall come back later to what this huge and enduring masterpiece has to tell us about the German identity in the 21st century.

Later, as Renaissance humanism began to spread in Europe north of the Alps in the 15th century, Germany saw a new momentum in literature and in art. Its spread was intimately connected with the spread of the new printing presses. Thus, for example, Sebastian Brandt's *Das Narrenschiff* – the Ship of Fools – describes the journey of a boatload of fools, steered by fools, towards the fools' realm of Narragonia. This vibrant and biting social satire, published in 1494, just a generation before Luther, was immensely popular well beyond the German lands. And in the world of art, three very different figures – all contemporaries who died within three years of each other – are yet more evidence of the sudden burst of German creativity: Matthias Grünewald, whose religious traditionalism produced the intense emotion of the Isenheim altarpiece at Colmar in Alsace – one of the most extraordinary pieces of Renaissance religious art anywhere in Europe; Tilman Riemenschneider, the woodcarver and sculptor whose figures, sometimes religious, sometimes ordinary folk, are quite astonishingly lifelike; and, best known of the three and surely the greatest artist of the northern Renaissance, Albrecht Dürer, whose prolific output of paintings, portraits and prints made him rich and famous well beyond Germany when he was still in his twenties.

But it was Luther who gave Germany a new and truly distinctive Kultur whose imprint on much of German creativity ever since is impossible to miss. Not that this cultural impetus was limited to the Lutheran or Protestant areas of Germany; and other influences, especially from the Italian baroque were clearly of major importance too, particularly in Catholic religious architecture and in music. But Luther, as we have already noted, stabilised the language – above all through his translation of the Bible, which has the same literary standing in Germany that the 1611 Authorised Version of the Bible has in English.[10] He was also a gifted religious poet and almost certainly had a strong sense of melody; he composed many hymns, and in the case of his most famous – 'Ein feste Burg ist unser Gott' – A Safe Stronghold Our God Is Still – he may well have also composed the tune with which it is associated to this day. This instinct for the use of hymns with popular tunes that could move a congregation in worship was taken up by generations of successors, both poets and composers (including Heinrich Schütz and – above all – Johann Sebastian Bach).

Luther also strongly emphasised the role of education in equipping the individual to make life choices. The impact of this was eventually felt in all realms of cultural expression, not just the religious, and through all the German lands. There are literally dozens of examples of great German intellectual leaders – writers, philosophers, scientists – who grew up in the households of Lutheran pastors. This new German energy, both spiritual and intellectual, was so rich in its creativity that it evolved into something much more universal, whose impact has spread far beyond the German lands and beyond the German language.

Thus the contribution of Germany to human cultural enrichment has been immense and many-sided. Taken as a whole, it is unsurpassed by any of the other great Eurasian cultures. Down the centuries since Luther, and especially from the 18th century on, the wealth of creativity in art, in architecture, in philosophy, in science and in literature is astonishing; and in music its legacy reigns supreme to this day.

In the visual arts: from the riches of 16th century art (Cranach the Elder and Holbein the Younger), to the powerful romanticism of Caspar David Friedrich in the 19th century, and on to the widely influential expressionists of the 20th century, this was a tradition which, if not as rich as Italian, French, Spanish, Dutch or even English art, was nevertheless as intense as any of them. And in architecture and design: from the soaring brick Gothic churches of the north to the 18th century baroque splendours of Potsdam or the now beautifully restored Dresden and of such churches as Vierzehnheiligen or the Wieskirche; to the exquisite taste of the unhappy and disturbed Ludwig II of Bavaria (Neuschwanstein, Linderhof and Herrenchiemsee); to the monumental grandeur of Karl Friedrich Schinkel's Berlin (Unter den Linden); to the 1920s Bauhaus in Dessau (whose style and philosophy eventually spread throughout the world); not to mention hundreds of classically pretty town squares and country houses which have survived all the destruction of recent centuries – in so many ways this country is a treasure store of eye-catching architectural beauty and interest.

In philosophy: if France is the soil of rationalism (fundamentally Cartesian as it is to this day), and Britain is the home of empiricism and pragmatic utilitarianism (with John Locke and David Hume as its presiding geniuses), then Germany is the home of metaphysics and systems. 'I am therefore I think' – to reverse René Descartes's famous dictum – captures one pole of the German psyche, still in evidence in the 21st century. Kant is undoubtedly the subtlest, profoundest and strongest influence on German thought since Luther. But the roles of Georg Wilhelm Friedrich Hegel, Arthur Schopenhauer, Karl Marx, Friedrich Nietzsche, perhaps – though more controversially – Martin Heidegger, and in recent decades Jürgen Habermas, are crucial too. We will come back to the role of German philosophical thought in the evolution of the German consciousness and sense of identity at various points as we follow the German journey all the way into present times.

In its scientific achievement, another pole of German intellectual creativity is evident for all to see. Germany became enormously influential in anthropology, in archaeology, in classical scholarship, in theology and in historiography. It produced a large proportion of the leading mathematicians, physicists, chemists, medical scientists, metallurgists and biologists of the 19th century. It applied fundamental research to industrial production more effectively than any other country in the world. Over a century later the industrial machine of the German economy is still one of the most formidable in the world and by far the strongest in Europe. Germany also reflected more systematically on the social changes which were transforming modern human experience under the impact of the industrial revolution than any other country – leading the way in the creation of the new disciplines of sociology and psychology. Much that we now take for granted about the way we live, and about the way we think about the way we live, we owe to inquisitive German minds of the 19th and early 20th centuries.

In German literature, yet another pole of the cultural psyche comes to the fore: Romanticism was a phenomenon of English (and, later, French) culture, but it took on a peculiarly intense tone in Germany, whose literature from the late 18th century onwards is full of restless activity, combined sometimes with a sense of foreboding. 'Im Anfang war die Tat' – in the beginning was the deed – to quote the famous cry of Faust as he twists the opening words of St John's Gospel and rejects words, ideas and books, and embarks on his rampage through a life of experiences brought to him by the devil. In some ways he is as much 'Everyman' as he is a true German archetype – but the hero who acts (and sometimes destroys himself) has centre stage often in Schiller, Goethe, Kleist and on into the 20th century (in increasingly urban, proletarian and often antiheroic guises – in Heinrich Mann, Hermann Hesse, Alfred Döblin, Hans Fallada) – so often, indeed, that he has to be seen as a key leitmotiv of German self-understanding.

Then there is music – a realm of human creativity which to this day is a German dominated world. More than any other art form, Germans have seen music as expressing something of their innermost being. As the 19th century German historian Johann Gustav Droysen put it, at a time of rising German self-awareness and yearning, this was the 'most German of arts'.[11] It was the purest manifestation of German culture's depth, of its world-historical significance and of its power to speak to the human condition. ETA Hoffmann described Beethoven's electrifying Symphony No 5 as 'absolute music'. The essentially romantic idea that music can draw the human spirit into the absolute underpinned the German self-image as people of music – or even as *the* people of music – well into the 20th century (and perhaps even beyond). And indeed, who are the enduringly influential creative geniuses of music – and not just in Europe but increasingly throughout our globalized world? From Bach onwards and well into the 20th century (Richard Strauss's haunting *Four Last Songs*, for example, date from 1948), the power of the enormous heritage of German music to enthral is probably endless (although whether its creativity has now died out is a question we shall have to return to later). There are other great musical traditions of course – Italian, Russian, French, English – but none as rich, varied and universal in their resonance.

All of this makes up the German Kultur as it evolved towards the mid-20th century: rooted in the German language and yet also rich and varied, with both Protestant and Catholic influences clearly evident (especially in architecture and in music), and with Jewish brilliance on display in all fields (Moses Mendelssohn in philosophy; his grandson Felix Mendelssohn Bartholdy, Gustav Mahler or Arnold Schönberg in music; Heinrich Heine in literature; Max Liebermann in the visual arts – to name but a few).

So where in all this are the roots that nourished a growing sense of destiny in 19th century Germany?

The place where we have to begin is the cultural revolution unleashed by Luther. Philosophically, the Lutheran world view (with its doctrine of the two kingdoms) became more and more influential with the rise of Prussia in the 18th century. To be clear, although this was Protestant doctrine formulated as much to counter the institutional claims of the Roman Catholic Church as to bolster the claims of the princes, the practical implications of a two-kingdoms view of the world were far from alien in spirit to 18th century Catholic rulers. They, like their Protestant counterparts, sought to keep the institutional church subservient in practice and out of their political way. But Luther's doctrine also privatised the individual's spiritual life, and so gave a distinctively German impetus to a movement of the European spirit of the late 17th century whose impact on intellectual life – on the Kultur – was to change Germany for ever: the Enlightenment.

In a sense we are all children of the Enlightenment, whose roots lie back in the European Renaissance and in the Christian humanism which was pervasive in the atmosphere of Luther's time. Its momentum picked up from the second half of the 17th century, as the religious passions and confessional strife triggered by the Reformation started to peter out. Optimism about the power of reason to answer human questions and to meet human needs was spreading through Europe. For many this meant radically calling into question traditional religious assumptions about the nature of existence and therefore undermining the old certainties. In Germany, the enormous influence of Kant gave a distinctive cast to the Enlightenment, or – to give it the German term by which its particularly German manifestation became known – *Aufklärung*. If the French Enlightenment was more radically revolutionary (and anti-clerical), and the English and Scottish Enlightenments were economic and libertarian, the German Enlightenment was at once more metaphysical and more compatible with absolutism. As we have seen, Kant's answer to Luther's question about grace and salvation – that inner realm where each individual makes his or her life choices – was, in effect, yes: you make your own decisions, within the limits of what you know, about what you believe and how you live.

But in that case the question that needed an answer was one about commitment: what could you devote yourself to, in the absence of any demonstrable metaphysical certainties? This might be described as the post-Enlightenment – or post-Lutheran, or post-Kantian – question. It is as arguably as pressing today as ever, and we shall have to return to German angst about it at the dawn of the 21st century later.

In the Germany of the 18th and 19th centuries, there were various possible answers to this question. The first was the religious answer – the answer of personal Christian faith and commitment, represented particularly by the pietist movement in the Protestant regions. Pietism had much in common with movements for renewal in other Protestant countries; similar impulses were felt in England and America. It is easy – from the perspective of a highly secularised 21st century – to underestimate its power. In Germany, Pietism spread during the second half of the 17th century as the expression of a yearning for the pursuit of personal holiness (and can be seen in many ways as a reaction to the ossification of official church Lutheranism).

But it was not just a retreat from the world. From the late 17th century onwards, especially under the leading influence of Philipp Jakob Spener, a brilliant 17th century theologian whose writings were to have enormous influence on a whole generation of new leaders seeking renewal in religious life, Pietism developed a strong ethos of hope for the future. That hope was founded on the expectation of the coming millennial reign of Christ on earth. True to the activism integral to the biblical presentation of Christ's teaching, this expectation became the motive for utopian programmes of reform centred on the remarkable work of August Hermann Francke at the new University of Halle, which Spener had been influential in founding. This work included the establishment of a remarkable orphanage and schools programme in Halle as well as running theological education on pietist principles for Christian leaders both in Germany and further afield. Best known of all, Pietism produced Zinzendorf's Herrnhut community of families – a model which spread outside Germany, and particularly in America where they remain a presence on the social landscape in, for example, the Moravian communities of Pennsylvania.

In some cases there was also a strong mystical bent to this new zeal, which interacted with and drew on other non-biblical mystical sources of inspiration (including Jewish cabalistic teachings). But what all these religious experiences had in common was a yearning for a real inner fulfilment – a personal commitment which would – to use a timeless phrase from the 20th century English poet TS Eliot – cost not less than everything. Its impact on German culture was profound, and went well beyond those who made personal pietistic commitments. Particularly in East Prussia, with the blessing and encouragement of Friedrich Wilhelm I, it was pietists who pioneered universal education, established homes for the poor and ran the theological faculty at Königsberg. No less a figure than Kant was influenced by and clearly respected the pietist teachers he knew there. Pietists were also very influential in Prussian military life: many of the army chaplains appointed under Friedrich Wilhelm were pietists. Their influence helped foster a strong sense of vocation and to instil discipline and a culture of dutifulness amongst the officer corps. This ethos set a tone, not only in the military but also in the bureaucracy, which endured into the 20th century.

But the inevitable truth was that Pietism was always going to be something of a minority calling. It would never take centre stage in the cultural life of Germany. Its underlying weakness was that for all its spiritual intensity and its commitment to social action, the rationalist and inquisitive spirit of the Enlightenment was always likely to be alien to it; yet it was that spirit which set the intellectual mood of the age. There was never any likelihood of a reversion to pre-Enlightenment patterns of faith and metaphysical certainty.

Other movements of the human spirit would, come the 19th century, contest the rationalism of the Enlightenment, notably Romanticism. And pietistic mysticism was indeed one of the streams that fed much 19th century German thought. In particular, the influence of pietist metaphysics and mysticism on two figures whom we shall shortly look at in the context of Germany's growing sense of destiny – Friedrich Hölderlin and, even more importantly, Hegel – is demonstrable. Nevertheless, the Romantic reaction against Enlightenment rationalism was for the most part a long way removed from anything that could be described as orthodox Christian belief. The Romantics would never be good witnesses to the truth as the pietists understood it.

The fact is that Christian theology and praxis had lost the initiative. The theologian and philosopher Friedrich Schleiermacher wrote his highly influential 'Der christliche Glaube nach den Grundsätzen der evangelischen Kirche' – the Christian Faith According to the Principles of the Evangelical Church – in the 1820/30s. In it he argued that religion was a reflection of a deep human instinct for dependency, and that Christianity was an expression of that dependency rather than an objective metaphysical or even historical truth. As the 19th century wore on, others would set utopian themes at the heart of more political gospels. There were certainly some who journeyed from a mystical romanticism into – or even back into – orthodox Christianity. But it was often Catholicism which became their new home (not that the Catholicism they embraced was any more rationalist than pietist Protestantism, but it did offer the warmth of 'mother church' in a way that Protestantism by its essence could not).[12]

By the outbreak of the First World War there were very few creative intellectuals going into church leadership or exploring credible and authentic approaches to Christian theology in a post-Enlightenment thought-world. A quiet pietist holiness continued of course to strengthen the ordinary Christian lives of many individuals, including many in significant positions of influence (as it still does for some today). Its influence amongst the Prussian military was particularly notable: Alfred von Schlieffen, author of the notorious military strategy which was deployed at the outbreak of the First World War, was one such figure. Several of the Valkyrie conspirators in the Second World War were imbued with similarly deep pietist convictions.

But intellectual leadership was another matter: the running was being made by philosophers and poets, not by theologians. It is striking that when a young Dietrich Bonhoeffer – he who was to become in his short life the greatest German theologian of his time (as well as a courageous opponent from within of the Third Reich) – announced that he was opting for the career of a Christian pastor, the response of his highly educated family was one of amazement that he should contemplate hiding his light under a bushel in this way.

For the fact was that from the 18th century onwards – in Germany as elsewhere – other quite different ways were being explored to find spiritual rootedness in the absence of the traditional metaphysical certainties.

One way lay through the rediscovery of the ancient heritage of Greece and Rome. As the century wore on, more and more of the educated and the well-born of Europe made their pilgrimage to Italy – from the English *milordi* to German researchers: above all there was Johann Joachim Winckelmann, the brilliant son of a cobbler who, with the support of his highly intellectual aristocratic employer, was able to visit Rome, where he ended up spending several years researching the ancient ruins and the treasures of Greek and Roman civilisation. His 1764 masterpiece *Die Geschichte der Kunst des Althertums* – The History of the Art of Antiquity – became a bestseller not only in Germany but across Europe.

Rome had always been a destination for Christian pilgrimage, of course – Luther had been there, and been outraged by its worldliness and corruption. Others more easy-going than he were seduced by the sights, the splendours and perhaps as much as anything by the light of the Italian sun. But Winckelmann opened up the world of ancient Rome with its traces all around of past grandeur. Nor was it just Rome: although few made it at that time to Greece (which was further away and which was still under Ottoman rule), the remains of Greek civilisation in southern Italy entranced those who ventured that far. The love affair with classical Greece and Italy soon drew in an excited Goethe. It is hard for us to recover the newness of this: we are too used to easy travel and too familiar with the sights they were seeing for the very first time (and without all the convenience and the clutter of modern tourism).

For Goethe, the experience was transforming, as is clear

from his *Italienische Reise* – his reflections on his Italian
sojourn. And in his second novel, *Wilhelm Meisters Lehrjahre*
– Wilhelm Meister's Education – he captures something of the
ecstasy of the Italian sunlight and warmth in one of the most
famous lines in all German poetry (which became as much a
cliché as, say, Wordsworth's daffodils) when the tomboy circus
girl Mignon with her strangely hermaphroditic quality sings:

Kennst du das Land wo die Zitronen blühn,
Im dunklen Laub die Gold-Orangen glühen,
Ein sanfter Wind vom blauen Himmel weht,
Die Myrte still und hoch der Lorbeer steht,
Kennst du es wohl?
Dahin! Dahin
Möcht' ich mit dir, o mein Geliebter, zieh'n!

(Do you know the land where the lemon trees blossom,
where the golden oranges glow in the dark foliage, where a
gentle wind blows from the blue sky, and where the myrtle
is silent and the laurel stands tall? Do you know it well?
Thither, thither would I go with you, my beloved!)

But behind the captivation and the excitement was a more
serious philosophical – indeed, metaphysical – question: what
did all those ancient stories of gods and humans tell us about
the nature of the world and of human experience? Was this
some paradise we had left and lost? Could we – should we –
rediscover our rootedness in that ancient civilisation? Could
we learn more about the good, the beautiful and the true from
them than from the tired and desiccated Christian culture of
Northern Europe?

Some were certainly tempted to dally – to see in the ancient myths an old/new inspiration for humanity in the demystified age of the Enlightenment. Somehow the difference between the pale northern light and the strong warm southern light was all the difference between an austere, rigid culture weakened by centuries of medieval and Reformation metaphysics and dogma, and the aesthetically powerful experience of classical antiquity. Schiller's 1788 poem 'Die Götter Griechenlands' – the gods of Greece – captures the sense of loss:

Da ihr noch die schöne Welt regieret,
an der Freude leichtem Gängelband
Glücklichere Menschenalter führtet,
schöne Wesen aus dem Fabelland!
Ach! da euer Wonnedienst noch glänzte
Wie ganz anders, anders war es da!
Da man deine Tempel noch bekränzte,
Venus Amathusia!

(When you still reigned over the beautiful world, and led humanity in happier times on the gentle leash of joy, o beautiful ones from that fabled world, ah! how different, how utterly different it was, when it was still such glorious bliss to serve you, when your temple was still garlanded with wreaths, o Venus Amathusia!)

Yet for the most part they understood that it was over. Greece and Rome might provide a treasure trove of motifs for art, architecture and literature. But they could hardly be a focus of commitment or any meaningful answer to that post-Enlightenment question about commitment. Heinrich

Heine, nearly 40 years later, writes a much more dreamlike and ghostly poem on the same theme, with the dose of satire so characteristic of him. But he also hints at a different way of looking for truth: the Romantic search for meaning in nature:

Vollblühender Mond! In deinem Licht,
Wie fließendes Gold, erglänzt das Meer,
Wie Tagesklarheit, doch dämmrig verzaubert,
Liegts über der weiten Strandesfläche,
Und am hellblauen, sternlosen Himmel
Schweben die weißen Wolken,
Wie kolossale Götterbilder
Von leuchtendem Marmor.
[…]
Also sprach ich, und sichtbar erröteten
Droben die blassen Wolkengestalten,
Und schauten mich an wie Sterbende,
Schmerzenverklärt, und schwanden plötzlich.
Der Mond verbarg sich eben
Unter Gewölk, das dunkler heranzog;
Hochaufrauschte das Meer,
Und siegreich traten hervor am Himmel
Die ewigen Sterne.

(O moon in full bloom! In your light the sea gleams like flowing gold, like clear daylight, and yet duskily entranced, it lies along the broad strand; while in the light blue, starless sky the white clouds float like colossal statues of the gods, in gleaming marble … Thus I spoke, and above me the pale forms in the clouds blushed and looked at me like those who were dying, transfigured by pain, disappearing suddenly. The moon hid itself at that moment behind clouds which came on darker; the sea rose up high and, victorious in the heavens, came forth the eternal stars.)

So the answer of the Romantics, not just in Germany, was that art which celebrated the mysteriousness of nature, which was awed by the presence of the sublime, helped human beings to see themselves as part of that wider being. Such art could become in effect the new religion. Art could open the human spirit to the beautiful and the sublime and enable it to achieve wholeness – so Schiller argued in his writings on aesthetics. There were others too, all active over about two decades from around the time of the French Revolution. The remarkable flowering of German Romanticism had much in common with its contemporary British equivalent: the sense of the power and beauty of nature as evidence of, or gateway to – or even as actually being – the divine. This sense infuses the writings of Hölderlin and Novalis as it does those of Wordsworth and Coleridge (both of whom travelled in Germany in 1798). But in Germany, much more so than in Britain or France, the Romantics were closely involved in a wider philosophical movement of reflection – on the self's relation to the other, and on the nature of the absolute of which the self was just a part.

Perhaps no poet anywhere at the time was so absorbed by this identity of the human and the natural as Friedrich Hölderlin. This sad figure with his pietist background wrote intense, jagged poetry, far ahead of its time, his tones anticipating 20th century poetry. For him the Greek phrase *hen kai pan* – the one and all, or the oneness in all – became a watchword. *Hen kai pan* was the goal of art and the only answer to the human thirst for meaning. Tragically, he suffered what must have been some form of schizophrenic breakdown in his mid-thirties, living on for another four decades reclusively in a tower by the River Neckar in Tübingen, visited irregularly by only a few of his former friends. But after his death his poetry came to be treasured more and more as time went by. As a poet, he is arguably the greatest of them all. Yet somehow his fate is symbolic of a failure – the end of a road that sought ultimate meaning, a sort of religion, in art.

The reality was that these young idealists from educated backgrounds were as disconnected from ordinary life in the new century as were their English contemporaries. In the end the high road of Romanticism proved to be a lonely road which led further and further into the inner recesses of the soul. *Weltverwandlung durch Menschenverwandlung*[13] – changing the world by changing human beings – was no more possible through art than through Pietism. The Romantic hope was always going to be a vain aspiration – especially as society was now changing profoundly under the early impact of urbanisation. Very few of the bourgeoisie, which increasingly made up the new readerships and new audiences, were likely to be ready to climb to the mountain top where all would be one because the one was in the all.

The rise of an educated and urban bourgeoisie in Germany had its roots in Luther's social revolution. For with or without renewal of the inner life, Lutheranism's impact on the German *Kultur* through its commitment to education was profound and path-breaking. This emphasis on education arose originally from Luther's determination that every person should be able to read and interpret the Bible for themselves and reach their own life decisions. But education inevitably opened up broader vistas, especially after the dawn of the Enlightenment. Eighteenth century Prussia became the first state in Europe to introduce compulsory education, with a focus on the basic skills needed for a trained military and for work in an increasingly organised society in the early stages of mechanisation (as well as on what might be called the social skills needed for life in an ordered society). Education was – it might be argued – becoming not only a vehicle for the Kultur but also for the *Zivilisation* (this very German term carries connotations of mechanisation, monetization and materialism) whose emergence was inevitable with the onset of urbanisation and the industrial revolution. Both the artists and – later on, as we shall see – the völkisch nationalists saw Zivilisation as the degradation of real culture/Kultur. But it was the inevitable product of broad-based education. The post-Enlightenment century was not after all to be the century of the artist, but of the engineer. And this too was a legacy of Luther.

Yet as any Lutheran, Aufklärer or Romantic clearly understood, a technical education for industrial life did not make a whole person and left a spiritual void. Moreover, it did nothing to build a sense of community. Zivilisation has always been ambiguous (it raises the same questions today both in an Asia obsessed with technical progress and in a Europe unsure how to compete with it, as we shall see towards the end of this story). In 19th century Germany the question of community identity was being brought into sharper focus by the achievement of political identity. It was clear that there was no unifying religious expression that could fill the void. But if it was not going to be Christian faith (or individual religious renewal) that furnished the bonds of community, it was certainly not going to be the autonomous Kantian will or the Romantic's pursuit of the sublime either – these might work for the intellectual elite but not for the emerging Zivilisation). The risk was that something else would fill it.

One possible answer was socialism – whether the utopian and visionary kind represented by the Russian anarchists who were becoming influential at the time, or what Marx and Engels called scientific socialism (i.e. based on analysis of the forces at work in existing economic relationships). Marx was part historical determinist, part Romantic revolted by the alienation and suffering he and Engels documented, and part Promethean optimist who saw the proletariat defiantly seizing and realising its own utopian future. But the stark lesson of the 20th century is that even when it triumphs, socialism proves unable to inspire the human spirit for long, and all too rapidly dissolves into horrendous terror or soul-destroying bureaucracy. In 19th century Germany its prospects for inspiring the broad mass of urban workers were remote. This was partly because Bismarck had pulled the teeth from any genuinely revolutionary fervour amongst the industrial working classes with his insurance system. But also, the workers' party, the Socialist Party, although – and perhaps even because – it became politically significant as the largest party in the Reichstag, was too institutionalised and bureaucratic to be a real agitator for radical change. Mainstream socialism succumbed to the same fate as Lutheranism.

What filled the void, for many at all levels of society, was an emerging sense of the German destiny – that the German culture had a special richness rooted in the soil of ancient German traditions, that the German identity was being established on the world stage with a special mission, and that in the world-historical evolution of the human spirit this was now the German age.

There were several strands to all this. Historians were beginning systematically to investigate the past – both the classical past of the Ancient Greeks and the Romans and also the German past from Arminius to the high Middle Ages and the onset of the Reformation. Of ground breaking importance was the work of Leopold von Ranke, writing in the mid-19th century. This great historiographer and historian was, throughout his life, a pious Lutheran. His work on the Germany of the 15th and 16th centuries established a narrative about the emerging German identity which was crucial in the 19th century search for a German polity with real – i.e. historically rooted – cultural legitimacy.

Ranke famously defined the task of history as being to investigate the past 'wie es eigentlich gewesen' – as it really was. This is sometimes misunderstood as a rejection of the role of interpretation or evaluation in historical narrative. But it is generally recognised that this is neither desirable nor even possible. Rather, Ranke's objective was to present historical periods and events as far as possible on their own terms – and in particular without bringing to the task some form of Hegelian assumption about the nature of progress in human history. In fact, though, his narrative about the development of the German national identity focused strongly on the impact of the failure to achieve a comprehensive Reformation. This is a clear example of history seen through a prism – in this case, the prism of a 19th century understanding of national identity (and indeed a Prussian, Protestant perspective rather than an Austrian, Catholic one).

There was, secondly, a newly discovered (or rediscovered)

pride in the culture embodied in the German language – the rediscovery of its ancient myth-making and story-telling traditions. In a sense this was, once again, a delayed outworking of Luther's cultural revolution. This journey of discovery had already begun by the time Ranke was at work. Once again, it was a figure from a pious Lutheran background, Johann Gottfried Herder, who played a decisive role in this renewal. He studied under Kant in Königsberg, but was never happy with the cold rationalism of the Aufklärung, preferring a sense of the mystical which took him away from the confines of an East Prussian austerity, on journeyings via Paris, Strassburg and Weimar into a thought-world shared with the young Goethe as well as Schiller. His was a world of ancient myth – of the Old Testament, of the Greek myths and of the Old Norse and German stories as well. Herder's reverence for all things Gothic and for the popular folk stories and poems of the culture became a hugely influential inspiration for writers in the early 19th century – notably Achim von Arnim and Clemens Brentano. Their collection of folk songs in *Des Knaben Wunderhorn* – The Boy's Magic Horn – was published in 1805–8 and was in turn inspiration for several German composers over the rest of the century, above all for Mahler who repeatedly used the poems in song settings and in his symphonies.

Herder's celebration of the German language as the embodiment of this ancient and authentic culture went with a belief in the central role of the people. It was the voice of ordinary people – the common voice – which was the source of a homespun wisdom, based on real experience of life and on its rootedness in ancient mythical truths. This was new: the people – *das Volk* – was not just an uneducated rabble, but the essence of the nation and the creator of its culture. None of this was unique: British and French poets and artists too were reaching back into their medieval hinterlands for inspiration. The difference was that the Germans were discovering their identity more fully for the first time. This was an awakening which seemed full of mysterious possibilities.

Hölderlin, for one, sensed this. He, like others, knew that the old religion of antiquity – with its roots, as he saw, all the way back in the Indus Valley – was gone. And yet what those ancient gods symbolised was still mysteriously real and looking for new embodiment. And for him it was Germania – the innocent, receptive, feminine spirit nourished in the German soil – that would awaken to this priestly task. In 'Germanien', written at the turn of the 19th century, he sees a mysterious destiny for Germany. Here, the spirit of the old gods, represented by the image of an eagle that has flown over the land from far to the south and east, sings to the young, immature, feminine spirit of Germany:

Du bist es, auserwählt,
Alliebend und ein schweres Glück
Bist du zu tragen stark geworden,
Seit damals, da im Walde versteckt und blühendem Mohn
Voll süßen Schlummers, trunkene, meiner du
Nicht achtetest, lang, ehe noch Geringere fühlten
Der Jungfrau Stolz und staunten, wes du wärst und woher,
Doch du es selbst nicht wußtest. Ich mißkannte dich nicht,
Und heimlich, da du träumtest, ließ ich
Am Mittag scheidend dir ein Freundeszeichen,
Die Blume des Mundes zurück und du redetest einsam.
Doch Fülle der goldenen Worte sandtest du auch

Glückselige! mit den Strömen, und sie quillen unerschöpflich
In die Gegenden all. […]

(It is you who have been chosen: you have grown strong to
carry a heavy fortune in love for all – since the time when
you drowsed intoxicated, hidden in the woods amongst the
flowering poppies, not heeding me for a long while, even
before other lesser ones felt a maidenly pride and were
astonished at whose you were and where you came from –
although you yourself did not know. But I did not mistake
you, and whilst you dreamt I secretly left you at noon a
parting sign of friendship – the bloom of your mouth, and
you spoke alone. Yet, blessed, you also sent forth a golden
fullness of words with the streams which poured inex-
haustibly through all the regions around. […])

This subtle, difficult and almost untranslatable poetry was
taken up – controversially – by Heidegger in 1934 at a time
when he was a public intellectual figure within the Third
Reich. Whether or not Heidegger misappropriated Hölderlin
for his own highly complex theories of being, and whether or
not his association with the Third Reich automatically vitiated
his views (as it certainly has done for many), the truth is that
Hölderlin's poem needs to be seen in the context of its own
time and of Hölderlin's own philosophy and spirituality. For
him, poetry was the medium of truth about the oneness of all
being; and the priestly – and vulnerable – role of Germania
was to divine and to proclaim that truth for the future, for
an age that had left the ancient world behind it and risked
being lost without a new experience of the gods. 'Die Blume
des Mundes' – the flower of the mouth – is the gift of poetry,

the language which brings divine and mortal into one. And it was Germany's calling to share that language of mystical union with others – the regions all around.

But Hölderlin was a lone voice in his own inner wilderness. His perception of Germany as feminine was at variance with a *Deutschtum* – a German-ness – which was increasingly seen in very masculine terms. At the same time, others shared with him a more general sense that in a mysterious way the future would belong to Germany. What they meant by this was very different from Hölderlin's vision of a creative, harmonious, priestly, receptive role. But there were many who did see this as a spiritual commitment, a mission, a destiny; and this sense grew as the 19th century advanced.

The sense of destiny was underpinned by a view of world history that owed much to the work of Hegel, who should surely stand on almost as prominent a pedestal as Kant. Hegel was apparently eclipsed for a time by others – notably Marx – but has been increasingly recognised in recent decades for what he was: a – or even the – fundamental alternative (or counterpoint) to Kant, whose relevance to modern debates about the politics of identity in a globalising world is as profound as ever. Where Kant was sceptical about any metaphysical certainty and immovably focused on the rational, autonomous individual subject, Hegel was on a very different journey. He was not alone in seeking to cut through the veil of perception to an absolute that subsumed the self in a wider, all-embracing whole. As the light of the Aufklärung seemed to be growing dim, this was the quest of Romantics such as Hölderlin, Novalis and Friedrich Schlegel as they sought to experience and express that mysterious oneness of everything. But it was Hegel who turned the Absolute into the 'world spirit' which was actualising itself in human history through a phased historical momentum.

For Hegel there was an overall pattern to history that had conceptual affinities to the Christian doctrine of the fall and redemption: history had seen an age of innocence when people lived in unity and harmony with each other and their environment; followed by a fall which was the experience of Christendom and then of the Enlightenment – Kant's age of the spiritual autonomy of the individual subject without reference to, or integration with, community or nature. The third and final phase was now imminent: out of the culture of Germany would come a redemption which would see a new and higher unity achieved, which is the only real freedom for humanity. This was not a smooth, gradualist process of continuous improvement but a conflictual process in which evil and suffering would play a necessary part. The individual was not absolute, and the purpose of the individual was realised in serving the wider whole (which, in Hegel's thought, could however bear an uncomfortable resemblance to the actual Prussian state).

Although Hegel's reputation went into decline in the decades after his death, he had unleashed a probably endless debate about the individual, the community, progress, the state and social justice, which has certainly not lost in intensity or relevance in the midst of rapid world-historical change in the 21st century. He is often seen as little more than an apologist for the status quo and the Prussian state. But this is only partly fair: he saw history as an over-arching process which would culminate in a universality of human experience never before known. Nevertheless, it was he who argued explicitly that this momentum had reached its final phase in his time and that this would be the Germanic age.

The ugly racial and cultural Darwinism that became more and more vocal later on in the century was not unique to Germany, and it would certainly not be fair to blame this on Hegel (let alone on Herder or Hölderlin). But he gave it a philosophical substratum which was of the highest pedigree, and it was uniquely German. It is hard to imagine Hegel having flourished in the empiricist world of British thought or in the rationalist Cartesian world of French thought.

As we have seen, all of this developed alongside a growing national consciousness with its self-perceived victimhood. So several strands come together: the sense of victimhood underpins the insecure aggressiveness of the new Reich. A Hegelian sense of historical momentum underpins the Reich's sense of destiny. And this destiny would be worked out with a sense of duty which traced its origins a long way back, perhaps even finding an early resonance in that oath of the Teutonic Knights which demanded commitment even unto death.

So this was the awakening of Germania in the thought world of the 19th century – a theme that was in an important sense profoundly un-Lutheran (and even more un-Kantian), but which was at the same time quite distinctively German. It owed much to the Romantic movement of the late 18th and early 19th centuries; and its presiding philosophical genius was Hegel. This awakening fed what came to be recognised as the völkisch movement of the German spirit – of which more later. There was much in this movement's anti-urban, backward-looking celebration of traditional pastoral life and lore that had clear parallels in contemporary English artists, writers and musicians. But these were never in hock to aggressive national aspirations, first to unity and then to recognition on the world stage (Britain already had both). In Germany, on the other hand, this became the low road of Romanticism as the century wore on. That low road took German self-expression through a terrain of memories, dreams and – in the end – nightmares, as we shall see in a later chapter.

But first, in the next chapter, we need to look at the self-awareness of this newly awaking Germania. For this became in effect the awakening of the *Volk* – or, more precisely, of a völkisch understanding of the Volk and of its identity – with all its sinister undertones and eventually terrible outworking.

5

Dem Deutschen Volke

'*WIR SIND EIN VOLK!*' We are one people. This was the slogan carried on banners in the demonstrations during the heady days of 1989, as ever larger numbers of East Germans took to the streets of their cities to demand their freedom. When the Bundestag of the newly reunited Federal Republic moved into the newly remodelled Reichstag which had stood in ruins since the day it had been set on fire in 1933, it met in a building which retained, prominently over the neo-classical columns of its entrance portico, the words '*Dem deutschen Volke*'. It was as if the word had come out of quarantine: ever since May 1945 it had been a sensitive term which few Germans had been comfortable using.

The Reichstag had opened in 1894, at the height of the Wil-helmine era. Its heavy, over fussy style was that of a new nation determined to out-compete its older European neighbours. It was there to make a statement. By that time the meaning of the word '*Volk*' had taken on an assertive superiority for many in Germany, including many of its leaders, which was eventually to take the nation into the abyss. Now, more than a century later, the Volk has lost all those 'völkisch' connotations – and indeed the very use of the word begs questions about what the Volk is, a generation after reunification, for the new Germany in the new Europe. But that is for a later chapter. For now we need only note that the cry for reunification in 1989 – 'Wir sind ein Volk' – and the surviving dedication of the Reichstag – 'Dem deutschen Volke' – completely stripped, as they now are, of all those Second and Third Reich resonances – were the end of a centuries-old journey of self-discovery.

In the time of Friedrich Barbarossa there was no German people. 'Deutsch' simply referred to a language (which was, to be exact, a series of dialects rather than a single standardised language, as we have already noted). Only slowly did it come to define a people with an identity beyond the fact that they spoke this language. The language had a geography: gradually those lands where the language was spoken came to be identified as the German lands. And the language gave voice to stories and songs which made for a common heritage. Over time those who shared this heritage came to be seen and to see themselves as a people – or, to use the term which became fashionable in the 19th century, a race. The concept of race, as used in the 19th century throughout much of Europe, carried increasingly biological overtones, under the influence of vulgar Darwinist texts. But it is worth noting that the concept can trace its origins in the Spanish self-understanding as 'la raza' – a term which connoted an exclusive purity, over against the Moors and later the Native Americans. The supremacist tone was inescapable. (Even as late as the 1950s, the Spanish national day was called the 'Dia de la Raza' – until it was changed to the more straightforward 'Dia de la Hispanidad'.)

For Germany this was to be a journey with many twists and turns and some dangerous digressions, which took it eventually through the valley of the shadow of death. The start of the journey has no clear marker, but an early milestone was the first known reference, in 1474, to the Holy Roman Empire as 'Deutscher Nation' – of the German Nation – which became its official name in 1512. Then came Luther, whose legacy was to have a profound impact, both helping and hindering the development of this emerging German identity. The 18th century saw the discovery – led by Herder – of cultural identity in the language, traditions and history of the German lands. It saw the beginnings of modern historical studies. It also saw the beginnings of the yearning for freedom and for political identity – manifest perhaps above all in the works of Schiller.

Then came the French Revolution. Many of Germany's young thinkers and poets reacted excitedly to the French Rev- olution, just as their English contemporaries did ('bliss it was, that dawn to be alive ...' as Wordsworth famously wrote in *The Prelude*). Others were more cautious – Schiller, for example, despite the fact that he was already well known as a passionate advocate of liberty, having composed his 'Ode to Joy' in 1786. As for the older Goethe, he was predictably hostile. The grand old philosopher of the age – Kant – welcomed the enthusiasm of the young whilst denying that violent revolution could ever be morally appropriate.

Even amongst the enthusiasts, disillusionment soon set in. Beethoven famously scratched out his dedication to the Eroica symphony on hearing that Napoleon had crowned himself emperor in Paris. The experience of conquest and occupation by the Napoleonic armies was to fan the flames of a new movement of the German spirit, a *Volksbewegung* which brought a new consciousness of the people's identity as a people.

It expressed a pride in the history, traditions and destiny of the German people. As we have seen, this pride did not materialise out of nothing. Voices from the 16th century onwards – including that of Luther himself – proclaim ever more loudly that the German cultural identity (or at least Protestant Germany's identity) is rooted in the German language. Gradually during the 19th century this new consciousness took on for many an assertive, even supremacist, tone. This was what came to be called the 'völkisch' movement. If there is a key date which, at least retrospectively, is often seen as the start of such a völkisch tendency in German self-expression – a point when it was given very public voice at a politically sensitive time by a major thought leader – it is when the philosopher Johann Gottlieb Fichte delivered his *Reden an die deutsche Nation* (Addresses to the German Nation) in 1808, in a Berlin under French occupation. For him, the German language was the bearer of a culture tracing its origins to the time of the Hermannsschlacht – Arminius's battle – which was the achievement of a people who preferred freedom even to all the benefits of the Roman Empire. That culture was uniquely well fitted to realise a fully free society and nation, a German destiny which he expresses in almost mystical terms.

This was a plea for a culturally rooted national pride – and for education (*Bildung*) in that culture to build national self-confidence. After 1945 it was often seen as a sinister early step on a path that led to Nazism. But a sense of national destiny was increasingly part of the atmosphere in Britain and in France too; and that it should be felt in Germany at this time, and express itself in assertively patriotic terms, is hardly surprising, especially given the denial of German identity and given what the German lands had been subjected to by the armies of Napoleon.

What is true is that from then on, it gathered momentum: every reverse gave it further animus, every triumph gave it further impetus. It fed on a perceived sense of victimisation which the growing consciousness of Germany's history nurtured – in a narrative that saw Canossa as the primal moment of humiliation, the religious wars of the 16th and 17th centuries as Germany's great tragedy, and the ambitions of the French as a continuing existential threat. And it was in danger of undergoing some very unattractive mutations. From the start it was communitarian and at the same time exclusive.

The Enlightenment had focused on the subjective, the autonomous self, rather than the communal whole, let alone any collective or 'absolute' spirit. Now the 'I' was becoming 'we'. At first the 'we' is a common humanity – with Schiller and Beethoven in the vanguard. But then the 'we' also becomes 'and therefore not you'. And especially not the Jews. It becomes more exclusive. Not only does it encourage the sacralisation of the ancient past and of the German lands, but it also becomes aggressive and defensive in tone, under the impact of defeat and occupation.

In 1803 Mme de Stael – the vibrant, intelligent daughter of Louis XIV's finance minister, who had survived the turmoil of the Revolution – visited the Weimar of Goethe and Schiller and then the Berlin of Fichte and of August Wilhelm Schlegel. Her experience of the richness of German intellectual life was transforming for her, and by the time she left, she was determined to write a book which would open the eyes of the French to what she saw as a culture more rooted in the people and the land, more pure, more alive, more in tune with the human spirit than what she saw as the superficial, urban, stereotyped literary world of Paris.

The result, first published in Paris in 1810, was *De l'Allemagne* – On Germany. As a showcase of German creativity in the turbulent and exciting years around the turn of the century, it is remarkably perceptive. It is far from being a naive or superficial paeon of praise written in exuberant infatuation. It is an exercise in comparative analysis of two cultures formed in very different social and political environments, and it is shrewd and perceptive. Its implicit political messages were also clear: on the one hand, the despotism of France was stifling the creativity of the human spirit; whilst the fragmentation of German political life was causing a vacuum in the centre of Europe which was stifling the national consciousness. Goethe, who first read the work in 1814, after the Napoleonic tide had receded from Germany, remarked that if it had been available in 1810, it would have had a major impact on the forces of liberation.

It did not appear then because the French censors clamped down and banned it, seizing and destroying the printing blocks (and forcing the publisher into bankruptcy). Although there was nothing explicitly critical of either the Emperor or the regime in it, they were certainly correct in reading between the lines. It was finally published successfully in 1813, and went on to become hugely influential in the development of the French Romantic movement in the next few decades.

What *De l'Allemagne* did not do was to foresee the dangerous possibilities in that German spirit which had so captivated Germaine de Stael. Those possibilities were being stirred even as she wrote by defeat and humiliation at the hands of Napoleon. They were given voice in patriotic songs with a violent streak – as evidenced notoriously in the work of Ernst Moritz Arndt. He was an ardent anti-French polemicist who had, like so many, begun by welcoming the French Revolution, but then turned violently against it as the Terror unfolded in France and the French armies invaded the German states. He set a new tone with his enormously popular 1813 poem 'Was ist des Deutschen Vaterland?':

> Was ist des Deutschen Vaterland?
> Ist's Preußenland? Ist's Schwabenland?
> Ist's wo am Rhein die Rebe blüht?
> Ist's wo am Belt die Möwe zieht?
> O nein, nein, nein!
> Sein Vaterland muß größer sein! …

> (What is the German's fatherland? Is it Prussia? Is it Swabia? Is it where the vine blossoms by the Rhine? Is it where the seagull flies by the Belt?[14] No, no, no! His fatherland must be greater than that!)

And successive verses ask the question of other parts of the German lands – including Austria, the Tyrol and even Switzerland. Having thus celebrated the geographical extent of a greater Germany, the poem then goes on to laud its Kultur – its language, its loyalty and courage, and its divinely ordained destiny:

> Was ist des Deutschen Vaterland?
> So nenne endlich mir das Land!
> So weit die deutsche Zunge klingt,
> Und Gott im Himmel Lieder singt:
> Das soll es sein! Das soll es sein!
> Das, wackrer Deutscher, nenne dein!

Das ist des Deutschen Vaterland
Wo Eide schwört der Druck der Hand,
Wo Treue hell vom Auge blitzt
Und Liebe warm im Herzen sitzt.
Das soll es sein! Das soll es sein!
Das, wackrer Deutscher, nenne dein!

Das ist des Deutschen Vaterland
Wo Zorn vertilgt den welschen Tand,
Wo jeder Franzmann heißet Feind,
Wo jeder Deutscher heißet Freund.
Das soll es sein! Das soll es sein!
Das soll das ganze Deutschland sein!

Das ganze Deutschland soll es sein!
O Gott vom Himmel sieh darein
Und gib uns rechten deutschen Mut,
Dass wir es lieben treu und gut!
Das soll es sein! Das soll es sein!
Das soll das ganze Deutschland sein!

(What is the German's fatherland? Give me its name at last!
Wherever the German tongue is heard and God in heaven
sings lieder, that's what it must be; that, O brave German,
is what it must be! Where a handshake is an oath, where
loyalty shines from the eye, and where hearts are warm with
love, that's where it must be; that, O brave German, you
must call your own! That is the German's fatherland, where
anger wipes out foreign frivolities, where every French-
man counts as an enemy, where every German counts as
a friend. That it must be, that should all of Germany be! O

God in heaven, look down on us and give us true German courage, that we may love it well and truly. That it must be, that should all of Germany be!)

Arndt mixed his francophobia with a strong dose of an anti-Semitism which was growing in German public discourse in direct proportion to the growth of this aggressive patriotism. If the French were the enemy without, the Jews were the alien – and therefore at least potentially the enemy – within (for good measure, he despised the Poles as well). He lived a long life, dying at the age of 90 and showered with eulogies by the German establishment, not long before the (at least partial) realisation of his hopes in the Second Reich.

Arndt was not alone in his ambition for Germany and his sense that Germany's time had come. Friedrich Jahn, for example, saw the gymnastics education which he founded as a way to create a healthy and confident nationalist spirit, schooled in the ancient German virtues, in the wake of defeat at the hands of Napoleon. One way and another, a strain was emerging in German public life that was assertively patriotic, very male, convinced of its cultural superiority to its effete neighbours, convinced therefore of its destiny to play a central role on the European stage, resentful of past mistreatment, and sure that its time had now come.

One contemporary writer saw the dangers in all this. Heinrich Heine, that perceptive and sardonic observer of German culture, wrote a riposte to de Stael's book, which he published first in French in 1833, and soon after that in German. Deliberately, he entitled the French version *De l'Allemagne.* Where de Stael admires German mysticism, romanticism and folklore, Heine sees obscurantism, parochialism and the denial of Enlightenment freedom. What he feared, though, was not just a failure to face modernity – a failure which was all too convenient for Germany's principalities. He foresaw, in words that seem like an uncanny prophecy of the 20th century, the violence which the völkisch turn in the German spirit would unleash:

> The (German) philosopher of nature will be terrible because he puts himself in touch with the original powers of the land; he conjures up the hidden forces of tradition, evoking all that Germanic pantheism, and awakening the thirst for combat which we find in the ancient Germans – the thirst to fight, not to destroy or even to win, but simply to fight … And thought precedes action as lightning precedes thunder. Yet in Germany even the thunder is essentially German – not very nimble, it comes rumbling on rather slowly. But it will come. And when you hear a crash such has never been heard before in the history of the world, know that this German thunder will have at last reached its goal. At the noise, eagles will fall dead from the heights; lions in the remotest deserts of Africa will slink away into their regal lairs, their tails between their legs. A drama will be played out in Germany beside which the French Revolution will be nothing more than an innocent idyll.

These words were published exactly 100 years before the birth of the Third Reich.

But Heine was writing in Paris, where he lived for the last 25 years of his life. His politics were radical – he knew Karl Marx and shared with him a dislike of bourgeois norms and attitudes – and he had no real empathy with the yearning which underlay the völkisch tendency, the yearning for a strong political unity which would nurture and solidify German cultural identity. Yet the yearning was real, and the only question was about what or who would give it spiritual leadership – about what form the völkisch movement would take.

It did not have to be the way of Arndt. It is worth looking carefully (and without doing so through the prism of the 20th century) at one popular poetic manifestation of this yearning from the time before the Second Reich which has survived – at least in part – through all the upheavals and the tragedy of the next 150 years. This is the poem, written in 1841 by a librarian, literature professor and poet named Heinrich von Fallersleben, at a time when the hope and expectation of a new unified and free Germany was at its height. It became Germany's national anthem:

Deutschland, Deutschland über alles,
Über alles in der Welt,
Wenn es stets zu Schutz und Trutze
Brüderlich zusammenhält.
Von der Maas bis an die Memel,
Von der Etsch bis an den Belt,
Deutschland, Deutschland über alles,
Über alles in der Welt!

Deutsche Frauen, deutsche Treue,
Deutscher Wein und deutscher Sang
Sollen in der Welt behalten
Ihren alten, schönen Klang,
Uns zu edler Tat begeistern
Unser ganzes Leben lang.

Deutsche Frauen, deutsche Treue,
Deutscher Wein und deutscher Sang!

Einigkeit und Recht und Freiheit
Für das deutsche Vaterland!
Danach lasst uns alle streben
Brüderlich mit Herz und Hand.
Einigkeit und Recht und Freiheit
Sind des Glückes Unterpfand;
Blüh' im Glanze dieses Glückes,
Blühe, deutsches Vaterland!

(Germany, Germany, above everything – above everything
else in the world, when it holds fast together like brothers
in protection and defiance: from the Meuse to the Memel,
from the Adige to the Belt, Germany above all things,
above everything in the world. German women, German
loyalty, German wine, German song – they should keep
the beautiful ring they have always had throughout the
world, and inspire us to noble deeds all our lives. Unity,
justice and freedom for the German fatherland! Let us all
strive for this as brothers, with our hearts and our hands.
Unity, justice and freedom are the pledge of happiness.
Flourish in the glow of this happiness: flourish, German
fatherland!)

Often wrongly seen as a piece of German expansionism,
this is in fact nothing more than a fervent plea for unity – for
what belongs together to come together, to borrow the mem-
orable phrase of West Germany's Willy Brandt at the time of
Germany's second reunification. The famous opening line is

not a call to arms and aggression: it is a call to the various German states to put the needs and hopes of Germany as a whole above their parochial and sectional interests. The geographic references in the first verse were rough markers of the area in which German or a version of it was the language of the people; they do not fit the present-day borders of Germany. The patronising reference to German women in the second verse certainly grates on the modern ear. But there is nothing in this poem that could be regarded as a hymn to expansion and there is no hint of racism or xenophobia.

This was a manifestation of what might be called the acceptable – or at least understandable – face of völkisch sentiment. It became the German national anthem in the Weimar Republic and regained that status in the West Germany of the 1950s, although there was an inevitable discomfort with the first two verses. After the second reunification, its third verse became the official national anthem of the new Germany. And its setting, right from the start, to the theme of Joseph Haydn's old anthem to the Hapsburg emperor – *'Gott erhalte den Kaiser'* – God Uphold the Kaiser – which he elaborated with lyrical beauty in the second movement of his string quartet Op 76 No 3, means that it surely holds the crown as the world's most beautiful national anthem.

Sadly, the völkisch tendency developed a different and more sinister temper, as the sense of destiny on the European stage became ever more potent in the second half of the 19th century. What had started as identity focused on language and hence on geography became ever more clearly an identity of race. The connection between the land and the race was what made a nation. Later on, in the 20th century, this would be encapsulated in an ideology of *'Blut und Boden'* – blood and soil – whose archetypal figure was the farmer whose whole being is linked inextricably to the land he lives and works on. Purity of blood came from generations of this intimate link to the land.

Historians played their part in this. In particular Heinrich Gotthard von Treitschke, prominent in the Wilhelmine period as both politician and historian, was a strident supporter of the colonial ambitions of the Second Reich and saw international relationships as a clash of cultures defined in racial terms. He was a strident supporter of the colonial ambitions of the Second Reich, which inevitably entailed a strongly anti-British stance. He was also overtly anti-Semitic. He influenced a generation of nationalist historians – including the military historian and general Friedrich von Bernhardi, whose inflammatory and popular 1911 book *Deutschland und der nächste Krieg* – Germany and the Next War – saw war as a 'divine business' and a biological necessity which accorded with the laws of nature. Friedrich Meinecke, who lived until 1954 and whose view of the Nazi period as an unfortunate aberration we have already noted, was also a student of Treitschke.

By the time of the First World War, indeed, the politics of race were firmly in the ascendant throughout much of Europe. For many, their race with all its purity was inevitably involved in a competition for survival with other races, in a world-historical struggle which came to be seen in Darwinian terms. Such aggressive ethnic competition became the stock in trade of nationalistic circles around Europe, including in particular both Germany and Russia. The German voice found expression in writers such as Paul de Lagarde and Julius Langbehn who, though virtually unknown these days, became highly influential in the Wilhelmine decades.

Lagarde was a university professor and expert in oriental and biblical studies. He was also a passionate believer in the superiority of German culture and in its world-historical destiny. Even more absolutely than Hegel, he argued for the all-embracing identity of the state which represented Deutschtum. He was profoundly disturbed by the actual circumstances of the Second Reich, which he believed had sold the Germans of Austria down the river. He believed Germany should seek to dominate and Germanise the east, removing the Slavs who were inconveniently in the way. He also (correctly) saw the failure of official Protestantism to provide any form of living, unifying cultural/religious bond for this Deutschtum: he argued for the creation of a new Germanic religion, based on a Christianity shorn of all its softness. Needless to say, his definition of the *Volk* had no room for those – notably the Jews – who were not ethnically part of it. His anti-Semitism was not only the rational outworking of a view which placed purity of blood at the heart of the national identity. It was also visceral, and was expressed with a new virulence which did not stop short of likening Jews to bacilli and calling for their expulsion and extirpation.

Julius Langbehn, an intelligent misfit from a poor background who never settled anywhere or with anyone for very long, was a disciple of Lagarde who went on to become the voice of an anti-intellectual, anti-modern populism which pitted the people – the *Volk* who were the true Germans – against the state which had in so many ways betrayed them, and pitted popular (German) art and expression against the scientific rationalism of urbanised modernity. Like Lagarde, he was strongly anti-Semitic (although more because he associated Jews with the urban modernity he despised than out of visceral dislike). His writings struck a chord with the disaffected young of the 1890s and achieved wide circulation. His influence on the Wandervogel youth movement is clear. It is worth noting that the Nazi party – which was in many ways itself a youth movement – found the ideas and the ethos of the Wandervogel and of the Jungdeutscher Orden (which occupied the same niche during the Weimar Republic) very congenial: the Nazis banned them and readily absorbed their members into the Hitler Youth.

These and other voices traded on the unease that seemed to lie just below the surface confidence of the Second Reich. From the successes of Bismarck against Denmark, Austria and then France in 1870, through the early successes of 1914, to the collapse in 1918 and the failures and the humiliations of Weimar, völkisch sentiment became ever louder, even as the sense of victimhood became ever more painful. In the end a particularly nasty version of it became part of the official creed from 1933 and made its inevitable demand on German culture – the demand for the surrender of all spiritual autonomy.

This outcome was not inevitable; there were plenty of other voices clamouring for attention in the late Wilhelmine period. Had it not been for the political misjudgements before and during the First World War, the social traumas of the Weimar Republic and the economic catastrophe of the Great Depression, all this völkisch ranting would have been an unpleasant footnote to German (and European) history. *Mein Kampf* would have been seen as what it was: the somewhat rambling credo of a gutter politician, instead of becoming the bible of a society. In their heyday, Marxists would often argue that this would be to fail to understand the deeper social and economic roots of the inevitable capitalist crisis. Some would even argue that the emergence and then collapse of the Third Reich was precisely the final collapse of capitalism that Marx had foreseen. But from the vantage point of a 21st century which has lost all faith in scientific socialism, this looks wrong. The truth is much sadder: what happened was far from inevitable.

What was nurturing the German spirit in the second half of the 19th century and in the run up to 1914 was certainly not simply an unadulterated diet of völkisch literature and art. Indeed, German culture of the period could hardly be described as overwhelmingly or even mainly völkisch. It is absurd to read back into the creativity of that period the approved opinions of the Third Reich – let alone to look for harbingers of it in any and all art that was influential in previous decades. Thus, for example, it is a distortion to suggest – as it has been – that Brahms contributed to the völkisch climate because his enormously successful *German Requiem* carried that title and used texts from the Lutheran Bible; or that Anton Bruckner's works have a sinister undertone just because they were so much in favour with Nazi cultural ideologues such as Alfred Rosenberg.

Rather, this was the time when bourgeois taste was increasingly influential: this was the great era of innocent and beautiful lieder flowing from pens of the Romantic poets and of the great composers – Schubert, Schumann, Brahms, Wolf – and of richly melodious instrumental music, in chamber form and on the grand scale, from Liszt, Brahms, Mahler, Bruckner and others. Concert going became a habit and composers became celebrities; Brahms, the northerner from Hamburg, was lionised in Vienna and became very wealthy (a reminder, incidentally, that the German identity was not coterminous with the new German political entity and that Vienna was still one of the most important centres of German cultural life). Mahler suffered continually from anti-Semitic backbiting; but the fact remained that he was a highly successful composer and conductor.

Beethoven, perhaps above all, turned music into a powerful means of individual spiritual expression. In his work music becomes the sound – often the tortured sound – of the human spirit, whether of the composer, the performer or the listener. It couldn't be composed to order or serve just as congenial background music. Beethoven cast a long shadow: all subsequent composers had to come to terms with him. Several even of the greatest remained in awe of him throughout their creative lives. The individual's relationship to music took on an intensity which – particularly in Germany (and in Russia, a country whose culture has so many touch points with German experience, for all the obvious differences) – influenced the spiritual mood throughout the 19th and into the 20th century, through and beyond the Second World War.

So German composers and musicologists from the late 18th century onwards began to articulate a high calling for German music. The music was popular with the bourgeoisie: that much was obvious. But at a deeper level, they argued, German music spoke to the spirit: its calling was not just to be beautiful but to have meaning: and as such it was universal. A theologian named Johann Karl Friedrich Triest, writing at the turn of the 19th century, made the case: Bach was the Gothic foundation for a German absolute music which would later import some of the sensuality of Italian music, thus creating a unique synthesis that would meet the human need for a balance of the sensuous and the structured. Schumann saw the power of this music in the coming together of Bach and

Beethoven: the musicologist Franz Brendel saw the pinnacle of art as represented by the music of Wolfgang Amadeus Mozart. All this has obvious echoes of the vision of Hölderlin and the other Romantic poets: indeed, both Triest and Schumann saw this music as being the vehicle of – or even as being – poetry, in the same effectively religious sense as Hölderlin did in his 'Germanien'. The difference is that the music clearly did speak to a wide audience – far more so than did the poetry.

As in the world of music, literature too was increasingly responsive to the tastes of the bourgeoisie. German authors wrote realist novels which reflected bourgeois values and aspirations, or they provided escapist opportunities which offered a frisson of excitement. Much of this was well observed, often poignant – especially the novels of the greatest of them, Theodor Fontane, whose subtle and acute portrayals of life in bourgeois Berlin and in his beloved Brandenburg homeland of the late 19th century have a universal but ordinary human resonance about them, rather in the way that Jane Austen does. As other examples – different from Fontane but, like him, not nearly well enough known to an English speaking audience – the Austrian Adalbert Stifter or the Swiss Gottfried Keller both wrote with an intricacy and a lyricism about the development of the inner life of the sensitive young man to the point of maturity and reconciliation with the world.

None of these could be easily adopted as standard-bearers for a new and völkisch Germany: Fontane was a Prussian who lived and wrote through the early decades of the Second Reich, but who was always ambivalent about the pretensions and the militarism of the new Berlin society, especially after the fall of Bismarck; Stifter did not live to see Austria excluded from the Second Reich, but would surely in any event never have succumbed to any form of crass völkisch nationalism; and Keller was Swiss, a citizen of a country that had centuries before gone its own way and formed a strong political identity of its own.

But in their different ways they spoke to the German bourgeois spirit with a delicate, personal touch which was at once reassuring about the natural order of things and at the same time gently probing and stretching. Fontane wrote of its foibles and its tragedies in such masterpieces of observation as *Effi Briest* or *Irrungen, Wirrungen* – Delusions, Confusions. Stifter and Keller wrote of its possibilities (Stifter's *Der Nachsommer* – Indian Summer – and Keller's *Der Grüne Heinrich* – Green Henry; both were Bildungsromane of the highest quality and in the best tradition of Goethe's *Wilhelm Meisters Lehrjahre*).

Alternatively, the bourgeoisie could also indulge in the blatant escapism of the hugely popular Karl May, who opened a vista on a make-believe world of the Wild West which his readers could enjoy without ever going there or coming into contact with its reality. Or they could experience the ghostly natural world of Theodor Storm's *Der Schimmelreiter* – The Rider of the White Horse – from the comfort of their armchair. Not much in all this was socially challenging. Not since Heine had written his 1844 poem on the revolt of the Silesian weavers (which was first published by Karl Marx) was there a major literary figure who focused on the plight of the urban underclass. Compared with the towering figures of Charles Dickens or of Émile Zola in English and French literature, there was relatively little realist description of the social and human costs to the new urban and industrialised poor. Georg Büchner was only 23 when he died in 1837, leaving in his uncompleted *Woyzeck* only an inkling of what might have been. Only around the end of the century did Gerhart Haupt-mann begin to fill this gap with plays such as his immensely successful debut *Vor Sonnenaufgang* – Before Sunrise – which explores the destructive consequences of alcoholism in a peasant family made newly rich by the discovery of coal on their land; or *Die Weber* – The Weavers of Silesia – which tells the story of the Silesian revolt which had so moved Heine half a century earlier.

So by and large, the literary diet of the bourgeoisie was comfortable, reassuring and consistent with its understanding of the order of things. Nevertheless, there were omens of trouble in the German literature of those decades. The bestselling novel of the last half of the century was Gustav Freytag's *Soll und Haben* – Debit and Credit. It tells the story of an aristocratic family in feckless decline, of Jewish entrepreneurs on the make, and – in the person of its hero – the good bourgeois who finds himself in the end, settling in to an honourable, orderly career in a solid business.

Not all the characters in this novel conform to the stereotypes, but most do. To be clear, these were not just German stereotypes: the declining aristocratic family features in Anton Chekhov, in Anthony Trollope, in Giuseppe Tomasi di Lampedusa. And the mercenary and devious Jew has a long pedigree in European literature. But the contrast between *Soll und Haben* and, say, Trollope's *The Way We Live Now* is striking: the latter is a highly satirical critique of a whole society, whereas the former is a Bildungsroman for the bourgeoisie. The novel as a whole confirms a view of the Jews as being hard, if not impossible, to integrate reliably into the bourgeois life which was so essential to the wellbeing of the Volk. It also underscores Freytag's belief that 'die freie Arbeit allein das Leben der Völker groß und sicher und dauerhaft macht' – working freely is the only way to ensure greatness, security and durability in the life of peoples. Looking back after Auschwitz, this phrase cannot help remind us of the cynical words above the entry gate: *Arbeit macht frei*.

If *Soll und Haben* was the single most popular novel for much of the period of the Second Reich, the most important was published at the dawn of the new century – Thomas Mann's *Buddenbrooks*. This remarkable work charts the decline over several generations of a Hanseatic merchant family and thus gives voice to the increasing unease of the time, as it exposes the inner hollowness of the new Germany's spiritual life. The confidence of Freytag has drained away, and the nagging question for a mind far too sophisticated and cultivated to succumb to the sort of nonsense purveyed by the likes of Langbehn was: what would fill the vacuum? The novel introduces a note of religious hope at the end (rather like Chekhov's ending to *Uncle Vanya*). Is this real? No more than it is for Chekhov.

For Mann the question was whether art could provide the answer. Mann was strongly influenced by the man who became the most important philosophical influence after Kant and Hegel on the makers of German culture in the Second Reich: Arthur Schopenhauer. Not only Mann himself but Wagner and Nietzsche were deeply affected by Schopenhauer's world view, set out in his central work, *Die Welt als Wille und Vorstellung* – The World as Will and Representation. This had been published long before, in 1819, but came into its own only gradually during the following decades. For Schopenhauer the individual will is an inevitable source of suffering and dissatisfaction. The way out of this existential dilemma, for those who recognise it, lies in aesthetic contemplation which allows the individual to dissolve the boundaries of autonomy and perception and to – as it were – lose him/herself in the blind will which animates and directs the cosmos. Art – especially music, particularly when it is wordless – is the way to this release. Schopenhauer's sublimation of the individual self is entirely alien to Kant, and his Buddhist-like view of experience is alien to Hegel's optimism about human progress.

But it could not realistically be the basis for a broad German cultural identity, particularly in the context of the new and assertive Second Reich. And in the end Mann could not live with the detachment from reality which was implied by Schopenhauer's ontology: the world was just too intrusive. Schopenhauer's famous opening line to his great work – 'die Welt ist meine Vorstellung' – the world is my representation – pointed the way to a spiritual blind alley, as Mann was to recognise.

Mann was not the first to come under the spell of Schopenhauer. For Wagner too, it had earlier been a call to art – a call to sublimate (and at the same time celebrate) the inevitable imperfection of human loves and desires in music. Schopenhauer's influence on him is unmistakable – particularly in *Tristan und Isolde* (in which the night is the realm where the two lovers dissolve their selves in a shared bliss which culminates in death) and in *Die Meistersinger von Nürnberg* (in which Hans Sachs comes to recognise the power of song – the power of art – to overcome the illusions and transience of experience).

But for Wagner his art was always far more than aesthetic contemplation: it was about grand themes which did not always fit conveniently with Schopenhauerian life-denial. They were about human fulfilment through carnal love; about redemption through sacrifice; about the charismatic example of the simple, naive, trusting hero; about the corruption of power and its inevitable doom. On top of all that, Wagner the passionate German saw his work as almost a liturgy or a sacrament of the German spirit.

Of all the great German artists of the 19th century, Wagner is the most important – but also misunderstood – source of völkisch inspiration in the 20th century. Hans Sachs sings of art as the preserver of German culture against threats from outside:

Ehrt eure deutschen Meister!
Dann bannt ihr gute Geister;
Und gebt ihr ihrem Wirken Gunst,
Zerging' im Dunst
Das heil'ge röm'sche Reich,
Uns bliebe gleich
Die heil'ge deutsche Kunst!

(Honour your German master [craftsmen and artists]! Then you will have good spirits at your command, and if you let them work, then even if the Holy Roman Empire should vanish into the mist, our holy German art would still remain!)

Notoriously, Wagner was a rabid anti-Semite, such that some have seen – with no objective justification – figures like Alberich, Beckmesser, Klingsor and Kundry as intended representatives of Jewish corruption of the pure German race. Notoriously, too, Hitler himself was profoundly moved by his operas – especially *Lohengrin*, which he saw numerous times when living his anonymous and pathetic existence in Vienna before the First World War. Although ironically almost nothing in the themes that are explored in Wagner's operas is consistent with the Nazi programme, the overall sensory and emotional impact of these operas created the perfect mood, the perfect atmosphere for the new Germany of the Third Reich. In *Tannhäuser, Lohengrin* and *Die Meistersinger von Nürnberg*, Wagner conjures up a largely legendary German past implicitly purer and truer than the mechanical, contaminated and failing present, and wholly suited to the Third Reich's aim of a thorough-going völkisch reconstruction of German culture in support of its geo-strategic aims.

Wagner's association with the sad and quintessentially romantic figure of Ludwig II of Bavaria is the first stage in the development of something of a German mystique about himself; Bayreuth is his apogee. Its role as a place for the influential to see and be seen has endured from its first opening in 1876 to the present day. But Wagner saw Bayreuth as a centre of German spiritual nourishment and renewal. It was to be as much a pilgrimage centre as an opera house. Yet this was always going to be unrealistic – even with the halo it later acquired from Hitler personally. Few people then or since were likely to become the sort of quasi-religious adepts that Wagner sought – for all the glorious power of his music. But his attraction for Adolf Hitler and for Alfred Rosenberg was obvious – even if other Nazi leaders found his music long and tedious, just as others have before and since.

Friedrich Nietzsche too came under the spell of Schopenhauer. But his initial fascination with the blind, cosmic will of Schopenhauer soon evolved in a quite different direction which at first brush might seem to be the perfect support for the völkisch ethos of Nazism. The will to power, not aesthetic contemplation, was the way of release. His is an existential and individual response which is utterly different from Schopenhauer's resignation or Wagner's sacralisation of the German spirit. Famously, Nietzsche was first entranced and then repulsed by Wagner. His Übermensch is a natural outsider who cannot be co-opted by the existing order (or any order) in the way he saw Wagner enjoying his success at Bayreuth. Unlike Wagner, Nietzsche is neither völkisch nor anti-Semitic. His philosophy is not interested in sacralising Germany as if it had a chosen destiny; he has a much wider relevance to the human process of self-discovery in an increasingly urbanised, de-sacralised, transactional world. But it is no surprise at all that his ideas came to be treated as manna from heaven by Nazi ideologues in a Germany which felt cornered and abused in the first half of the next century.

Nietzsche would have been disgusted by Leni Riefenstahl's film *Triumph des Willens*. Kleist would have been appalled by the use the Nazis made of his *Hermannsschlacht* (of which more in the next chapter), although perhaps Heine would not have been surprised by the burning of his works. In general, it is an unfair use of perfect hindsight to lay the catastrophe at the door of the great thinkers and artists of 19th century Germany. Writers like Lagarde and Langbehn, on the other hand, represent a perversion of the Romantic instinct which was overtly and full-bloodedly völkisch; they were virulently anti-Semitic, and they championed the Führer principle and Germany's eastern destiny. Hitler's *Mein Kampf* has all these ideas in it – and none of them is original.

And what about the voice of Christianity in a supposedly Christian culture? Had it been silenced by the

Enlightenment? Who was sounding the authentic note of the Christian gospel in the new economic, social and political reality which was the Second Reich? How was institutional Christian religious life responding to the spiritual yearnings of the age?

The Enlightenment had certainly posed a fundamental challenge for Christianity, in Germany as elsewhere. Kant had apparently set the limits of any serious theological or ethical engagement. In 1835 David Strauss published his *Das Leben Jesu kritisch bearbeitet* – The Life of Jesus Critically Examined – which argued that the miraculous elements in the gospel records were nothing but myth. This book was a sensation throughout Europe but especially in Germany: it seemed to cut away the historical underpinnings of Christianity, just as completely as Kant had denied the possibility of ontological certainty. Then in 1859 Darwin seemed to demolish any claim to special status for human beings, with the publication of *The Origin of Species*. Could any claim to special revelation survive this onslaught?

Indeed, throughout the 19th century, Germany saw a sustained intellectual attack on orthodox Christian doctrine which was arguably more intense than anywhere else in 19th century Europe. This was not because the spirit of Enlightenment rationalism had carried the field: it did not, as we have seen. But neither the Romantics who sought union with the mysterious absolute, nor Hegel who saw the absolute as revealing itself in the sweep of history, turned to orthodox Christianity as a basis for their philosophies. Friedrich Schleiermacher seemed at one level to be a vocal defender of religious faith: but in truth he wrapped the religious sense of ultimate dependence in Christian terminology rather than claiming objective truth for Christian doctrine: this was of course not so far at all from the Romantics.

Then there was a series of writers who developed an explicit hostility to Christianity on the additional grounds that the very ethic which Christ stood for was a weak, degenerative principle, inconsistent with the real thrust of human endeavour. Ludwig Feuerbach opened the way for this new line of attack with his *Das Wesen des Christentums* – The Essence of Christianity – which followed in the wake of Strauss's work in 1841 and had a similarly sensational impact. Feuerbach's thesis, simply put, was that humans had created God, not the other way round. If that was true, then humans could mould God to their purposes – and had done so: this was the argument of Nietzsche, articulated with a virulence which can still astonish, even today. Christianity was not merely untrue, not merely corrupt, but actually dangerous because it was the ethic of weakness. Others such as Lagarde developed this in a specifically völkisch variant: Christianity was incompatible with Germany's destiny of strength and dominance. (It is ironic – but perhaps not surprising – that so many of the thinkers who undermined traditional Christian faith over these decades had backgrounds of strong Protestant observance and/or theological studies: Hölderlin, Hegel, Schleiermacher, Strauss, Feuerbach, Lagarde and Nietzsche.)

By the end of the 19th century the voice of the institutional churches varied from being abrasively supportive of the völkisch tendency (particularly in the Prussian church: notoriously, the court chaplain to Kaiser Wilhelm II was vocally anti-Semitic and called for a Germany purified of modern capitalism which he saw as intimately related to the presence of Jews in society) to the more inward orientation of the

Reformed Churches and the more universalist focus and sacramental life of the Catholic Church. At one end of the spectrum, the danger was that this would end in the ridiculous German Christian movement of the Third Reich: at the other end, the danger was of a quietism which led to silence when they should have spoken out.

The more that völkisch ideas were in the ascendant, the less it would be possible to be neutral – as both religion and art would discover. The journey of Thomas Mann shows that there was to be no middle ground – no way of inner purity which could avoid the choice between compromise and opposition. *Buddenbrooks* came out of his own background life experience in Lübeck: it tells the story of the decline and fall of a great Hanseatic family. The old energies are sapped by the loss of the inner and outer conviction which had once been the bedrock of the family's energy and success in a classic Lutheran world of two kingdoms.

It is no surprise that he never wrote anything like it again. His *Betrachtungen eines Unpolitischen* – Considerations by an Unpolitical Person – was written during the First World War. It shows how even an artistic intellectual could be seduced by the romance of the new Germany in its hour of trial. This book is a profoundly interesting insight into the mind of Germany in this time of trial: it is full of the resentment felt by the victim (as well as battling with Thomas's brother Heinrich, whose realist novels with their focus on the antihero were in Thomas's disparaging view '*Zivilisationsliteratur*'). Far from being just a period piece, it expresses a mood which can be recognised in the 21st century – in the new Russia, for example, or in China.

Mann quickly regretted the *Betrachtungen*. In the aftermath of the war – in the cold light of defeat and humiliation, he wrote *Der Zauberberg* – The Magic Mountain – which shows its protagonist Castorp, after his kaleidoscopic *Bildung* on the mountain, being conscripted into probable death in the trenches as he comes down to the 'flatland' of the unromantic real world of war. The mountain – symbol of the purity of art – is also now, in the wake of the intrusive realities of the war, the symbol of the divorce of art from reality which can no longer be accepted. This was an artistic intellectual's loss of innocence.

Then comes *Doktor Faustus*, written in exile during the Second World War. Adrian Leverkühn is an artistic figure who seeks to break out of the constraints of the accepted rules of music. He knowingly contracts syphilis (the disease that brought down Nietzsche) and in so doing signs the Faustian pact with the devil – inspiration in return for madness. His friend and foil – the worthy, conventional Serenus Zeitblom – acts in effect as Apollo to Leverkühn's Dionysius. At one level this was a complex metaphor for the moral collapse of Germany and the roles played in that disaster by the various competing themes of German culture as it had developed in the journey towards the Third Reich. But it is also more than that: it is the recognition of the reality of evil in human affairs and of the continuing and universal relevance of the myth of the pact with the devil in a desacralised world. It is, moreover, a recognition that art can no more guarantee redemption than religion can. Leverkühn is a composer, and it is no surprise that Mann makes music the vehicle for his parable about the redemptive failure of art. As we shall see, if any art was going to speak to the German soul in the dark night that was coming in the Third Reich, it would have to be music – the most German of arts. But no: the interior life, post Luther and post Kant, is a blind alley. One of Luther's two kingdoms is deserted.

Or perhaps not deserted but instead insecure, emotional, angry at the modern world and the spiritual alienation which it brings. German expressionist art and film before and after the First World War, together with the hard-edged music of the early Strauss (*Salome* and *Elektra*) or of Schönberg, were part of a Europe-wide phenomenon: a jarring reaction to the machine society. It had something in common with the Romantic reaction a century before – with the difference that whereas the Romantics saw the rationalist individualism of the Enlightenment as isolating, this time it was the machine culture and völkisch nationalism that repelled. It is small wonder that all this creativity should come to be considered *'entartet'* – degenerate – in the Third Reich.

For some it was the other of Luther's two kingdoms that needed attention. The class structure and capitalism, not foreigners and outsiders, were the enemy. To artists and writers such as Brecht and Weill, the truth was about individuals crushed by the system. There was no question of a German *Sonderweg* or special destiny – unless it was to be in the vanguard of the inevitable revolution which would destroy the system. But that revolution had already occurred in a country which scientific socialist analysis would have seen as far less ready for it than Germany, and Stalin was fundamentally uninterested in fomenting revolution abroad.

Brecht is one of the greatest poets and most influential playwrights of the 20th century; his influence has been immense and enduring. But he did not live long enough to see the terminal decay of socialism in the post-war German Democratic Republic (let alone the moral vacuum left in

post-communist Russia). The failure of utopian socialism –
whether 'scientific' or just plain revolutionary – to nurture the
spirit and to answer the questions 'who am I?' and/or 'who
are we?' did not become finally clear in Germany until the
1980s (although arguably it was already obvious in the Russia
of the 1930s). As a possible alternative to the völkisch path in
Weimar Germany, it was in any case already being corrupted
by the cynical manipulation of the German Communist Party
for Soviet purposes.

In 1933 what Joseph Goebbels called 'das völkische Zeitalter' – the völkisch age – arrived. 'Das Einzelindividuum wird
ersetzt durch die Gemeinschaft des Volkes', he continued –
the individual is replaced by the community of the people.
And cultural activity like everything else would have to fit in
with and serve what he described – in a clever, and perverted,
Kantian reference – as the 'Volk als Ding an sich' – the people
as the essential thing.[15]

In practice there were four choices for German culture.
There were those who threw in their lot with the new dispensation: the German Christians, Leni Riefenstahl, the
sculptor Arno Breker. Others accepted roles in public life
or in academia, and were in varying degrees uncomfortable
with the ambiguity: Martin Heidegger, Wilhelm Furtwängler,
Werner Heisenberg (both the latter two were the subjects of
poignant plays from the 1980s which explored the ambiguity
and the risks of self-deception involved). Yet others went into
exile, either literally (Bertolt Brecht and Kurt Weill, Heinrich
and Thomas Mann) or into what was later called internal
exile – i.e. keeping their heads down (Ernst Jünger, Gerhart
Hauptmann and, after an initial dalliance, Richard Strauss).
Finally, there were the small handful who risked their lives in

opposition: Bonhoeffer, the Scholl family, the Kreisau circle, Stauffenberg and his co-conspirators. On the night before he committed suicide after the failure of the Valkyrie plot, Henning von Tresckow quoted the Biblical story of Abraham bargaining with God over the fate of Sodom: for the sake of just a few good people, would he not spare the city from total destruction?

By that time, the memories and the dreams which had nurtured the German spirit as it journeyed towards Goebbels' '*völkische Zeitalter*' were turning into terrible nightmares, as we shall see in the next chapter.

6

Memories, Dreams and Nightmares

AS THE YEARNING and the sense of destiny grew stronger, German self-expression drew more and more on memories and dreams – memories which were gilded in the afterglow, and dreams which were set in the lands they had lived in from ancient times.

The memories that thrilled the popular spirit in the new Second Reich had been reawakened by the cultural repossession, from Herder onwards, of the history and lore of the German lands. In particular, there were two figures from Germany's deep past who took on new life: Arminius/Hermann and Friedrich Barbarossa. Monuments, both physical and poetic, were devoted to them, and these tributes to two figures who had taken on semi-mythic status reveal all too clearly their symbolic power for the new Germany as it sought its place in world history.

Arminius was promoted to national hero during the last decades of the 19th century. Well before that, in the midst of the Napoleonic Wars and at a time when Germans were suffering one defeat after another, Kleist had written his play *Die Hermannsschlacht*. Kleist meant it to serve as a call for resistance, but during his short and tortured life it was not even published. By the time it was published in 1821, the Napoleonic menace had gone. Not until 1860 was it performed, and even then without success. But after unification its popularity grew rapidly and performances multiplied. By the time of the First World War it was being staged in Berlin in the presence of the royal family and performances would be interrupted by news from the front. Not surprisingly, the play had its apogee during the Third Reich, to whom it was a gift from one of the 19th century's greatest literary figures. Since the Second World War it has only rarely been performed, and typically with politically correct reinterpretations that determinedly seek to break the link with Germany's recent past.

The play portrays Hermann as the somewhat reluctant leader who has to be talked into taking arms against the militarily superior Romans. Their duplicity in providing advice and support to his tribal rivals is given an added twist by the amorous approaches of a Roman legate to his wife – a lock of whose blonde Germanic hair the Roman secretly steals. Roman treachery and savagery in a German village finally unites the various tribes, and the legions are lured to the disaster in the Teutoburg forest.

It is not a great play, but the contemporary resonances were obvious enough. No one could mistake the anti-French tone. For the wary and squabbling tribes, read: the disunited German states. For the devious Romans, read: the French. Both before and after the Franco-Prussian war and unification, resentful hostility to the French was the order of the day. The huge statue of Hermann – the *Hermannsdenkmal* – outside the pretty town of Detmold stands 53 metres high from its base to the tip of the battle sword he holds high in the heavens.[16] The personal vision of one dedicated sculptor, Ernst von Bandel – who worked on it for over 30 years, living at the site for long periods of time – it was completed in 1875. Significantly, however, whilst it commemorates a victory against Roman legions, the figure of Hermann is facing not south towards Italy but south-west – towards France. On a tablet at the base of the statue, France is described as the 'Erz-feind' – the arch-enemy.

The elevation of the battle of the Teutoburg forest as a defining moment of national glory did not go unchallenged. While Kleist celebrated the *Hermannsschlacht*, Heine sent up any attempt to turn this into a national epic in his *Deutschland, ein Wintermärchen* – Germany, A Winter's Tale. Heine, like Kleist, was an outsider – but for completely different reasons. Kleist was from a distinguished Prussian military family. Heine was from a Jewish background, a politically radical admirer of much that Napoleon had accomplished in the parts of Germany which came under French control. He spent much of his adult life in Paris. His satirical journey through the stiflingly conservative Germany of 1844, in the period before the failed revolutions of 1848, includes a stopover at the site where the *Hermannsdenkmal* was being constructed:

Das ist der Teutoburger Wald,
Den Tacitus beschrieben,
Das ist der klassische Morast,
Wo Varus steckengeblieben.

Hier schlug ihn der Cheruskerfürst,
Der Hermann, der edle Recke;
Die deutsche Nationalität,
Die siegte in diesem Drecke.

Wenn Hermann nicht die Schlacht gewann
Mit seinen blonden Horden,
So gäb' es deutsche Freiheit nicht mehr,
Wir wären römisch geworden!
[...]
Wir hätten einen Nero jetzt,
Statt Landesväter drei Dutzend,
Wir schnitten uns die Adern auf,
Den Schergen der Knechtschaft trutzend.
[...]
Gottlob! Der Hermann gewann die Schlacht,
Die Römer wurden vertrieben,
Varus mit seinen Legionen erlag,
Und wir sind Deutsche geblieben.
[...]
O Hermann, dir verdanken wir das!
Drum wird dir, wie sich gebühret,
Zu Detmold ein Monument gesetzt;
Hab selber subskribieret.

(This is the Teutoburg forest described by Tacitus; this is
the classic marsh where Varus got bogged down. Here he
was beaten by the prince of the Cherusci, Hermann, that
noble warlord; German nationhood was victorious in this
muck. If Hermann and his blond hordes hadn't won the
battle, then German freedom would be no more: we would
have become Roman ... Now we would have had a Nero,
instead of three dozen local princes whom we call fathers of
our lands; we would have slit our veins to defy the hench-
men of slavery ... But thanks be to God! Hermann won
and the Romans were driven out; Varus and his legions

were defeated and we remained Germans ... Hermann, we owe you thanks, and as is fitting we are putting up a monument near Detmold – I have donated to it myself!)

Heine's satirical verses did nothing to stop Arminius becoming a folk hero of the late 19th century. And nor was Arminius alone: he was joined in the pantheon by Friedrich Barbarossa who had been one of the last of the medieval German emperors to have had real power over the German lands. Now, as we have seen, he was said to be asleep in a cave in the Harz Mountains. He would one day return to punish the crimes of those responsible for the people's misfortunes. By the 19th century the legend had begun to take on new life, as part of the recovery of interest in – indeed, a fascination with – Germany's medieval past. Germany was of course not alone in this: there are obvious parallels in both English literature – Ossian, the novels of Walter Scott, the legend of King Arthur – and in French, in Victor Hugo's *Notre Dame de Paris*, for example. The difference is that in the Germany of the Second Reich this legend became a powerful defining myth for the new identity.

Even before unification, the Romantics had focused their hopes for a newly unified Germany, purified and strengthened, on the legend of Barbarossa. Friedrich Rückert, a prolific poet whose work has a fluent grace which proved an inspiration to many great German composers from Schubert to Mahler, wrote the easy-flowing verses which came to define the Barbarossa legend in the popular mind of the 19th century:

Der alte Barbarossa,
Der Kaiser Friederich,

Im unterirdschen Schlosse
Hält er verzaubert sich.

Er ist niemals gestorben,
Er lebt darin noch jetzt;
Er hat im Schloß verborgen
Im Schlaf sich hingesetzt.

Er hat hinabgenommen
Des Reiches Herrlichkeit,
Und wird einst wiederkommen
Mit ihr, zu seiner Zeit.
[...]

(Old Barbarossa, Emperor Friedrich, keeps himself entranced in an underground castle. He never died, but lives
there still; hidden in the castle, he sat down to sleep. He
took with him the glory of the empire, and will one day
return with it, when his time comes ...)

More emotionally charged was the 1829 play *Kaiser Friedrich Barbarossa* by a young German dramatist named Christian Dietrich Grabbe, which explores the complex relationship
of this colourful medieval figure with his main political rival,
Heinrich (known as *Der Löwe* – the Lion). Grabbe's plays
centred on themes which spoke loudly to the new German
nationalism – he also wrote a *Hermannsschlacht*, as well as a
play about Napoleon's famous last 100 days. His style, strongly
influenced by Shakespeare and by the Sturm und Drang of
the previous generation, was often grandiose to the point of
being almost unperformable (although in some ways his use

of short and rapidly changing scenes prefigured more modern dramatic techniques). By the dawn of the 20th century his *Barbarossa* became more regularly staged. His themes (and his anti-Semitism) would later make him a favourite of the Nazi cultural ideologues.

Barbarossa was becoming established as a sort of presiding genius or protecting angel of the Second Reich. He appears in Berlin on the victory column, which was designed in 1863 originally to celebrate the defeat of Denmark over the Schleswig-Holstein question, but was finally completed in 1873, by which time the French had been defeated and the Second Reich had been born. He also appears in the mosaics in the old tower of the Kaiser Wilhelm I Memorial Church, built in the early 1890s. The linkage of the great Kaiser of the first Reich with the new Kaisers of the Second Reich was of course deliberate. Some patriotic writers were sufficiently carried away to suggest that these new – and distinctly unromantic – figures were living evidence of the truth of the legend that Barbarossa had indeed wakened in Germany's hour of need. Old Kaiser Wilhelm I was even nicknamed, affectionately but significantly, *Barbablanca* – white beard – in a conscious reference back to his great predecessor. Barbarossa's image could be said to have had the same sort of effect on a patriotic Germany in the run-up to the First World War as Lawrence Olivier playing Henry V at Agincourt had on Britain in the Second World War.

At the same time as the Memorial Church was being completed in Berlin, a huge monument was erected in the Harz Mountains in Thuringia, on the site of the old Kyffhäuser castle. Barbarossa is portrayed as a heavy, brooding figure, awakening from his long slumber; above him is an 11 metre high equestrian statue of Kaiser Wilhelm I and above that is a 57 metre high tower, with an imperial crown at its top. The tower soars above its wooded surroundings and is visible for miles. The point being made by this monumental (and scarcely beautiful) configuration was neither subtle nor understated. Old Kaiser Wilhelm was the father of the new Reich, which would be as glorious as the old one had been in Friedrich's time.

It is striking that at the Kyffhäuser site Barbarossa faces east, not south. So much of the energy of the Holy Roman emperors was focused on Italy; and, as we have seen, Barbarossa had always been drawn southwards to Italy in his military campaigning. But by the time of the Second Reich German yearnings had shifted eastwards. This reflected the influence of Prussian instincts inherited from the time of the Teutonic Knights. The east was the heartland of the Kingdom of Prussia; its eastern lands were the bastion of a conservative society which became hugely influential in German public life for a hundred years after the failure of the 1848 revolutions (as we have seen). This society had had the psychology of a land surrounded by enemies for centuries – long before the united Germany of the Second Reich had it. Then in the 1870s no less than 15 defensive forts were constructed around Königsberg, which were paid for out of French reparations after the Franco-Prussian war. And in the 20th century it voted more strongly for the Nazis than anywhere else in Germany.

The loss of the eastern lands after 1945 has spread a haze of nostalgia over 700 years of an eastward drive which was a strange mixture of civilising mission, fear of the Asiatic hordes and a yearning for spacious land to cultivate. Here, more than anywhere else in Germany – and precisely because it was land that had to be won from others in armed conflict – was where the sense of 'Blut und Boden' had real power over the German imagination. Images of the east were images of pretty towns settled by Germans, amid fields made fruitful by their *Kulturarbeit* (an almost untranslatable word which speaks of the sense that all the disciplined, dutiful expertise they could muster was invested in the work), and surrounded by undulating landscapes of woods and lakes – and of epic battles lost and won against the Slavs. Symbolic of this German eastern drive was the fortress of Marienburg – the great citadel of the Teutonic knights from the 13th to the 16th centuries. Allowed to go to wrack and ruin in succeeding centuries, it was heavily restored by a 19th century Germany out to assert its ancient roots. Kaiser Wilhelm II triumphantly celebrated its completion in 1903. It was seriously damaged in the Second World War, as the SS used it to try to block the advancing Red Army. It has since been beautifully restored once more – by the Poles in whose country it now stands.

Hitler, writing in *Mein Kampf*, was completely clear about this strategic shift of focus, basing it not only on the need for Lebensraum but also on an explicit ethnic Darwinism (neither of which he originated, as we shall see):

Damit ziehen wir Nationalsozialisten bewußt einen Strich unter die außenpolitische Richtung unserer Vorkriegszeit. Wir setzen dort an, wo man vor sechs Jahrhunderten endete. Wir stoppen den ewigen Germanenzug nach dem Süden und Westen Europas und weisen den Blick nach dem Land im Osten. Wir schließen endlich ab die Kolonial- und Handelspolitik der Vorkriegszeit und gehen über zur Bodenpolitik der Zukunft.

(So we National Socialists consciously draw a line under the foreign policy direction of the pre-war period. We take up where we broke off 600 years ago. We stop the endless German movement to the south and west, and turn our gaze towards the land in the east. We finish with the colonial and trading policies of the pre-war period and adopt the policy of the soil of the future.)

He underscored this strategic shift when he used Barbarossa's name for his great eastern campaign – the invasion of the Soviet Union. The eastward facing monument to Barbarossa shows that Hitler did not conjure this strategy out of thin air; he was tapping into a root of the new German identity which had been planted in the soil of East Prussia centuries before. After the Second World War some wanted to blow up the Kyffhäuser monument; perhaps surprisingly, the local Russian commander refused to allow this. But in any case, the horrendous failure of Operation Barbarossa killed off the myth of Friedrich Barbarossa in the German consciousness for ever.

The backdrop to the myth of Barbarossa – as also to Arminius – was the wooded landscape of Germany. All countries' identities are influenced by their geography, even those that have become highly urbanised. For the British, the sea is still a defining force in the folk memory; for Russia, the steppes; for China, the great rivers. For the Germans, there have been equally strong memories and images; above all, relating to the woods. They have infused the German consciousness, one way or another, down the centuries and left their mark on the German psyche, culture and history. Heine had once said that the secret religion of the Germans was pantheism – a comment which is misleading at one level but which perhaps highlighted an important truth about the German soul.

Germany is, even today, a land of woods. Despite a population density as high as Britain's and double that of France, woods cover a higher proportion of the land than in France and three times higher than in Britain. The woods have always had a double meaning in the folk memory. They are where Germans go for recreation; and they are where sinister and violent things happen.

From Arminius onwards the woods are ever present in the German story. For Tacitus, writing about the disaster, the woods of Germany were endless, impenetrable and treacherous. For the Germans, though, they were by the same token a source of protection. When Luther is held for his own safety in the Wartburg castle on the orders of the Elector of Saxony, he looks out over the rolling, wooded hills of Thuringia. The woods were also a setting for pleasure. Paintings by German artists from Cranach onwards are often of hunting scenes, set in the woods. From the late 19th century onwards, they are the setting for hiking – the sport of the new Zivilisation, as the hugely successful Wandervogel movement led rambling groups of the nation's youth out of the cities and into the woods to refresh their spirits by getting close to nature again.

But they are also the setting for things more sinister. In the popular mind in rural communities they were the home of spirits which were at best unpredictable and mischievous. And for the 19th century Romantics, with their strong sense of the mystery and the awe of nature, the woods were the place where that encounter with nature often occurred – as evidenced, for example, by some of Caspar David Friedrich's most evocative paintings. Wooded hills with swirling mists or in the moonlight, sometimes with gothic ruins merging into the natural environment: these seemed at the time (and seem now) to capture something about the German psyche as surely as the landscape paintings of John Constable – his almost exact contemporary – capture the English soul with their mostly more workaday themes and colours.

The woods set the scene for all kinds of strange encounters. The treasure chest of folklore from the woods was a source of inspiration perhaps above all for the Brothers Grimm. These two brothers worked together as academics all their lives. As students at the University of Marburg they were introduced by their professor to Arnim and Brentano, the collectors of *Des Knaben Wunderhorn*, and through them to the legacy of Herder. The fascination with German folklore never left them. In 1812 they published the first version of their own collection, *Kinder- und Hausmärchen* – stories for children and the home. Subsequent versions added more stories, and their fame spread. Many of the stories have become part of the patrimony of the world: 'Little Red Riding Hood', 'Hänsel and Gretel', 'Snow White', 'Cinderella', 'The Frog Prince', 'Sleeping Beauty' and so on. Their influence on German culture was profound: *Kinder- und Hausmärchen* became part of the teaching curriculum in Prussia, and later the Nazi cultural ideologues called for every household to own a copy. Indeed, for much of the period since the Second Reich it was the second most popular book in Germany after the Bible.

It has often been noted that there is a streak of violence in many of these stories; in their original forms, they can – for today's sensibilities at least – seem unsuitable for the children who were meant to be their audience. 'Little Red Riding Hood' and 'Hänsel and Gretel' – to cite but two – have an element of cruelty and violence which is unmistakable: and the versions of 'Snow White' and of 'The Frog Prince' which we know today have been carefully sanitised (particularly by Disney).

The woods are the background to so many of these stories because they were the background to the life of a rural society. The deciduous forests of Germany, their clearings alternating with deep, dark woodland where wild animals and spirits lurked and where humans could easily get lost for ever, represented a constant existential threat. By the 19th century the atavistic fear of the forest was of course well on the wane; but it could still send a shiver down a child's spine. And perhaps even for urban, educated adults the appeal of these stories was that they tapped into deeply buried folk memories which could still give them nightmares.

There were other examples of the impact of the woods on German self-expression in the 19th century. Carl Maria von Weber's enormously popular opera *Der Freischütz*, premiered in 1821, was an instant success both in Germany and throughout Europe. Based once again on a German folklore story, it tells of the twists and turns in the efforts of the forester Max to win the hand of his true love, the daughter of the head forester. The plot takes him on a dangerous journey from his failure in a marksmanship contest through dalliance with the sinister Caspar, who has made some sort of Faustian pact with the devil and who offers to take him to the *Wolfsschlucht* – the wolf's glen – where an evil spirit will cast him magic bullets. The seventh and final bullet almost kills his beloved; but she is miraculously protected by supernatural power and the bullet claims Caspar instead, so that the devil claims his own. Max is required to prove his repentance and good faith for a full year, at the end of which the prince will allow him to wed his betrothed.

This plot is turned from trivial fairy tale into an emotionally charged masterpiece by Weber's extraordinary musical power. It conjures up a natural and supernatural struggle between good and evil, using motifs that were deeply embedded in the German psyche with its folk memories of the forests (as well as the Faustian pact – which we will come back to shortly). The Wolfsschlucht scene remains one of the most chilling musical portrayals of supernatural evil ever composed.

So the woods crowd in on the historical, the legendary and the wholly imaginary: Arminius in the Teutoburg forest; Barbarossa asleep in his cave; or the emotionally intense first act of Wagner's *Die Walküre* – of which more later. Last, and not the least sinister, Hitler spent most of his wartime days, not in Berlin, not in Berchtesgaden in his beloved mountains, but in the '*Wolfsschanze*' – the wolf's lair – deep in the forests of East Prussia. The echo of the '*Wolfschlucht*' is unmistakable.

The influence of *Der Freischütz* on the young Richard Wagner is clear. And it was he who paid the greatest musical tribute to the other great feature of the landscape to mould the German identity in the 19th century: the River Rhine. For him, it was the backdrop to his huge tragedy of *Der Ring des Nibelungen*. The remarkable 137 opening bars of *Das Rheingold* conjure up the ever-rolling stream, ultimately indifferent to the strivings and purposes of gods and humans, as nothing else could.

The Rhine had been the great central artery of Charlemagne's empire. After the split the Rhine became a focus for conflict – was it the artery of Germany or was it a border zone which the French would control? In the German consciousness the answer was always clear. Its strategic significance is shown by the number of fairy-tale castles along its course and nearby – including the spectacular Hoch Königsburg – now in French Alsace but carefully and extensively restored under the direction of Kaiser Wilhelm II in the first decade of the 20th century when Alsace was a *Reichsland* (imperial territory). Hoch Königsburg had originally been constructed in the 12th century under Friedrich Barbarossa's father to protect the western flank of the imperial domains. During the Thirty Years War it had been besieged by Swedish forces, overrun and burnt down; by the end of the 19th century, when it was gifted to Kaiser Wilhelm II personally by the local town, it was little more than a ruined hulk. Like the Marienburg, its restoration to renewed magnificence was part of the careful nurturing of the imperial myth during the Second Reich.

More than any other great river in Europe, the Rhine became the focus of Romantic attention. German writers produced hundreds of poems on the theme during the 19th century. Most were unexceptional; some have the same sort of folksiness – and quaintness – as, say, 'Old Father Thames' does in an English context. But some are much more than that. Two of them come from the pens of two of Germany's greatest literary figures.

Hölderlin's 1801 poem 'Der Rhein' has the same aura as his 'Germanien'. For him, the Rhine as it races from its mountainous sources, through woodlands and past treacherous cliffs before flowing calmly through cultivated land and orderly towns, tells of the human loss of the old gods and yet of the yearning for a spiritual elevation which can never be content with domesticity. He portrays the river as a demigod who escapes from primal turbulence and finds peace in nurturing the fertile creativity of the regions through which it flows. But this demigod never forgets his origins and cannot avoid the urge to strive for immortality: and yet the price of this yearning is the destruction of all he knows and loves:

Es haben an eigener
Unsterblichkeit die Götter genug, und bedürfen
Die Himmlischen eines Dings,
So sinds Heroën und Menschen
Und Sterbliche sonst. Denn weil
Die Seligsten nichts fühlen von selbst,
Muß wohl, wenn solches zu sagen
Erlaubt ist, in der Götter Namen
Teilnehmend fühlen ein Andrer,
Den brauchen Sie; jedoch ihr Gericht
Ist, daß sein eigenes Haus
Zerbreche der und das Liebste
Wie den Feind schelt und sich Vater und Kind
Begrabe unter den Trümmern,
Wenn einer, wie sie, sein will und nicht
Ungleiches dulden, der Schwärmer
[…]

(But the gods have immortality enough of their own. What the heavenly ones need is heroes, humans and other things mortal. Because the blessed ones feel nothing for themselves, they need – if one may speak thus – another who can feel for them. But their law is that one who would be like them must destroy his own house, curse as an enemy what he loves most, and bury his own father and child under the rubble – all this is in store for the dreamer who would be like them and not settle for anything less.)

Hölderlin's thought here is as always hard to express simply. But in this very German vision of the Rhine there is something of the human need for the absolute, the undivided, the eternal – but also a sense that to strive for equality with the gods involves a horrendous cost and is in the end as impossible as it is inevitable. Its strange foreshadowing of a looming German tragedy is – from a later vantage point – all the more poignant.

After Hölderlin comes the very different Heine, whose 1822 poem 'Die Loreley' draws on a story told originally by Brentano and turns it into the fable of a sort of siren who lures men to their death on the treacherous rocks at what is the narrowest part of the river Rhine between Switzerland and the North Sea. Where Hölderlin glimpses the possibility of the absolute – and of tragedy awaiting those who seek to grasp it – Heine's poem is a metaphor for the way in which the sinister lurks beneath the normality and even the beauty of life. Both sound a note of foreboding, of melancholy, which resonates with something deep within the German soul. Where Hölderlin writes with an almost 20th century complexity and involutedness, Heine paints his picture with simple, deft brushstrokes. Very different from Hölderlin's poem, Heine's 'Die Loreley' has the deceptive simplicity of a folk song written by a master. It is almost too well known:

Ich weiß nicht was soll es bedeuten,
Daß ich so traurig bin;
Ein Märchen aus alten Zeiten,

Das kommt mir nicht aus dem Sinn.

Die Luft ist kühl und es dunkelt,
Und ruhig fließt der Rhein;
Der Gipfel des Berges funkelt
Im Abendsonnenschein.

Die schönste Jungfrau sitzet
Dort oben wunderbar;
Ihr goldnes Geschmeide blitzet,
Sie kämmt ihr goldenes Haar.

Sie kämmt es mit goldenem Kamme,
Und singt ein Lied dabei;
Das hat eine wundersame,
Gewaltige Melodei.

Den Schiffer im kleinen Schiffe
Ergreift es mit wildem Weh;
Er schaut nicht die Felsenriffe,
Er schaut nur hinauf in die Höh.

Ich glaube, die Wellen verschlingen
Am Ende Schiffer und Kahn;
Und das hat mit ihrem Singen
Die Lore-Ley getan.

(I don't know what it should mean that I am so sad; I can't get this age-old story out of my mind. The air is cool and dusk is falling, and still flows the Rhine; the hilltop sparkles in the evening sunshine. There on the hill sits the most beautiful and mysterious young girl; lithe and golden she flashes as she combs her golden hair. She combs with a golden comb, singing as she does – a melody of marvellous power. A wild sadness seizes the boatman in his small boat; he doesn't see the rocky crags. All he does is gaze upwards – and I sense that the waves overwhelm him and his boat in the end; and all because of the singing of the Loreley.)

For Hölderlin, then, the Rhine is a metaphor for humanity's dangerous immortal yearnings, and for Heine it is a metaphor for the sinister lurking within the beautiful. From a later perspective they might both be regarded as unintentionally ominous.

But the Rhine soon became for 19th century Germans a symbol of a much more tangible threat to the fragile German identity – the threat of attack by its ancient enemy. Most significantly for the German sense of vulnerability and destiny in the late 19th century, the Rhine was celebrated in the poem known to all Germans as 'Die Wacht am Rhein' – on guard on the Rhine. Composed by a merchant from Swabia named Max Schneckenburger in 1840, at a time when the French government was publicly arguing that the Rhine ought to be its natural frontier, this poem gave voice to a powerful new spirit in Germany – a spirit nurtured by a combination of resentment of the long history of French incursions in the Rhineland and of fervour for unification. This spirit fuelled German hope and ambition in the decades leading up to the First World War.

The poem, set to a rousing tune by one Karl Wilhelm, director of music in Krefeld, became a sort of unofficial national anthem. Its words are inscribed on the Niederwald monument, near Rüdesheim on the Rhine, which was erected in 1883 to celebrate the founding of the Second Reich: there the figure of Germania holds the imperial crown and sword, and below her is a bas-relief of Kaiser Wilhelm I accompanied by the leading aristocratic and military figures of the new Reich – and the text of 'Die Wacht am Rhein':

Es braust ein Ruf wie Donnerhall,
Wie Schwertgeklirr und Wogenprall:
Zum Rhein, zum Rhein, zum deutschen Rhein,
Wer will des Stromes Hüter sein?

Lieb Vaterland, magst ruhig sein,
Lieb Vaterland, magst ruhig sein,
Fest steht und treu die Wacht, die Wacht am Rhein,
Fest steht und treu die Wacht, die Wacht am Rhein!
[…]

(A call sounds like thunder, like the clash of swords and the crash of waves: to the Rhine, to the German Rhine, who will protect the river? Beloved Fatherland, you can rest easy; the watch on the Rhine is firm and true! …)

From the mysterious complexity of Hölderlin to the uncanny simplicity of Heine – and thence to this. We shall see later how the völkisch spirit fed on brash trivia such as this. The poem was, needless to say, popular too in the Third Reich. As an ironic twist, in the wartime movie classic *Casablanca*, there is a famous scene in which German army officers are outsung in patriotic fervour by the French, led on by the immortal Rick Blaine played by Humphrey Bogart: the Germans sing 'Die Wacht am Rhein' whilst the French sing the Marseillaise – which, as we have seen, was originally the war song of the French invasion armies on the Rhine.

These landscapes and their myths and memories – the woods and the river – have been formative for the German psyche – and poignant because of their tragic undertone. And this German background was the specific setting for a mythical figure who came to play a major role in German self-understanding (and whose story has worldwide resonance because it was taken up in an artistic creation of the first order): Siegfried.

A complex saga with no pretensions to a historical core, and drawing on ancient German and Norse themes, the song of the *Nibelungs* attracted more and more attention from the early 19th century onwards. In the medieval version of the song known to writers such as Hegel (whose judgement that it has less universal human cultural significance than the Iliad is surely right), the story tells of the complicated relationships between Gunther, king of Burgundy; Siegfried, crown prince of Xanten; Kriemhild, sister of Gunther who eventually marries Siegfried; and Brünhild, an Icelandic queen subdued by Siegfried on behalf of Gunther, who finally marries her. Jealousy and suspicion lead to Siegfried's death at the hands of Hagen, a vassal of Gunther, with the apparent connivance of Gunther and the unwitting help of Kriemhild. Like Achilles, Siegfried enjoys a sort of magical protection, but, like him, he has one vulnerable point. Hagen stabs him in the back with a spear – an act which becomes a defining moment in German myth. He steals the treasure that had been Siegfried's, throwing it into the Rhine to prevent anyone from using it against him or Gunther. Kriemhild seeks revenge and demands that her brother deliver Hagen. But he and her other brothers refuse, because they have an obligation of total loyalty – the *Nibelungentreue* – to Hagen, as a vassal of the king. In the end, years later, Gunther's armies are drawn into a fight to the death with Kriemhild's armies, and Gunther and Hagen both come to a fiery end in the banqueting hall to which she has invited them. Kriemhild in her turn is slain for having violated her obligations both to guests and to kith and kin.

Wagner substantially changes and universalises the story. He borrows from Norse sagas to bring the gods into play, and he completely invents the role of the Rhinemaidens and their role in the opening and closing sequences of his Ring Cycle. Gunther and Kriemhild (who becomes Gutrune) have relatively modest roles, and the ending is not just the bloody defeat of Hagen and the Nibelungs – but the twilight of the gods, the *'ragnarok'*, or doom of all power. This was a distinctive feature of Norse mythology – the total fiery destruction of all things including the gods, which would however be the prelude to a new era of peace and plenty.

It would be all too easy to see this extraordinary and unique work as providing a natural source of energy for the aspirations of the Second Reich and then the Third Reich. But this would be to overlook its overwhelming pessimism about power: not only does Siegfried die, not only is Hagen defeated, but the gods too are consumed by fire. Wotan is constantly shown to be a flawed figure whose desire for power through the ring leads to the destruction of the world. Only the timeless river keeps rolling and the slaughter ends only when the ring returns to its invisible depths. If there is a hint of redemption in the very last bars of *Götterdämmerung*, it is only an unformed hope, and only possible because Brünnhilde has ridden into the flames in a final redemptive sacrifice. This version of 'ragnarok' is as far away as it is possible to be from the overweening swagger of the Second Reich and the dreadful ambition which drove the Third Reich to its own final immolation in May 1945. In Hitler's last testament there is not a trace of recognition of the corruption of power, let alone of evil, and let alone of any possibility of redemptive hope.

Between them, the original *Nibelungenlied* and Wagner's Ring Cycle provided the political culture of early 20th century Germany with much of the imagery it needed to engender enthusiasm and maintain morale in its increasingly dangerous and bloody international entanglements. Nibelungentreue in particular became almost a leitmotiv of foreign policy in the years before the First World War. In 1909 the then Chancellor, Bernhard von Bülow, invoked it explicitly to justify Germany's support for Austria-Hungary in one of the succession of Balkan crises which eventually led to the war. And it was in the spirit of Nibelungentreue that fatefully, on 5 July 1914, the Kaiser promised unconditional support to the Austrians in the wake of the assassination of his friend the Archduke Franz Ferdinand in Sarajevo. Later, Siegfried's name was given to the defensive line built on the Western Front during the winter of 1916/1917.

After defeat, the stab in the back becomes a leitmotiv of interwar politics – not used first by Hitler, but taken up enthusiastically by him in *Mein Kampf*. Erich Ludendorff was the first prominent figure to use the term. The army had not been defeated: it had been stabbed in the back (by the civilian politicians). As the *Dolchstoßlegende* – the myth of the stab in the back – gained currency in right wing and military circles, the link with Siegfried became established in the popular mind. If anything, the stab in the back with a dagger was an escalation of the outrage, in that the spear which kills Siegfried is at least visible to all, whereas the dagger is furtive and hidden, the weapon of duplicitous civilian politicians. Notoriously, the University of Vienna, for example, erected a memorial to its fallen heroes of the war in the form of a bust of the dead Siegfried, in a not so subtle reference to the stab in the back.

During the Second World War, Nibelungentreue and Siegfried's simple, trusting loyalty and heroism to the death were ruthlessly and regularly extolled – most cynically in the poignant and dreadful final weeks of Stalingrad, when Göring explicitly evoked the determination of the Nibelung army to fight to the very end:

Auch sie standen in einer Halle von Feuer und Brand und löschten den Durst mit dem eigenen Blut – aber kämpften und kämpften bis zum Letzten.

(They too stood in a hall ablaze with fire and quenched their thirst with their own blood – but fought and fought to the end.)

So powerful was the myth of Siegfried in the German popular mind that it was also used by those who resisted. Not coincidentally, the July 20 conspirators invoked the imagery of the Ring Cycle as they gave their plan to assassinate Hitler the codename *Die Walküre* – after Brünnhilde, whose sacrifice makes redemption possible. Later on, after the war was over, they were deemed to have died – as it says in a circular letter sent round by a victims' organisation in 1947 commemorating their deaths:

> … den Heldentod im freien, ehrenvollen Kampfe für Wahrheit und Recht, für des Deutschen Volkes Freiheit, für der Deutschen Waffen Reinheit und Ehre, als bewusste Sühne für das vor Gott verübte Unrecht unseres Volkes …

> (… a hero's death in a free and honourable struggle for truth and justice, for the freedom of the German people, for the purity and honour of German arms, and as a deliberate atonement for the injustice perpetrated by our people in the eyes of God …)

Hitler thought not only that the sixth army at Stalingrad should have fought to the very end like the Nibelung armies – and should have taken their own lives rather than surrendering – but that this was the duty of the German people as a whole. The Allies had demanded unconditional surrender – not least to avoid any repetition of the Dolchstoßlegende. As far as Hitler was concerned, there could be no surrender, conditional or otherwise. The result was indeed a sort of Götterdämmerung – the immolation of Germany itself.

Again, as for Barbarossa, the power of the myth of Siegfried was killed off at zero hour. The difference is that the myth itself lives on – perhaps, despite Hegel's view, even more so than the *Iliad* – because of the unsurpassable power of Wagner's music. But no longer as a political force.

Not all myth is ancient. Germany's dominant 18th century leader, Frederick the Great, became the subject of hero-worship even in his lifetime and still more after his death. He was certainly a convenient idol, for both the Second and Third Reichs. Being an early modern figure, rather than a medieval or a legendary one, he personally managed his persona, as Hitler would do so brilliantly later on. So this was the supreme ruler who ruled alone, but was at the same time the 'first servant of the state'; the philosophically enlightened but absolutist ruler; the atheist who would nevertheless have felt entirely comfortable with Luther's calling of the prince to rule; the musician who was a gifted flute player and competent composer; the brave soldier alongside his troops in battle; the leader who tired himself out travelling his domains talking to ordinary folk about their needs; the old man with his beloved whippets, living alone in his exquisite palace of Sanssouci at Potsdam.

After his death the halo became ever brighter. It is easy to see why. He was the hero who could appeal to every little boy who played toy soldiers, as well as to the elite who saw the new Germany pursuing its own special path – its Sonder-weg – into the 20th century; strong, organised, determined and ambitious, as well as cultured and civilised. On Berlin's famous boulevard Unter den Linden a magnificent and beautiful equestrian statue of him was erected in 1851, facing east towards the Prussian heartlands of his domains. By the First World War Frederick was firmly ensconced as the greatest leader the emerging Germany had known – the leader who would have spared the country from its humiliation at the hands of Napoleon, had he been alive at the time. No wonder Hitler used the myth of Frederick to draw parallels with his own position – as, for example, when he carefully stage managed the first meeting of the Reichstag after the fire in 1933 in the garrison church in Potsdam, where Frederick was buried. The statue on Unter den Linden survived the Second World War undamaged, but was removed by the East German authorities. And so Frederick became 'verehrt, verklärt' (honoured, transfigured) and – after Stunde Null – 'verdammt'.

As time went by the determination to cut off the past faded, and the East German government reinstated the statue on Unter den Linden in 1980, in its original position, facing east. And to this day, 'der alte Fritz' – unlike Arminius, Barbarossa and Siegfried – lives on as an image with the power to fascinate, as the creator of the beauty of Potsdam, as the archetype of the enlightened Platonic despot and as the first servant of the state which many in this democratic age still yearn for in their politicians, even though it is not quite what he was.

There is one more powerful German myth which takes as its starting point not the woods or the river or the lure of the east, nor the brilliance of historical success, but a rootless mountebank from an urban setting. But it becomes a metaphor for the way in which these German memories and dreams became a nightmare. Faust may have originally been an alchemist and showman, born around 1480 in the small and (to this day) undistinguished village of Knittlingen not far from Stuttgart. Probably intelligent and entrepreneurial, he travelled the towns and countryside of Germany making a living one way or another at fairs. He is a recognisable type from his gullible age. He would have had his look-alikes all over Europe. There was no reason why he should have achieved any notice at all – except that he goes down in legend as having sold his soul to the devil in return for all the powers and pleasures of this world.

What lies behind this cannot be known, but does not matter to the subsequent development of the Faust legend. Already by the late 16th century, Faust had become the protagonist of one of the first German novels. In England the story appeared in translation in 1592. Christopher Marlowe then took this legend and was the first to turn it into a great drama with a deep human resonance. But it is a quintessentially German theme, recurring like a leitmotiv in a culture obsessed with metaphysics, for which this figure becomes a sort of sinister alter ego. In particular, of course, Faust is the subject of Goethe's masterpiece, where he becomes a sort of Promethean Everyman – and provokes endless German debate about the inexhaustible ambiguity of his achievements and his fate. But the devil is there in the story; so too is Gretchen (and also based, like the original Faust legend itself, on a historical person). Her fate reminds us that the human tragedy of evil cannot simply be dissolved in metaphysical and political speculation as to what ends justify what means. Evil has consequences in individual human suffering.

This, Goethe's greatest work – and surely German literary culture's greatest – is so protean that no one can harness it. Certainly not the Nazis, who never felt able to make much ideological use of Goethe's *Faust*. In one sense, no single culture can own Faust – any more than Hamlet, for example. But in another sense, Germany was to live out this most German of myths – all the way to its apparently final conclusion, and perhaps beyond.

Goethe's Faust rejects religion and philosophy; he finds that the pursuit of ideal beauty does not bring satisfaction – and then right at the end he finds a morally flawed fulfilment in a civil engineering project which creates new and productive land. It is morally flawed because it involves the killing of an innocent old couple who are in the way. And how should we read the ambiguous apotheosis, in which Faust is taken up into a heaven empty of God where he finds a new kind of redemption in which the feminine plays the leading role? We shall come back to this in our final chapter. But for now it is worth noting how it calls into question (and in so doing calls attention to) the stereotypically male dominance in German culture – a dominance which is deeply rooted in German traditional iconography. This dominance was a striking element of völkisch imagery and is clearly reflected in the aggressively 'male' social psychology of an insecure Germany both as it came of age in the Second Reich and as it went amok in the Third Reich.

This male dominance has of course been true of all cultures (not just in Europe); is it more marked, and more aggressive, in German imagery than in other European cultures (or in Asian cultures)? On the one hand, the parallels in other literatures and cultures are obvious (the decline of Lady Macbeth, the overcoming of the ice maiden Turandot – which was a popular Peking Opera plot long before it became one of Puccini's great operas; or compare Effi Briest with Madame Bovary). Yet there is a degree of violence about German imagery which remains striking. In the *Nibelungenlied* Siegfried effectively rapes Brünhild to bring her under control. And Wagner moulds – or tames – Brünnhilde into a figure of appropriately heroic feminine loyalty to a dim-witted man she has good reason to despise. Yet something different happens in Goethe's drama: Gretchen has the last transfiguring word, and 'das Ewig-Weibliche zieht uns hinan' – the eternal feminine draws us on. Whatever this may mean, it is certainly not consistent with the very male-dominated imagery that came to nourish the German spirit in the tragic decades of the Second and Third Reichs.

Because the spiritual and moral questions posed by Faust are of universal resonance, it is no surprise that this story lives on in the human consciousness, in a way that Barbarossa and even Siegfried do not. The enduring fascination with the man who sells his soul – who prefers power or pleasure now to the bliss of eternity, whose thirst for experience can never be satisfied, for whom doing is more important than being, for whom this life is the be-all and the end-all – has inspired writers and composers from Marlowe to the present day. Goethe's great creation inspired several operas (by Berlioz, Gounod, Boito and Busoni), Murnau's classic 1926 film and Thomas Mann's *Doktor Faustus* (as we have already seen). The word 'Faustian' has entered the vocabulary. It is one of the richest and most enduring gifts of German culture to humanity.

Faust's resonance in 20th century Germany is obvious. These German memories, and the dreams they nourished, turned into a hellish nightmare. Barbarossa and Siegfried were used aggressively by the insecure leadership of a new and insecure nation to bolster confidence in dealing with real and perceived enemies all round. Failure in the First World War gave renewed impetus to the deeply rooted sense of victimhood, escape from which seemed to lie in the Faustian pact with the devil – who then certainly claimed his own.

7

The Pact with the Devil

WE LIVE IN A NEW MILLENNIUM, at a time when no one under the age of around 75 can have any clear memory of the Second World War. In 50 years, no one will be alive who has any memory of it and few will have any memory of parents who had memories of it. What will people then think of this episode in human history? The facts will of course still speak for themselves – both the mind-numbing statistics of destruction and death, and the individual stories of horror. And historians will sometimes ask: was it unique? To which the answer is, in the end: yes.

Yes, even though many other terrible things were done in the 20th century (and before, though inevitably on a smaller scale and less well documented). If the criterion were simply the number of man-made deaths, then the Soviet Union under Stalin might well have as much to answer for as Nazi Germany; and Chinese history over the 200 years to the death of Mao (the Tai Ping rebellion, the Boxer rebellion, the Japanese occupation and the Great Leap Forward, in particular) saw millions upon millions of violent deaths. If the criterion were to be a combination of scale and deliberately targeted annihilation of particular groups – then the Soviet Union, again, would compete strongly for this dreadful prize. Furthermore, Cambodia is a more recent and horrific example: so is Rwanda. In both cases the percentage of the population involved was comparable to some of the worst European experiences in the Second World War. And what of the Armenian genocide, which even today, as a successor state on the territory of the Ottoman Empire, the Republic of Turkey cannot bring itself to acknowledge?

So where lies the uniqueness? Or is uniqueness only in the eye of the beholder? No: virtually everyone (and certainly virtually every German) would acknowledge the uniqueness of this extraordinary period; and we should all hope that our descendants in 50 years time will have no cause to revise that judgement. But as they look back on events of more than a century before, they will probably look on with as much bemusement as horror. Indeed, we already know this feeling: when we look at the old newsreel footage of Nazi rallies, it is hard to put ourselves in the place of those who were present, hard to empathise with their obvious emotion. Hitler's rants seem rasping, tedious, even comic. Göring looks ridiculous as he struts about in his fancy uniforms. Yet a young girl bursts into tears as Hitler passes by and he pats her on the cheek in a fatherly way. And boys salute in earnest as they show off their prowess in sport before the grandees. Even allowing for Goebbels' intelligence and propaganda skills, Hitler's charisma clearly wasn't just invented for the cameras. But it is hard, by now, to sense where its power lay.

Yet the bemusement will surely soon give way to something else – as it does for us, even now, seventy-five years after Stunde Null. For them, as for us, no matter how familiar they think they are with what happened, when they look afresh at the facts, they will surely be struck by a sense of awe: at the sheer scale and nature of the expansionist ambitions of Nazi Germany; at the possibility that they might actually have succeeded in establishing their thousand-year Reich; at the brutality and the efficiency of its aggression; at the Holocaust; at how few resisted and at their lonely, apparently pointless, bravery; at the final Götterdämmerung; and then at the very emptiness of it all – the complete absence of any legacy left behind by the Nazis that had any value whatsoever.

For the brutal aggression of their ambitions was surely unique: different – if not in kind, then certainly in scale – from anything that had gone on before in human history. Neither the Prussian state nor the Second Reich had behaved that way. Not that they had been peaceful neighbours in Europe, of course: but Germany's aims and tactics in the 19th century and in the First World War were very different from those of the Third Reich. If there were omens in earlier German behaviour, then they were to be seen in the German colonies, and in Belgium as the army executed the Schlieffen Plan in the first weeks of war in 1914. But these episodes were not at all unique in the story of human aggression; and their scale was as nothing compared with what was to come.

There had been times before when peoples had embarked on sudden, aggressive and astonishingly rapid international expansion: the Arabs Muslims in the 7th century; the Mongols in the 13th century; much more recently, the French under Napoleon. The first was a missionary conquest motivated by religious zeal; the second had no clear purpose or goal, other than bounty and tribute; the third had a mixture of motives, but was clearly animated by the spirit and energy of the French Revolution. The international ambitions of Soviet Communism were similarly broad to begin with; in both cases the ideology had at its core a conviction that they had a mission to break up old structures and to advance human progress. Then there was the phenomenon of Japan's 20th century expansion. This was certainly different; no missionary zeal, no ideological drive motivated their occupation of China. What they sought was an empire they would dominate politically and economically. The so-called 'Co-Prosperity Sphere' in South East Asia was never about Lebensraum.

All this was different from the ambition of Nazi Germany – which was not merely to dominate Europe, but to take whole swathes of land to the east and Germanise them by massive resettlement and the use of brutal force. Even this might be argued to have a precedent in some of the behaviour of incoming Europeans towards existing inhabitants in the New World; but the sheer scale of Nazi ambition, based on a blatant and brutal ethnic Darwinism, and the explicit government intent, make it completely different in kind.

Could they ever have succeeded?

It is certainly too easy to presume that Operation Barbarossa was doomed to failure from the start. It is inevitable that parallels are drawn between the fate of the Wehrmacht and of Napoleon's Grande Armée. Both were disastrously weakened by Russia's famous General Winter. On top of this, a combination of German planning failures and strategy mistakes, together with the Soviet Union's success in shifting production of materiel to the east and its brutal single-mindedness in mobilising its massive demographic reserves, meant that by the end of 1942 the German effort was probably doomed. And yet other scenarios can be painted with very different outcomes. Not least: what if the Japanese had opted for a northern strike in late 1941? Since the beginning of the century influential voices in Japan had been pushing for this. In the end they lost out, partly as a result of the bruising experience of fighting with Soviet troops in 1939. But what if they had prevailed? Would the United States have entered the war without being attacked? Could the Soviet Union then have withstood a war on two fronts? What in that case would Britain's lonely defiance on the western edge of Europe have amounted to?

This did not happen: instead Japan embarked not only on its lightening campaign through the British and Dutch colonial empires but also on its all-or-nothing gamble of a strike against the United States itself. This brought the United States into the war, and did make the final outcome inevitable. Even then, we might ask, what if Hitler had not declared war on the United States? In fact, surely, sooner or later US involvement in the European war was inevitable. But the counterfactual is a reminder that at least until the winter of 1942/43, the war against the Third Reich was, to borrow Wellington's famous saying about Waterloo, a close run thing. Even later on, when the ultimate result seemed clear at least in retrospect, the Wehrmacht fought and fought with a frightening determination and discipline, which meant that in almost every major encounter on virtually all fronts, their opponents' losses were higher than theirs.

Meanwhile, the infamous *Generalplan Ost*, with its aim to colonise and ethnically cleanse Eastern Europe, set out the terrifying scenario the Nazis were planning for in the wake of military success. Its pseudo-scientific classification of different races into those with greater or lesser capacity for Germanisation (with Estonians, Latvians, Czechs towards one end of the scale, and Poles – and of course Jews – at the other) sends a shiver down the spine. The explicit targeting of percentages of populations to be removed or eliminated one way or another has no parallel (even the deportations instigated by Stalin at various stages before, during and after the War, horrendous though they were, did not reach the scale envisaged in the Nazi plan). It is breathtaking in its sinister arrogance.

Could it ever have been implemented as planned? Maybe not: for one thing, there was never any likelihood that there would be enough Germans to settle in the vast areas to be conquered by the Wehrmacht. And in general, the plans for Germanisation and resettlement had a complexity about them that would have demanded unflinching efficiency – something the Wehrmacht, and even more the SS *Einsatzgruppen* regularly demonstrated – but which would have had to be kept up over decades by the bureaucracy of local government (which was often no more efficient or less corrupt under the Third Reich than in many other countries before or since). Nevertheless, they certainly made a start in Poland in particular: words are inadequate to express what that country experienced at the hands of Germans in the annexed west and in the rump colonial government area around Warsaw. In general, this brutal mindset conditioned behaviour on the fighting fronts, behind the lines, and in the numerous prisoner-of-war and concentration camps. The pattern is clear – from the grand schemes of the Generalplan Ost to the actions of the Einsatzgruppen to the awareness and therefore the compliance of the Wehrmacht.

They came close to succeeding completely in one key component of the Generalplan Ost – the methodical liquidation of European Jewry. As we have seen, anti-Semitism had not been unique to Germany; it was not even unusually virulent there. Anti-Semitism was part of the back-chat of bourgeois and aristocratic society – but so it was in Britain, and certainly in France. But the Jews became increasingly identified in too many peoples' minds with both capitalism and bolshevism: the former became a bête noire of the völkisch movement in the later decades of the 19th century; the latter became the bête noire of the right in the Weimar years. One way and another, the Jews became an easy target. Hitler made them a monstrous cause célèbre, and the Nazis became increasingly radical and thoroughgoing in their campaigns to marginalise and then eradicate European Jewry.

To stand in the attractive drawing room where the Wannsee Conference was held in January 1942 is to feel an inner chill to this day. Outside there is a terrace and then a lawn which drops away down to the lakeside. It is a beautiful setting for what would now be called an off-site. They drank champagne in the evening and got down to business round a conference table the next day. What did these people think they were doing? – not so much Reinhard Heydrich and the other Nazi leaders involved (who had presumably deliberately and without qualm made their Faustian bargain), but the civil servants who arranged the event and secretarialised it – what did they think they were doing? What was all this meticulous classification about – categories for mixed marriages of Jews and non-Jews, for the children of such marriages, for the grandchildren. Didn't any of them see the absurdity of it all, if not the evil? Or were they so involved in fashioning the process such that it could run well with clear decision rules that the process became the only thing that mattered?

The statistics alone do not convey the full horror. It is the individual stories – or even just the names of those whose stories are unknown (from Yad Vashem) – or children's drawings of life in the camps (from the synagogue in Prague) – which compel attention. In the early stages, the Einsatzgruppen had found it slow going – and sometimes hard to stomach, given the close proximity to their victims. Christabel Bielenberg, in her remarkable memoir of the life of a British/Irish woman married to a German, tells of a chance conversation on a train in the winter of 1944/45 with a Latvian who was an SS man. He had been in Poland, rounding up and shooting Jews:

> What do you say when I tell you that a little boy, no older than my youngest brother, stood there to attention and asked me 'Do I stand straight enough, Uncle?' Yes, he asked that of me; and once an old man stepped forward, he had long hair and a beard, a priest of some sort, I suppose. Anyway, he came to us slowly across the grass, slowly step by step, and within a few feet of the guns he stopped and looked at us one after another, a straight, deep, dark, terrible look. 'My children,' he said, 'God is watching what you do.' He turned from us then, and someone shot him in the back before he had gone a few steps.

The experience was slowly destroying this Latvian; and we know he was not alone in this.

So the process was industrialised, to increase efficiency and to put more distance between the killers and the killed at the moment of death. Hence the gas chambers. The programme was carried out with a persistence well into the winter and spring of 1944/45, long after it was clear that Germany was in full retreat in the war, and needed every resource it could muster in its defence. From platform 17 at Grunewald station in the wooded suburbs of west Berlin the transport trains took the deported Jews away: there are now plaques there which show the numbers week by week through the war. The last ones were being herded into the wagons on 27 March 1945, even as the Red Army was closing in on Berlin.

Platform 17 was at one side of a busy commuter station, within a stone's throw of people's homes – affluent suburban villas (many of them inhabited by wealthy Jews before the war). There is no record of any protest. As we know, there were few voices raised in protest, anywhere in Germany. Famously, a group of non-Jewish women forced the Gestapo to release their Jewish husbands who had been rounded up for deportation from Berlin by their stubborn and noisy protests outside the house where they were being held in the Rosenstraße. But this was exceptional. There are individual stories of families who risked their own lives sheltering Jews on the run. But why so few? Christabel Bielenberg tells of one occasion when she was asked to give refuge to a Jewish couple: she does so for two nights but, in the interests of her own family's safety, cannot do so for longer. She never learns what happens to them after they leave, but her memoir suggests that she lived with the discomfort of this decision for the rest of her life.

Why, in general, was resistance to the regime so rare – even by the growing numbers who thought that it was leading Germany to disaster (though not necessarily that it was all inherently evil)? Part of the answer is of course that the regime had a wide measure of approval for its early achievements and at least some of its objectives. If Hitler had died after the fall of France in the summer of 1940, he might have lived on as a national hero – as a leader of genius seen as having outshone even Bismarck. Later, as the clouds darkened, that widespread approval became more and more a cowed obedience, as people's horizons narrowed to the daily tasks of survival and their fears for the future became more and more focused on the bombing and on the coming of the Russians. We have already looked at the culture of dutiful obedience, which certainly played its part in this. But they were also living in a police state where any protest was dealt with mercilessly: in this respect, Nazi Germany was hardly different from other regimes where totalitarian governments rule by terror – from the Soviet Union under Stalin, through Saddam Hussein's Iraq to North Korea.

All the more remarkable, then, are the few lonely stories of resistance which stand out from this grey background of supine support. The most celebrated are the small group of students and their philosophy professor at Munich University, known as the White Rose. They distributed leaflets calling for the overthrow of a regime whose odious behaviour they had seen as medical students sent to the eastern front in late 1942. They did not last long: Hans and Sophie Scholl were caught in the act of distributing the sixth of the group's leaflets. Others were soon rounded up. They faced the infamous Nazi judge Roland Freisler, and most were executed after the inevitable convictions for sedition.

There were others too, less well known: for example Otto and Elise Hampel, a middle aged working class couple whose brave protest might have been largely unknown were it not for the novel based on their story which Hans Fallada wrote in 1947: *Jeder stirbt für sich allein* – Each Person Dies Alone – which appeared in English under the disappointingly bland title *Alone in Berlin*. They write unsigned postcards calling for the removal of Hitler and the regime and leave them in public places such as the hallways of apartment blocks in Berlin. Most of their postcards are dutifully handed in to the police, and they are meticulously tracked by an investigating officer. They are eventually caught, imprisoned and meet their deaths without knowing whether their actions have achieved anything at all. Indeed, we know that they didn't – except that they lit a small candle for humanity in the midst of the moral blackness of the Third Reich.

The churches had a mixed record. In Protestantism, the pro-regime German Christians were a small, noisy minority; the oppositional Confessing Church was also small, and whilst its leaders showed great personal bravery – which in some cases cost them their lives – the fact is that the vast majority of pastors and of congregations were quiescent. Far too few spoke out against the obvious abuses of human rights that were taking place daily under their noses. The Catholic Church produced its heroes in, for example, Bishop Galen of Münster and Bishop Preysing of Berlin. The papal encyclical 'Mit brennender Sorge' – with burning concern – which was read out in all Catholic Churches on Palm Sunday 1937, was an outspoken attack on racial ideologies that elevated one race above others. But of the millions who attended Protestant services of worship or Catholic masses every Sunday, there were few who even quietly lifted a finger for their Jewish neighbours. Even fewer were vocal in protest. But the story of the White Rose demonstrates that there were some: its members included committed Protestants, Catholics and one (converted) Orthodox. So too does the record of Dietrich Bonhoeffer, as we shall shortly see.

Within wider society too, there were those who resisted. They were not a homogeneous group: many – like Stauffen-berg and the majority of his co-conspirators – were from the traditional social and military elite; others like Julius Leber and Wilhelm Leuschner were social democrats. Others were communists. Carl Goerdeler was a civil servant, from a family of civil servants. Their approaches to the regime and its replacement were as varied as their backgrounds: many sought to turn the social clock back to something a lot more like the Wilhelmine era than the Weimar Republic. Many had begun as supporters of the Third Reich. Some were not immune to anti-Semitic prejudice. A few never succumbed to Hitler's dreams in the first place, and either out of deep Christian commitment or an unwavering belief in the country's right to a democratic future (or to a socialist or communist one) worked covertly for change.

From the vantage point of the 21st century (and in the context of some of the questions about identity that the modern Germany faces), one of the most interesting – and poignant – of these groups is what became known as the Kreisau circle (named by the Gestapo after the country estate of one of its leaders, Graf Helmuth James von Moltke). The circle centred on Moltke and on Peter Yorck von Wartenburg, both scions of great Prussian Junker families who had featured prominently in 19th century German history. Moltke was amongst the very few who regarded the fall of France in 1940 as an unam-biguous evil, not as a cause for exhilaration. Their thinking about a new order after the demise of the Third Reich would seem outmoded in some ways (particularly in that it was conditioned by the widespread sense that the parliamentary system of the Weimar Republic had been part of the cause of Germany's social and moral breakdown and of Nazism's success). But what was striking was, firstly, their commitment to a new order which fostered self-determination and public responsibility – in other words, giving real moral content to the concept of citizenship, and in effect upholding a Kantian rather than a Hegelian view of society; and secondly, their commitment to and advocacy of a united European governance within which regional entities with cohesive cultural and historical identities could exist together in trust and at peace. The issues they wrestled with have an obvious and continuing relevance in the modern Germany and the modern Europe. The Kreisau circle is much more than just a historical curiosity, more than just a footnote in the story of the Third Reich.

Best known of all of these establishment efforts to bring about change before it was too late was of course the Valkyrie plot to assassinate Hitler on 20 July 1944. The consequences of failure are well known – and indeed were recognised by the conspirators, who went to their deaths with unrepentant bravery. Hundreds lost their lives as the Gestapo rounded up more and more of those who had been involved not just centrally but tangentially. The whole episode has been subject to endless analysis in the post-war years, focusing on what some have seen as the amateurism of the attempt, the motives of the ringleaders, and on what chances they would have had of extracting what they would have considered a reasonable peace deal from the Allies. One way and another, they have often had a mixed press. But the fact remains that they knew that Germany was heading towards catastrophe, were prepared to do something about this, and knew that they were running grave personal risk. It is a telling fact too that in the immediate aftermath of the attempt there was an upsurge in support for Hitler: indeed, for two decades after the end of the war, a sizeable proportion of German public opinion held the conspirators to be traitors who had violated their oath of obedience to the Führer.

All in all, there were too few. Too few of the young, too few ordinary citizens, too few in the churches, too few from the establishment. Yet there were some. Tresckow's prayer seemed to go unanswered. But Germany now had a new kind of heroism to honour which may not have been perfect, but which was utterly different from the false völkisch heroes of the Third Reich. In Valhalla, the temple to the heroes of Deutschtum which stands in neo-classical splendour high above the banks of the Danube just downstream from Regensburg, there is now a bust of Sophie Scholl alongside the hundreds of others of the great and the good of German history.

Amongst the writings left behind by Dietrich Bonhoeffer was a masterpiece which will surely endure as long as there is a Christian tradition to nurture: *Nachfolge* – translated as *The Cost of Discipleship* – which remains to this day one of the most challenging meditations on the implications of Christian commitment that has ever been written. Its specific relevance to the circumstances of the Third Reich was clear. In this book which was first published in 1937, Bonhoeffer dismisses outright the Lutheran doctrine of the two kingdoms which, as we have seen, had conditioned so much of German thought and behaviour for four centuries:

Jesus aber ist diese Unterscheidung zwischen mir als Privatperson und als Träger des Amtes als maßgeblich für mein Handeln fremd. Er sagt uns darüber kein Wort. Er redet seine Nachfolger an als solche, die alles verlassen hatten, um ihm nachzufolgen. 'Privates' und 'Amtliches' sollte ganz und gar dem Gebot Jesu unterworfen sein. Jesu Wort hatte sie ungeteilt in Anspruch genommen.

(But any idea that a separation between myself as a private person and in my public responsibilities could be relevant to the way I act is completely alien to Jesus. He says not a word about this. He speaks to his disciples as people who have left everything to follow him. 'Private' and 'official' were both to be completely subjected to Jesus's command. Jesus's word claimed them both, whole and undivided.)

From this he concludes that the love which Christ stood for cannot be absorbed in or reduced to or equated with patriotism or friendship or professional responsibility, and that no Christian should ever give an unconditional oath of loyalty to anyone – the reference to the Wehrmacht pledge is unmistakable. During the later stages of the war Bonhoeffer walked a perilous path of undercover resistance. He ultimately paid the price of his position: he was executed at Flossenbürg prison in April 1945. Right up to the end the regime was ruthless in dealing with its opponents.

For Nazism, the Germanisation of the east and the elimination of the Jews and others was all underpinned by an ethnic Darwinism which meant that German identity had to be asserted in a struggle to the death. If Germany lost the historic struggle with the Slavs, then it deserved to go under. This is yet another aspect of its uniqueness. Increasingly explicitly, Hitler saw the fate of Germany as one and the same as the fate of Nazism, as his own fate. This was a new and heightened version of the arrogance of '*Après moi le déluge*'. Others before and since have preferred death to surrender. But there are surely no parallels to this leader who staked the future of a whole people – a whole culture – on a fight to the death with his chosen enemy; who, when the enemy was gaining the upper hand, used his extraordinary ability to command obedience to order a defence to the last; and who, when the defence became increasingly hopeless, still refused to contemplate surrender. Yet he himself escaped the hero's death he demanded of everyone else, by taking a very different way out.

This was indeed the twilight of the gods – the Old Norse 'ragnarok' being played out to its fiery end. Can we imagine Hitler responding to an A-bomb being dropped on a German city the way the Emperor of Japan did? Hardly. For him nothing was worthy of survival in defeat. Indeed, as Nazi Germany approached its end, the violence became even more intense. The rate of bombing of German cities increased in intensity from the summer of 1944 onwards. More German soldiers died per month in early 1945 then in any other month of the war (even including Stalingrad). In no sense was the violence winding down in the spring of 1945 – to the contrary, in fact – even though it was clear, at least from the early new year, that the Third Reich was doomed. Even after 8th May the agony was nowhere near over. Through reprisals and especially during the forced deportations of Germans from the now lost eastern lands, over two million died after the end of the war. This really was a moral and physical collapse so huge and so total as to be without precedent.

Were there any enduring achievements at all from those 12 terrible years? Was there anything at all of positive value that the Third Reich bequeathed to humanity, to set against all the slaughter and destruction?

To 21st century minds it seems crass, offensive and immoral even to ask about positive results from such unspeakable evil. But what is striking – not to say chilling – is that even if the question is actually asked, there seems so little to say. Some Autobahns? The idea of the Volkswagen? Some buildings of architectural merit, perhaps (the Olympic stadium in Berlin, what was formerly Goering's Air Ministry and is now the Federal Government Finance Ministry, or the Haus der Kunst in Munich)? The very idea that such things are all that can be proposed for the credit balance somehow underscores even more strongly the moral bankruptcy of the whole enterprise. How could a network of roads, a concept car and a few buildings be all there was to show for 12 years of extraordinary upheaval in the life of what had been one of the greatest cultures of the world?

How did culture fare under the weight of all this? Answer: it shrivelled as the regime brought it under the control of its ideology through the establishment of the *Reichskulturkammer* (the Reich Chamber of Culture), whose President was Goebbels. It is no answer to point to the undoubted brilliance of *Der Triumph des Willens*, whose claim to be great art is irredeemably vitiated by its purpose. It is no answer either to point to recordings of beautiful performances by the Berlin Philharmonic Orchestra under Furtwängler's direction. These simply beg the question he was confronted with at his Nuremberg interrogation: how could you possibly compartmentalise an interior world of aesthetics in the context of the realities of the Third Reich? Ronald Harwood's 1995 play *Taking Sides*, about Furtwängler's interrogation by an American army colonel, who has little knowledge of his sophisticated musical world, brilliantly exposes the deep ambiguity of Furtwängler's position – and by extension of any claim that culture might somehow humanise hard spirits and thereby redeem them.

The Third Reich produced its politically acceptable art, for sure, some of which bore a marked resemblance to the so-called socialist realist art that was endorsed in the Soviet Union. It was wholesome, bland, undemanding: gone was the energy and tension of expressionism. There was no great poetry or literature either: the contrast with the Soviet Union under Stalin is stark. Where were the equivalents of Anna Akhmatova, Alexander Blok, Mikhail Bulgakov, Osip Mandelstam, Boris Pasternak, Marina Tsvetaeva and others? All of these wrote under the sometimes appalling conditions of the Soviet Union: their secret was that their spirits were never suborned, and so their creativity endured, in some cases at great personal cost. Compared with this outpouring, Nazi Germany was virtually silent.

Perhaps unsurprisingly, it was in that realm of creativity where Germans had for so long believed in the absoluteness and the universality, in the poetic or even religious significance of their art – music – that there was more to show. Furtwängler had indeed worked hard to preserve the humanising power of music (and indeed to protect Jewish musicians). Inevitably, music like all other human creativity was suborned by a regime which regarded jazz as degenerate and demanded music to support the prescribed völkisch mood. But there were composers of genius living in the Third Reich – Richard Strauss above all, but also Paul Hindemith and the Austrian Anton Webern. Hindemith was a controversial figure in the German musical establishment of the time, and although he benefitted for some years from Furtwängler's protection, he eventually emigrated in 1938. Webern's music was condemned as degenerate and banned, although he continued to compose demanding, Schönberg-influenced music. That he had thrown his lot in with the regime did not help him much, although he was able to get some of his work performed in Switzerland. And Carl Orff's hugely successful *Carmina Burana* was premiered in Frankfurt in 1936.

But Germany's greatest 20th century composer, Richard Strauss, is the most intriguing case: after stepping down from an uncomfortable public role as head of the *Reichsmusikkammer* (the Reich Chamber of Music) in 1935, he retired to a more private life – but one in which, in his seventies, he seemed to experience a new momentum of creativity. At least one of his works, the 1938 opera *Friedenstag* – day of peace – represents a clear if indirect appeal against war. After the war began, unsurprisingly, it was never performed again in the Third Reich. But his final opera, *Capriccio*, is a light-hearted look at various forms of human expression in music, dance and poetry – composed and then performed in Munich, in the gradually darkening months of 1942.

Strauss is perhaps the exception who proves the rule. Or rather, he points to the exception which is music. After all, the concerts did keep going. The government invested significantly in musical performance; and Bayreuth seemed to enjoy more favour than ever, not least a result of Hitler's personal love of Wagner's operas. That the 'most German of arts' continued to be part of German life throughout the Third Reich tells us something about some of the continuities in German spirituality – and perhaps too about the universality of its music – that we will need to reflect on later when we consider the German search for identity in the new era of the 21st century.

Meanwhile, the broader truth about the spiritual atmosphere of the Third Reich is that it was not one in which true creativity could find enough oxygen. Neither literature nor the visual arts had left anything much of value. Nor indeed did the fundamental science of the period: much of the glorious era of German excellence in discovery and invention was now over (not least because the Jews who had been so strongly represented in the scientific academy were gone). Perhaps the truth is that the dearth of art and science in those years is the clearest signal of the emptiness of the evil that overcame Germany. The silence cries out all the more because of what had gone before.

Evil: even today, we do not use the word lightly. Indeed, it is striking that the word has not lost its power, even in a secularised, demystified age. To call an act or a person evil is to use strong, unsettling language. It is an absolute judgement, so we should pause on it. What makes for evil? What is it? Perhaps we can only begin to find the answer if we recognise that it is inextricably bound up with the self. Self-aware beings are capable of respecting others as ends in themselves (to put the matter in Kant's terms), or of receiving and giving love (to use the still more challenging, and more intimate, terms of Bonhoeffer's *Nachfolge*). But the self is also capable of a self-love, or self-centredness, that sees others only as obstacles or instruments; and the fact is that we human beings are a mixture of both: respect and manipulation; love and self-love. We know, in effect, what it is both to accept and to reject Kant's categorical imperative.

This rejection – this explicit rejection – is the essence of evil. Using Bonhoeffer's terms, the result is the opposite of love. Where love gives, this takes. Where love shows compassion, this shows callous indifference or worse. Where love forgives, this seeks revenge. Where love is ready for sacrifice, this asserts itself against all comers. If goodness is generated by love, then evil is generated by this self-centredness which is the absence of love. Yet self-centredness is part of all of us. So we all know – in ourselves – about evil, though much of the time we may be only partially honest in facing this truth about ourselves. Which is why the judgement about the Third Reich is unsettling. Self-centredness was the very essence of the Third Reich: its self-understanding entailed an entirely explicit rejection of the value of others. This utter rejection of respect, of love, was what was at the root of its evil. If we are unsettled by this, it is in part because we recognise that the Third Reich was at one end of a spectrum at some point on which we all find ourselves somewhere. In judging it to be evil, we judge ourselves.

Or to put the point differently, the Third Reich was not in a class of its own. Its leaders were not automata: they were human beings. We know little enough of the inner person in the case of ordinary acquaintances and friends. We know very little indeed – perhaps virtually nothing – of the inner man in the case of someone like Hitler. But he was a human being. He was enthralled by the music of Wagner – that much he had in common with many of us. By his own testimony, and by the evidence of those who knew him when she was alive, he clearly loved his mother; her death from breast cancer when he was 18 deeply shook him. There are many human beings for whom this is a familiar experience. He kept a portrait of his mother at his bedside throughout his life, even in the bunker in Berlin. In gratitude to the (Jewish) family doctor who had cared for her through to the end, he sent him one of his own watercolours from Vienna. It is this humanity that gives the evil its excruciating mystery. There is something that we share with him. We know what self-centredness is, even if ours is limited, humdrum, and often balanced by better instincts of care and love. We are indeed stupefied by such extreme, such megalomaniac self-centredness – a self-centredness which, in the limit, creates its own world within the mind, inhabited by type-cast devils and enemies, and which excludes or warps all facts and experiences that clash with its own inner reality. But we are stupefied precisely because he and we are on the same spectrum, even if a long way apart. Which is, furthermore, why the history of the Third Reich will not be just of academic interest even in 50 years time.

So what gives rise to this self-centredness? Partly, of course, history: human histories of wrongs we believe were done to us – sometimes unremembered or distorted and deeply buried in the subconscious. As we have seen, the abused who turns abuser is one of the oldest patterns in human experience, not only in our personal histories, but in our community histories too. The communities of which we are a part have often carried folk-memories of wrongs suffered or rights denied. Down the ages and right into present times these histories have been used as excuses for violence, for revenge, for war. The Third Reich was the epitome of this pervasive human instinct. People were carried away by it; a whole culture was perverted by it; the Führer himself seemed to embody it. Hitler remains an extreme – and still astonishing – example of just how far megalomaniac self-centredness can go, as at the end he condemns his people – after all the horrors they (not to mention the rest of Europe) have endured – for proving unworthy of him. This, if anything, was surely evil.

But this begs the inevitable question: where lies the guilt? Just with one man? Right to the end he had the power to stop it or to keep going to the end. The thrall of duty 'unto death' worked right up to the end. Yet of course the guilt does not either begin or end with one man. There were the Nazi bigwigs, and then the thousands who made up the SS, the mid-level party functionaries, the prison guards and so on. Indeed, the circle widens well beyond those – as it always does in human affairs.

When does it start? And who is involved? Plainly not just in January 1933, when a small group of the aristocratic and military elite thought they could co-opt and control Hitler: and not just the relatively small group who formed the leadership from then until May 1945. Like a tree whose branches spread wide and whose roots go deep, guilt for what happened spread out amongst many and went down deep into the past.

It is clear that those who led had too many ready followers; and there were too many who were complicit because they knew but did nothing; and too many who did not know, but were uneasy and did nothing. Too many walked by on the other side. Max Frisch's 1953 play *Biedermann und die Brandstifter* – entitled *The Fire-raisers* in English – is a vivid dark comedy about arsonists and the gullibility of their victims, an obvious parable of the readiness of the worthy citizens of the Third Reich to go along with what in the end burnt their world down around them.

Is this the same as the collective guilt of a whole society, of a whole people? Certainly, too many were too ready, in both East and West Germany after the war, to allow guilt to be displaced onto others. Particularly in the West, the process of Vergangenheitsbewältigung – overcoming the past – was a painful discovery of the extent of active and passive involvement.

But no: that does not add up to collective guilt, if that means that everyone was (and is) guilty just by being born into that culture. And no, if that leads us to turn a blind eye to the sins of others who contributed to the disaster, both in the run up to the Second World War and during it.

Which leads to the uncomfortable reflection that there are victims on all sides, even in a war which undoubtedly had to be fought against an undoubted evil. There is the inescapable question of the sins of others in the distant and the more recent past: the sense of victimhood was not conjured up out of nothing. In particular, the victors at Versailles could have avoided their crass vindictiveness. Stalin clearly carries much blame: the Molotov-Ribbentrop pact in 1939 gave Hitler the free hand he wanted, both in the west and in Poland (and Russian behaviour in Poland ran the Germans a close competition in brutality). And why for example was Pope Pius XII, with all his influence in Catholic Germany, so cautious in his public utterances? He who had been so closely involved in the drafting of his predecessor's encyclical *Mit brennender Sorge* never publicly and explicitly condemned the Nazi treatment of Jews, despite been urged on several occasions by the Americans to do so.

Then what about the deeds of war? There is probably no such thing as a morally clean war, and the Second World War was certainly no such thing. At least with the perspective of a new century and of those who were not personally involved we can ask questions more freely about who were victims – of deliberate targeting of civilians, of reprisals and of forced deportations.

First: the Allied bombing campaign. The use of this new tool of war as a deliberate means of spreading terror and causing social breakdown was, of course, begun by Nazi Germany (Guernica, Warsaw, Rotterdam, Coventry, London, Stalingrad). The Allies began to respond in kind with increasing might and ferocity – particularly from July 1943 (the first major attack which created a firestorm in Hamburg). Neither the German nor the Allied use of bombing can be remotely interpreted simply as legitimate targeting of productive infrastructure. There was some unease, and some vocal opposition, in Britain (enough to ensure that Bomber Command – unlike Fighter Command – never got a campaign medal, despite the bravery of those who flew and despite the horrendous casualty rate). But the campaign continued all the way through to April 1945, led with obsessive and unrepentant determination by Bomber Harris, and indeed increased in intensity right up to the end – after there was any conceivable military justification. The attack on Dresden (February 1945) is infamous. The attacks on Pforzheim (February 1945 – which produced a casualty rate amongst inhabitants of at least 20 per cent, the highest of any attack), Würzburg and Magdeburg (March 1945) or Halberstadt and Potsdam (April 1945) are just other and later examples of what would surely now be considered war crimes.

How do we judge this now? In the words of one Briton old enough to remember: 'All they had to do was surrender'.[17] Maybe it is too easy now to underestimate the hatred and disgust (fuelled in the East by the unspeakable atrocities committed by Germans and in the West by the savagery of the fighting in the aftermath of D-day and by the discovery of the horrors in the concentration camps). In any case, almost to the end there was ambiguity and uncertainty; there were few who would have been willing to take any risk with the eventual outcome against a foe who seemed determined to go all the way to the end, in order to reduce the number of civilian deaths – let alone to preserve beautiful baroque buildings.

Or do we have to say that wrong is not justified by evil? More died in the air raids on Stalingrad than in Dresden; but that is surely no kind of justification. (In London, when a statue of Bomber Harris was erected in front of the RAF Church of St Clement Danes in 1992 there were widespread protests. When a much more prominent memorial to the young men of Bomber Command was built at Hyde Park Corner in 2012, there was quiet and respectful acceptance of its elegant propriety: an overdue catharsis?)

Then secondly: what of the behaviour of the Allies as they invaded the German lands from late 1944 onwards? In recent years this has attracted perhaps more attention by German writers than the bombing campaigns. The rape of hundreds of thousands of women by the Red Army was an atavistic rampage which the authorities did little to control. And French behaviour in Freudenstadt was little better. Both had been occupied by Germany, of course; both had built up deep reserves of hatred. But what kind of a vengeance was this? Again, there is no monopoly of guilt.

And thirdly: the deportations. Some 16.5 million Germans were expelled from the eastern lands, mostly under merciless conditions. Over 2 million died, as an outworking of resentments and hatreds built up over the years throughout Eastern Europe. One particular episode, the torpedoing of the 'Wilhelm Gustloff' in January 1945, has become iconic in the German mind. This ship, named after the founder of the Swiss branch of the Nazi party who had been assassinated in 1936 and proclaimed a hero and martyr by the Third

Reich, was sunk by a Soviet submarine as it left Königsberg in January 1945 with thousands of refugees on board. To this day, it remains the world's worst maritime catastrophe. (One young woman missed the ship because her sister was ill; they saw it sink just outside the harbour at Königsberg – and then boarded the next ship to leave.)[18]

These deaths lie at the door not just of the Russians but of Poles, Czechs and others. Once again, the evil perpetrated by Germans on them may explain, but cannot justify the response. Once again, there is no monopoly of guilt. The trouble with the doctrine of an eye for an eye is that it is never the end of the matter. All human history cries out that retaliation provokes retaliation. Hitler lived and breathed this principle: he used it against the Jews on Kristallnacht and in the Warsaw Ghetto; he envisaged that underground resistance fighters ('werewolves') would carry on the fight after the fall of Berlin, and that even if it took a few generations, Germany would get its revenge against the Slavs.

But what happened was something strangely different. At least in this sense – that a law of human nature was abrogated – Stunde Null meant something truly significant, as we shall see in the next chapter.

8

Remnants, Renewal, Redemption, Reconciliation

IT SEEMED ALL TOO OBVIOUS at the time that Stunde Null was the end of all that had been. It was not obvious at all that it might be the beginning of something new. The devastation was so widespread, the trauma so shocking, the challenge of restoring a functioning society so mountainous: it would have been easy to despair. Over 150 cities lay largely in ruins; transport systems, power and water supplies were badly damaged; the currency was worthless; food was scarce in many urban areas; infant mortality rose sharply; millions of people were displaced.

Only in recent decades, particularly after reunification, has a fuller story of the suffering come to be told – of the brutality of the deportations, of the rapes and murders (particularly in the east), of arbitrary arrests and unexplained disappearances. But even at the time writers such as Heinrich Böll and Wolfgang Borchert caught the mood – sometimes stoic, sometimes despairing. Borchert's play *Draußen vor der Tür* – Outside the Door – tells of a soldier returning from the eastern front who finds his wife in bed with another man, his parents dead having rejected denazification and been thrown out of their home, and his now prosperous former commanding officer refusing to have anything to do with him. In *Der Engel schwieg* – The Angel was Silent – Böll tells the story of a soldier return- ing to a bombed out city, bringing news of the execution (for desertion) of his comrade – to a wife who is herself dying of stomach cancer. The unscrupulous brother-in-law of the dying woman grabs her husband's will in order to ensure that he, and not some charity, benefits from the proceeds after her death. The soldier hitches up with a woman who has lost her child and together they embark on the struggle of daily living amongst the ruins. It is a grim picture, although there is light in the story in the solidifying relationship between the soldier and the woman, who end by planning for marriage.

Both Bochert and Böll reflect the reality of the millions who found their energy and attention wholly taken up with the daily tasks of survival. All too many were slow to come to terms with what happened. The traumas of the returning soldiers were not the only source of anguish. There were ten- sions between the Easterners who had lost everything and those whom they found themselves amongst. And there were the horrific facts of the death camps to deal with. Many, many people had memories of what they had done or not done which were hard to live with. Response mechanisms ranged from self-delusion to defensiveness to suppression and careful concealment. In many cases they were ordinary, humdrum stories of passivity: sins of omission rather than of commis- sion (though they were not the less sins for that). But some 12 million former members of the Nazi party faced detailed questionnaires about their activities. Of these a small percent- age had very clearly sold their souls to the devil: some of these – but only a very few – faced trial at Nuremberg. Others were in complicated and compromised positions, having – so to speak – supped with the devil with too short a spoon. The story of Werner Heisenberg is emblematic: the famous physicist and father of the uncertainty principle had a notoriously ambiguous role in the German nuclear weapons programme. Michael Frayn's compelling play about Heisenberg's controversial meeting with fellow scientist Nils Bohr in occupied Copenhagen has him relate in graphic terms his experience of the last days of the collapsing Reich:

Three days and three nights I travelled. Out of Württemberg, down through the Swabian Jura and the first foothills of the Alps. Across my ruined homeland. Was this what I'd chosen for it? This endless rubble? This perpetual smoke in the sky? These hungry faces? Was this my doing? And all the desperate people on the roads … The second night and suddenly there it is – the terrible familiar black tunic emerging from the twilight in front of me. On his lips as I stop – the one terrible familiar word. 'Deserter,' he says. He sounds as exhausted as I am. I give him the travel order I've written for myself. But there's hardly enough light in the sky to read by, and he's too weary to bother. He begins to open his holster instead … what comes into my mind this time is the packet of American cigarettes I've got in my pocket. And already it's in my hand – I'm holding it out to him. The most desperate solution to a problem yet … He closes the holster and takes the cigarettes instead … For 20 cigarettes he let me live. And on I went. Three days and three nights. Past the weeping children, the lost and hungry children, drafted to fight and then abandoned by their commanders. Past the starving slave-labourers walking home to France, to Poland, to

Estonia. Through Gammertingen and Biberach and Mem-mingen. Mindelheim, Kaufbeuren and Schöngau. Across my beloved homeland. My ruined and dishonoured and beloved homeland.

Against this background, few had time or energy for visions of a new future, or any sense of how a future could be built on anything that might have been valuable in the past. Engag-ingly, an old Catholic priest asked the British writer Stephen Spender if he could envisage the British zone becoming a dominion of the British Empire – a renewal of the Hanove-rian connexion?

And the victors had no agreed blueprint either. Stalin had a clear understanding of Russian interests; he was deter-mined to establish a sphere of influence – in effect a cordon sanitaire around the Soviet Union which would come under Moscow's control, and to ensure that Germany would never again be a threat. The cordon sanitaire was bad news for countries which shared a border with the Soviet Union, all of which eventually became puppet states with communist gov-ernments imposed on them one way or another, and some of which lost territory to direct incorporation in the Soviet Union. The country which lost the most territory in the east in this way was long-suffering Poland. Its compensation was the gain of about two thirds of East Prussia, together with the German lands east of the Oder-Neisse line – which meant that its western borders were once again as they had been a thousand years earlier.

But what all this would mean for Germany, and for Austria, was not immediately clear. Austria had been re-established as a separate country, reversing the Anschluss, and dignified as 'the first victim of Nazi aggression' – the dark irony of which would certainly not have been lost on anyone who remembered the welcome given to the Wehrmacht in 1938 and who compared its fate with that of the Czechs and then the Poles. Both Germany and Austria were zoned into Allied occupation areas. But Allied plans for neither were clear. For Stalin, Austria was in truth a sideshow, small and largely irrelevant to Russian interests; exporting the communist model as an objective in itself ranked low in his priorities. So a unified but neutral Austrian state was for the Russians a perfectly acceptable outcome – which is what was achieved eventually in 1955.

But Germany was a different matter. Even with the loss of 25 per cent of its territory, the country remained large – no longer the largest country by area in the European mainland, but still the largest by population and still what it always had been: the centre of Europe. Stalin seemed for a while to be prepared to countenance a unified but neutral (and neutered) Germany. Was this a sustainable proposition? Like Austria, Germany had no common border with the Soviet Union. But could the Soviet Union have ensured a pliant state without bringing Germany much more closely into its orbit than genuine neutrality would have implied? Even then, could it keep the behemoth in chains? In any event, Stalin had no certainty about the approach of the Western allies – especially the Americans. Would they countenance a unified but neutral state? How would they have responded to any manoeuvre to bring it closer to the Soviet sphere of influence?

Meanwhile, the Western allies, who had no clear and agreed view of what to do about Germany, awoke only gradually to the full implications of Russian realpolitik. As the Americans came to see the importance of helping a capitalist Germany onto its own feet – launching first the Marshall Plan and then the currency reform which rescued the German economy from near collapse – the Soviet Zone moved to establish separate arrangements for its government and for its economic system. The broad truth is that neither side had initially been planning for what actually happened: yet neither was too discomfited by the result either. Amidst the jockeying of the Western allies and the Soviet Union in the late 1940s, a divided Germany emerged – with an ideological fault-line splitting the country, as religious fault-lines had done 400 years before. The division looked set to be permanent, offering two very different visions of a resurrected Germany. It stabilised a balance of power which was rapidly turning into a so-called cold war. Once again a front line of European history ran through the German lands. Once again, therefore, the whole question of the German identity and of its place in post-war Europe was in dispute.

So was the question of whether there had to be a clean and total break with the past or not – and if not, what in the past represented foundations that were sound enough to rebuild on. The Soviet Occupation Zone and the three Western zones (which were merged in two stages – in 1947 and in 1949 – into one) pursued very different strategies. The Russians imported German communists from Moscow to introduce Soviet style political and socio-economic reforms. Large numbers of ex-Nazis and other potential sources of opposition were rounded up and many were deported to the Soviet Union. This was to be a new society, newly founded. The West too saw denazification and re-education programmes; but there was no equivalent to the radical social engineering or to the large-scale arrests and deportations in the East. Allied zeal gave way gradually to a pragmatism whose end can broadly be described as the creation of a self-governing, self-sustaining open society that would be part of the US sphere of influence and would not be a nuisance to the rest of Europe.

This meant that the continuities with the past were bound to be more evident, at least on the surface, in the West than in the East. Many people were able to evolve from pasts imprinted one way or another by the Third Reich, into citizens with a new basis for respectability, apparently at ease in the new democratic post-war reality. Countless individual lives must have undergone such remoulding. The story of August Winnig, a modestly influential figure in pre-war völkisch thought, has more twists and turns than most, perhaps. But it illustrates how Stunde Null was not after all the end for many who had shared at least some of the outlook of the Third Reich. Winnig, both before and after the First World War, had been active in SPD politics; during the turbulent early years of the Weimar Republic he was for a while governor of East Prussia. But he became increasingly conservative, nationalist and anti-parliamentarian in his orientation, publishing *Das Reich als Republik* – The Reich as a Republic – in 1928, whose opening sentence used the phrase the Nazis were to make so prominent in their rhetoric: *'Blut und Boden sind das Schicksal der Völker'* – blood and soil are the destiny of peoples. His views on the Jews were by that time the typical pseudo-historical racist clichés of the nationalist right. Winnig never joined the Nazi party; instead he moved in the direction of a Christian conservatism which may have brought him into contact with some figures from the 1944 conspiracy: but whatever those contacts actually amounted to, he survived the subsequent persecution. He became an early member of the new post-war

Christlich Demokratische Union Deutschlands (CDU) – Christian Democratic Union of Germany. He received an honorary doctorate in theology from Göttingen and was decorated by the Adenauer government. After he died in 1956, a school was named in his honour (as was a street in his home town in the East, after reunification).

Such remoulded continuities were widespread in individual people's stories. The convenience of it all was obvious: it enabled the individual and the community to get on with life. Nevertheless, both East and West faced the question of what to do about the past: both about the overwhelming fact of the Third Reich but also about the earlier past – the Second Reich. Frederick the Great, the religious wars, Martin Luther and all the way back to Arminius. How could they appropriate the culture without appropriating the evil? How was the German identity to be thought about now? In the East the official position took refuge for a while in the view that it had done away with the past and that the culture – or at least some of it – could be disembodied from its context. In the West the question of both history and culture would be the cause of much open agonising in ensuing decades. In the end neither could avoid it; in the end the country came face to face with it individually and collectively, as we shall see.

Meanwhile, it is worth noting that Austria had embarked on a journey as a result of the post-war settlement that led finally to the creation of a separate Austrian identity. The country that had styled itself 'German Austria' at the end of the First World War, and which had been far from unhappy about its incorporation as the *'Ostmark'* – the eastern march – of the Third Reich, was now the Republic of Austria, pure and simple. Over time surveys showed a steady rise towards an eventually large majority of the population seeing themselves as Austrian rather than German or even as Austrian Germans. This identity was not of course manufactured from scratch – given its exclusion from the Second Reich and the long history of Habsburg governance, its Catholicism, and its memories of imperial dominance and of cosmopolitan cultural brilliance. In any case, the Swiss had shown the way to a separate identity centuries before. In 1946 Austria equipped itself with a new national anthem (with bland and unexceptionable words and music which – though attributed to Mozart – is surely less beautiful than Haydn's old hymn to the Kaiser). Its journey as an independent identity became irreversible.

And what of Germany? When the Federal Republic was born in 1949, it would have been understandable if there had been some nervousness about what this new self-governing German state would be like. The past history of German government had, after all, varied for almost a century between the unsatisfactory and the appalling – from the half-democracy of the Second Reich through the fissiparous and unstable Weimar Republic to the totalitarian regime of the Third Reich, which subverted and abolished the democratic process all too quickly and easily. So the structure was carefully designed to avoid either the representational fragmentation of Weimar or the excessive accumulation of power which made the Third Reich possible. The presidency was reduced to an essentially ceremonial office and was indirectly, rather than directly, elected. Strong regional *Länder* had already been re-established by the Western allies; thresholds for party representation at *Land* and at federal levels were introduced (the famous five per cent rule, which saw the ejection of the Freie Demokratische Partei (FDP) – Free Democratic Party, in the 2013 election); the system of so-called constructive no confidence votes was designed to prevent governments being brought down by votes of no confidence without a replacement being voted in – a weakness which had bedevilled the Weimar Republic; and a new *Verfassungsgericht* – constitutional court – was brought into being to police the operation of the respective levels of government in accordance with the Basic Law – which was passed in 1949 and which still does duty as Germany's effective constitution.

Later that year its rival, the German Democratic Republic (GDR), came into existence in the Soviet Zone, with a constitutional structure which in form looked somewhat like that of the Federal Republic to start with, but which evolved over the years in the predictable way of Soviet client states – allowing for a far greater degree of centralisation on the typical communist model. Later the *Länder* were abolished, and the primacy of the *Sozialistische Einheitspartei Deutschlands* (SED) – the Socialist Unity Party of Germany – was enshrined in the constitution by 1968. Thus there were two competing models of the new German post-war state. Both were predicated on the assumption of eventual reunification, and in the case of the Federal Republic on the non-recognition of the loss of the eastern lands. So for the first 40 years of its life, the Federal Republic was in competition for international recognition with another German state which offered a radically different approach to economic and social governance (and which also regarded the eastern question as resolved – i.e. it accepted the fate of East Prussia and the new borders of Poland).

Over those 40 years the Federal Republic proved to be the winner in a contest which was in a sense existential – as we can perhaps see more clearly with hindsight. Neither sought to claim that there were two separate German nations; and the GDR had a ruling ideology which at least theoretically assumed the eventual triumph of its own socio-economic system and the downfall of the other. In practice, of course, many began to assume that they would simply coexist for the indefinite future, as two states of what was still the one German nation. But the underlying truth was that the existence of each called into question the existence of the other. If one proved to be much more successful (both economically and politically), then the existence of the other would be put into play. This was a point that the realists in the Soviet leadership understood perfectly well: they knew by the 1970s that the GDR was losing the competition and that it would not survive if they were to leave it to its own devices.

In the end the Federal Republic became the new Germany, after reunification in 1990. And the fact is that almost 70 years after the end of the war, the new Germany of the 21st century has an extraordinarily successful record. It became, and is to this day, one of the powerful economic machines on the planet. It has developed a robust democracy under a constitution which has withstood the challenges of terrorism after the upheavals of 1968 – of which more later – and which has shown itself equal to the historic task of reunification. It successfully integrated itself into a new Europe: first – as West Germany – as a member of NATO and then as a founder member of the European Economic Community; and then – after the convulsions in East Europe and the incorporation of East Germany into the Federal Republic – into a new European Union of which Germany is once again the centre. Gone completely are the aggression, the expansionism and the militarism. Instead, Germany has a – indeed, reluctantly, the – leading role in the most ambitious European project yet: the eurozone, of which more later. By any reasonable standards, this is an astonishing achievement, which was completely unexpected and for which there are few if any parallels in human history. It would, in fact, be tempting for the dispassionate observer to conclude that the question of the German identity and of its place in Europe had been resolved.

Tempting, perhaps, but wrong. The journey from 1945 to the present has been far from plain sailing. The Germany which is on this journey cannot be said to have arrived. Germany's identity is still in question – no longer politically, for sure, but at the psychological or spiritual level; indeed, the question of its identity is related to a question about the new European identity on the world stage, as we shall see later. But before turning to this question in all its ramifications, it is necessary first to look at these achievements of the new republican Germany and acknowledge them for what they are.

To begin with the economics: the start of Germany's post-war economic boom begins in the depths of the economic crisis of the exceptionally cold winter of 1946/47. The old Reichsmark had become worthless, food was being hoarded by farmers, cigarettes and chocolate were the only trusted medium of exchange, and a human disaster was in the making. But this proved to be the turning point: the launch of the Marshall Plan and the currency reform which introduced the Deutschmark proved decisive. The former made huge funds available for Germany's reconstruction and the latter provided the basis for a sound monetary policy which would underpin an efficient market, a strong savings rate and long term investment. The contrast with conditions after the First World War is stark: then the new Weimar Republic was saddled with war reparations, and its middle classes were bankrupted by a hyperinflation which seared the psychology of a whole society. Now the emerging West German polity was launched with an impetus which created the basis for what became known as the *Wirtschaftswunder* – the economic miracle – in the 1950s and 1960s.

The experience of the Soviet Occupation Zone was dramatically different: not only was it not free to accept Marshall Plan assistance; not only did it undergo a completely separate currency reform which was an inevitable milestone on the journey towards establishment as a separate state; but in addition the Zone was forced to make vast reparations to the Soviet Union in the form of materials, production facilities and labour. In the end East Germany became the strongest economic performer in the Eastern bloc, just as West Germany became the most powerful economy in the West. But the relative weakness of the East – due largely to the intrinsic weakness of its planned, collectivised economy – was aggravated by this very different and far more unfavourable starting point.

Meanwhile, the West German economy took off. Throughout its first decade it grew at an average of 8 per cent (not as fast as that other defeated power – Japan – but twice as fast any other major economy in Europe). This performance was sufficiently strong to enable the Federal Republic to successfully absorb the enormous influx of Germans expelled from the eastern lands – some 12 million, or an increase of over 20 per cent in its total population. It involved the extensive reconstruction of over 150 cities rendered to varying degrees uninhabitable by wartime bombing, as well as corporate restructuring (notably the breakup of the great chemicals group IG Farben – which had been part of the backbone of the German war economy – into what became the three pillars of the German chemical and pharmaceutical industries: BASF, Hoechst and Bayer). Famously, British managers had got the Volkswagen factory at Wolfsburg going: it went on to produce one of the world's most successful cars – a car which became an icon of the new, modest, homely Germany. It was exported around the world, as perhaps the most visible sign of the effectiveness of an economy which was to become an export machine of unexampled power.

All of this was underpinned by an approach to employer-employee relations designed to encourage cooperation and avoid confrontation, known as *Mitbestimmung* – co-determination – and by Germany's two-tier educational system and its admired apprenticeship structure. In addition, the *Handelskammern* – chambers of commerce – were re-established, having been abolished by the Nazis. All companies, both the great names and the hundreds of thousands which made up Germany's world renowned *Mittelstand*, had to belong to their Handelskammer, which became well resourced, well administered and highly effective networks of business support for business. This social corporatism drew on older features of the German business scene as it had evolved since the 19th century. Whatever might be the case in an East Germany determined to start from a more radically clean break with the past, the West German economy was rebuilt on the basis of a much greater degree of continuity with traditional ways. So successful was its growth model that West Germany found itself becoming home to its famous *Gastarbeiter* – guest workers, increasing numbers of whom became permanent residents who would eventually have a major impact on the German identity.

Yet this was not business as usual. The West German economy was powered in a totally different way from the Third Reich economy – which had relied heavily on the government's drive for military expansion as its source of demand, and increasingly during the war on slave workers, not on guest workers, as a key source of labour. The economy of the Second Reich before the First World War, though export-oriented like the new Wirtschaftswunder (Germany had become the largest steel producer and exporter in Europe by 1914), also benefitted from massive naval construction as the country sought to challenge British supremacy on the seas.

This time German expansion was powered first by the need for reconstruction and then by exports, especially of manufactured goods. German engineering excellence dated from the 19th century; and although it had by no means always outclassed that of its enemies during the war,[19] it certainly showed its power in the post-war economy. German manufactured exports have triumphed in the global markets. Already by the time of reunification it had become the largest exporter in the world – a position which the German economy did not lose until 2010: even now it is still the second largest exporter after China and has much the strongest export orientation of any major developed manufacturing economy (as measured by exports as a percentage of economic output). Over 40 per cent of output is exported, compared with about 30 per cent in France or in Britain, and less than half that in the United States. As we shall see, there is lively debate about whether this export oriented growth model is sustainable, and about whether it is cause or consequence of weaknesses elsewhere in the eurozone. But for now we should simply note the fact of this extraordinary performance on the world stage.

The environment became tougher for West Germany – as for all other European economies (including, crucially, the GDR) – in the 1970s in the wake of the first oil shock. In the 1970s growth averaged less than 2 per cent; the Wirtschaftswunder was well and truly over. Then came the management challenge of reunification – of which more below – and the emergence of new markets particularly in Asia and in Eastern Europe which became highly competitive production bases. German performance stagnated and the economy seemed to lose its dynamism. In the 1990s German economic growth averaged only 1 per cent (behind a resurgent Britain for the first time since the war). The financial markets seemed now to be king, and financial engineering seemed to have more value than the real thing. The much vaunted Mitbestimmung seemed to prevent adjustments to a changing world. Some even began to see in Germany the new 'sick man' of Europe.

This was premature. In the early 21st century, Germany benefitted from the combination of a newly competitive exchange rate achieved through the introduction of the euro, together with labour market reforms achieved by a socialist-led coalition government under Gerhard Schröder (in a sort of national Mitbestimmung that became known as the Hartz reforms after the personnel director of Volkswagen who led the reform project). This was reinforced by an unrelenting drive for premium product quality by so many German producers. The result was that the country became the European partner of choice of the developing world. 'Vorsprung durch Technik' was the advertising slogan of Audi, used around the world: this phrase came to summarise the essence of what the country had to offer, especially to emerging markets hungry for German capital goods and German premium cars.

Perhaps the clearest evidence of the standing of German industry on the world stage is the overt readiness of the Chinese authorities to treat Germany as their main strategic priority in Europe – to the point of holding regular joint meetings of the two governments at cabinet and senior ministerial level, something not vouchsafed by the Chinese to any other European government. By any standards the German economy has travelled a long way from the ruins and rubble of 1945.

If currency reform and other structural changes introduced in the late 1940s were the bases for post-war economic success, then no less important were the constitutional and political reforms which were introduced at about the same time and which laid the foundations for the democratic success of the Federal Republic. In the coming decades it demonstrated beyond any doubt its robustness as a democratic polity. It produced a succession of stable governments from the very first moment when Konrad Adenauer was elected Chancellor by a majority of one vote (famously, he voted for himself). He then went on to win the only election in the life of the republic so far which produced an outright majority for the CDU and its sister party the Bavarian *Christliche Soziale Union* (CSU) – Christian Social Union. Adenauer dominated the political life of the republic until 1963, and for several years after that the CDU benefited from the halo effect, even though its position was weakening. From 1966 the country had the first of several experiences of government by a so-called grand coalition of the two major groups – CDU/CSU and the SPD – but even then the CDU held the chancellorship.

So when the close 1969 election resulted in the formation of a coalition of the SPD and the liberal FDP – with the SPD taking the chancellorship for the first time in the republic's history – this was a watershed: leadership passed from the CDU, who had never been out of the Chancellor's office since the beginning, to the Socialists under Willy Brandt. If one of the hallmarks of a healthy democracy is the ability for power to change hands constitutionally and peacefully, then this was the time when the Federal Republic passed that test. Overall, the colour of government has changed along a spectrum between right of centre and left of centre in response to shifts in the electoral sands in a way which is almost a classic sign of mature democracy at work: change has taken place at a frequency which is high enough to be evidence of real responsiveness to underlying popular demand, and yet low enough to allow for stability. Since 1949 Germany (first West Germany and then the unified country) has had eight Chancellors; by comparison, the US has had 12 presidents and the UK has had 14 prime ministers – and Italy has had over 60 governments – over the same period.

Brandt took office in the wake of one of those earthquake years that shake the world no more than a few times in a century. The troubles of Germany in 1968 were in many ways part of a much wider upheaval throughout the Western world. But in Germany there was an additional, and profoundly significant, dimension: it was the demand for honest confrontation with the sins of the past. The children wanted to know of their parents: what had they done in the time of the Nazis? This is the question for the next chapter: for now, in the wake of all this, we need to note the emergence of a significant terrorist challenge from the RAF (*Rote Armee Fraktion* – Red Army Faction). Similar challenges had to be faced in – for example – Italy or, for different reasons, in the United Kingdom. In the 1970s the republic proved able to withstand and eventually defeat the terrorist threat without serious compromise to its democratic processes and its legal principles. There were many critics at the time who condemned the government for some of its methods in dealing with terrorists and suspected terrorists: but whilst comparisons may not take away the sting of such attacks, it is nevertheless worth noting that the British, Italian, French and US governments had troubles of their own which were not always handled without compromise either. Germany's record stands comparison with others.

Then in 1989 it measured up to the historic political challenge of reunification. Since then, as the united Germany has faced complex new challenges resulting from developments within the European Union – specifically the travails of the eurozone – its constitutional robustness has continued to prove its worth. The Constitutional Court has more than once taken cases brought by those who argued that German government agreements related to the stabilisation of the eurozone were unconstitutional; and no government would have dared sidestep its verdict, whatever the consequences in the markets. West Germany was sometimes derided as nothing more than 'Deutschmark democracy'. This was hardly an adequate description of its public life, but it is certainly true that its self-esteem depended in part at least on its economic prowess and financial strength: there was no more revered institution in the Federal Republic than the Bundesbank. But there was also no more revered institution than the Constitutional Court. And whilst it is an open question what influence the Bundesbank will retain as time goes by in the eurozone, the Constitutional Court remains as authoritative and respected as ever. Its status is perhaps the surest sign of the fundamental robustness of the new Germany's political system. To look at images of the judges at the Karlsruhe Constitutional Court in their traditional gowns is inevitably to be reminded of images of Roland Freisler in the same gown. The Third Reich reduced Germany's judicial tradition to shame: the courts of the Federal Republic have amply restored its honour.

The other sign of the radically new is the status of the *Bundeswehr*: Germany's military is firmly and without question under parliamentary control (whereas in the Weimar era it had reported directly to the president), and its image in public life is somehow humdrum. Completely gone – almost as though it had never been – is the self-perceived glamour, the swagger, the prestige which the Wehrmacht enjoyed in the Third Reich, itself inherited from the dangerous symbiosis between the military, the upper classes and the big capitalists of the Second Reich.

The Federal Republic is now in its seventh decade: its public debate has been vibrant, often intense, sometimes acrimonious. Criticism in the public domain, in the media, amongst the intelligentsia, is vociferous, relentless and demanding. But the overwhelming truth is that democracy and the rule of law are now so deeply entrenched as to be beyond challenge. In the 21st century we take the stability and durability of the republic for granted, and we all too easily forget how unpredictable this outcome was in 1949, in the light of Germany's history then. In truth, we should recognise from this vantage point what an extraordinary transformation this has been in Europe's largest and historically most problematic country.

Over the decades of Germany's rise to prosperity as a mature democracy, there has been a parallel journey of integration by this new Germany into a new Europe. It can be seen as having had four phases to it. In the first, the new West Germany anchored itself in a Western Europe which was itself part of a US sphere of influence. Then, under Willy Brandt from 1969 onwards, this Germany moved to recognise the other Germany and to build a relationship with the Soviet sphere which accepted the new realities of Eastern Europe and sought peaceful – even constructive – coexistence. Twenty years later, on Helmut Kohl's watch, came the unexpected and historic window of opportunity in which the Federal Republic absorbed East Germany. Over the next two decades this was followed by the admission to a newly expanded European Union of three former Soviet Socialist Republics, several former Warsaw Pact members, and previously non-aligned but communist states of south-eastern Europe. And then there is a next phase – which is still unfinished business – whose dominating German figure (and European leader) is Angela Merkel: the consolidation of the eurozone as the core of the European Union.

The Western orientation of the Federal Republic in its early years bore the strong imprint of Adenauer the Rhinelander. For him, integration into an Atlantic alliance was effectively a means to protect Germany from itself. The constitutional position might have been focused on eventual reunification, and Bonn might have been chosen as a distinctly provisional capital. But as far as he was concerned, Berlin and Prussian militarism had been the source of much of Germany's tragedy. If the eastern lands and their Protestant culture were lost – at least for the time being – this created the freedom to turn west for cultural inspiration and stability.

This *Westpolitik* was based on two foundations: NATO membership to ensure an American strategic and military umbrella; and the European project. NATO had been set up under US leadership in 1949, in order – as its first Secretary

General put it – 'to keep the Americans in, the Russians out and the Germans down'. But in the context of an increasingly intense Cold War, and despite the clear reluctance of the French, Germany joined and was permitted to rearm in 1955.

In the European project the Bonn government played a leading role from the first, alongside France, in creating what became the European Coal and Steel Community and then the European Economic Community. This started life as an economic programme, but was never only that, especially in German minds. This was a journey of integration into a wider European whole for a traumatised German psyche that was deeply unsure of itself. Its geographical field of vision was one which looked to the regions of Europe with which the Rhinelander had always felt familiar. Indeed, this familiarity was underpinned by some ancient patterns: the original EEC of the six founding members covered a region of Europe which quite closely overlapped with the domains of Charlemagne's empire almost 1200 years before. It was a region where Adenauer felt at home.

So did the French: what became the Gaullist view of Europe – an integrated Western Europe with France in clear intellectual and cultural, and therefore political, leadership – is in fact traceable to origins in Louis XIV, via the French Revolution and Napoleon. Adenauer never felt the need to challenge this view of the world or of the implied place of West Germany in it. Not that for Adenauer this meant the dissolution of the German identity into this wider (West) European whole. It was the same Adenauer who insisted on the readoption of the 'Deutschlandlied' as the Federal Republic's national anthem. But he accepted that Germany should have the role of economic dynamo and not of political leadership in the emerging

European community. He was certainly content to leave the East Germans to their own devices; but there was ironically more of the Prussian authoritarian about his dominant role in the booming years of the Wirtschaftswunder than stereotypes about this Rhinelander would suggest. His homeland had, after all, come under Prussian administration well before the foundation of the Second Reich. He knew good administration when he saw it, and was not afraid of continuity with the German past, even with the recent past. He appointed Hans Globke – who notoriously had written an interpretation of the Nazi Nuremberg laws for use in the implementation of their Jewish policies – as his (highly effective) administrative chief. All in all, Adenauer was unmistakably a product of German culture quite as much as he was a European.

The attitude of the West German government to its Eastern neighbour was wholly consistent with this. Adenauer may have been content for the Federal Republic to have been cut loose from the Prussian east by the partition which looked as though it was becoming final in 1949. But that did not mean his government was prepared to acknowledge this settlement before the world. On the contrary, the rigid policy of his government was to refuse to have diplomatic relations with any country that recognised the German Democratic Republic. This policy was formulated explicitly in 1955 in the wake of the establishment of formal diplomatic relations with the Soviet Union – which of course did recognise the GDR – and defined the Soviet Union as a special case precisely because of its status as one of the occupying powers: other countries would be denied recognition by West Germany if they recognised the GDR.

The ground began to shift in the 1960s. For all the human anguish created by the building of the Berlin Wall in August

1961, the fact was that it saved the GDR from collapse through the haemorrhaging of human capital (to use an unattractive phrase whose only advantage is to draw attention to the economic rationale for it). After that the GDR began to enjoy what turned out to be its most successful two decades. Insofar as the basis for the West German policy towards the East had been that the Oder-Neisse line was not irrevocable and that the GDR was not permanent, this policy began to seem more and more unrealistic. More generally, there was a growing urge – not just on the part of West Germans – to have dealings with the Eastern bloc rather than simply sit behind the physical and psychological palisades of the Cold War. Non-recognition was not bringing any benefit to West Germany; nor was there any reason to believe that it was helping the people of East Germany. Trade was better than confrontation; it had a better prospect of softening the system in the Soviet bloc and perhaps eventually opening it up.

The turn came in 1969, when Willy Brandt made a more constructive relationship with the GDR the centrepiece of a new *Ostpolitik*, designed not so much to replace the old West-politik as to balance it. Brandt had a new and different kind of charisma. The image of him kneeling at the Warsaw ghetto monument was not only an important step in a journey of repentance for the past, but also a key moment in this new Eastern outreach. Treaties with the Soviet Union and with Poland recognised the post-war borders; treaties with other East European states followed. And then, after fierce dispute in the West German Bundestag, a treaty with East Germany was approved, under which each state recognised the other. Both at this point joined the United Nations.

The implementation of the *Ostpolitik* by no means removed all the friction in the relationship with the GDR. Nor did it put an end to the yearning for the recovery of lost lands on the part of the expellees from the East. But their influence was fading with the passing of time. Furthermore, the truth was that fewer and fewer West Germans really saw reunification as a major priority, even though it remained officially the goal of the Federal Republic and the Ostpolitik was intended to make it possible, at least over the longer term. Meanwhile, ironically, a mirror image of this discrepancy between official ideology and actual popular sentiment had formed on the other side of the border. According to East German ideology the GDR was a separate state of the German nation with its own (and superior) approach to building the new society; yet the people, most of whom could see the alternative on their televisions every day, yearned for access to the West.

Could the GDR have eventually succeeded? Could it have created a new society which was sufficiently prosperous to earn the loyalty of its citizens such that it no longer needed a wall to restrain them from leaving? Could it have developed a separate identity in the way that Austria has done?

In one sense, it is plainly true that the GDR could well have lasted indefinitely if the Soviet system as a whole had proven able to do so – if Russia had retained the self-confidence, as well as the military muscle, to ensure that its client states continued in its orbit. But at a deeper level, the answer to these questions is surely: no, for at least three reasons. For one thing – and this is much clearer in hindsight than it was at the time – a collectivist command and control approach to economic management was doomed to be less efficient than a market focused one which encouraged more entrepreneurialism and creativity. This is not the place to argue this in detail; and it is certainly not to say that the capitalist system which drove West German economic performance was trouble-free (which it plainly was not and is not – a point vociferously and continuously argued in the West Germany of 1968 through to 1989, and in a unified Germany down to the present day). But in the last analysis, the competition between the Western capitalist economic system and the planned Soviet system did result in a clear winner. Furthermore, the free flow at least of broadcast information from West to East Germany meant that this was bound to undermine confidence and trust in the East. Of course only a few were prepared to risk escape; far more people retreated into an intimate world of family and friends, genuflecting where needed to the official intonements of collective responsibility and aspiration. And if the information borders were porous then, how much more so would they have become just two decades or so later with the advent of the digital age. No: the GDR's project of developing a confident and sustainable new identity was doomed. If the end had not come in that watershed year of 1989, it would have come later.

Moreover, this was not just about economics and information. An older point was at issue too. The old divide between a subjectivist and a collectivist view of human identity – between Luther's or Kant's autonomous individual and the Hegelian corporate, between the person and the people – had not lost its relevance in the contest for the German soul. From the vantage point of the 21st century we are wiser about this than in a 20th century which saw more than one social experiment, in East Germany and elsewhere, in which the corporate dominated the individual. Human beings are not

just Lutheran or Kantian autonomous souls: they can be suborned through deep seated yearnings to belong – as too many
Germans were during the Third Reich – and they can be sub-
ordinated to imposed social goals, as were the East Germans.
But sooner or later the individual human spirit cries out and
demands to be set free. The chant during the demonstrations
in East German cities in the autumn of 1989 was 'Wir sind
ein Volk!' – We are one people. But this was not a demand for
reunification as a new collectivist aspiration; it was a denial of
the official identity of the GDR. Underlying it was a demand
for the freedom to determine their identity which the West
Germans enjoyed. (We will come back to the question of
whether there is a German identity, now that the separation is
over, and how that relates to individual autonomy on the one
hand and to an increasingly connected and global world on
the other.)

There was another specific problem for the GDR which
made it more vulnerable than it might otherwise have been:
Berlin. Right from the start the question of the governance of
Berlin was central to the question of Germany's future. A point
clearly understood by the Russians, it also became increasingly clear to the Americans: if Western Germany was going
to evolve separately from the East, with a new currency to
kick start economic growth, then in the absence of sustained
commitment by the Western allies, Berlin would fall completely under Soviet control. Yet the Americans well understood the symbolism in the four-power supervision of Berlin:
and as cooperation between the Russians and the other three
broke down, they understood the increasing importance of
West Berlin. In 1948/49 an event of far reaching significance
occurred – even more so than was apparent at the time: the

Berlin airlift. Stalin's attempt to squeeze the Western allies out of Berlin by cutting off all land access was his first significant mistake in handling the post-war settlement in Europe. It met with a determined and dramatic response which was plainly unexpected by the Russians. Feeding and supplying an urban population of over two million via an air bridge was an extraordinary logistical feat involving more than 200,000 flights over a year. The airlift not only broke the blockade; it triggered the emergence of separate local governments in West and East Berlin. Shortly afterwards the Federal Republic of Germany and the German Democratic Republic came into being, but with West Berlin as an island in the midst of the GDR.

West Berlin remained a problem for the GDR throughout its existence. Anything that happened in Berlin happened in full view of the world – whether it was the brutal suppression of East Berlin workers in June 1953, or the construction of the Wall and the subsequent dramatic escape attempts, or Kennedy's famous visit which effectively sealed American commitment to the city and all that it stood for: 'All free men, wherever they may live, are citizens of Berlin, and therefore, as a free man, I take pride in the words "Ich bin ein Berliner"'. For the first time Germans appeared in the eyes of the whole world as victims and as symbols of freedom. And in the East the psychological impact of the wall was something the GDR would never recover from. For a young student named Angela Merkel, its construction was her first political moment. Who knows what would have happened if West Berlin had been abandoned? Who knows what would have eventually happened to an enclave which was economically dependent on generous life support from the West Germans and strategically dependent on an indefinite military commitment by the Western Allies? But the fact is that its presence, and the ugly artificiality of the Wall snaking its way through a European city, somehow revealed the artificiality of the whole East German project as nothing else could have.

In truth, the alternative way offered by the GDR could never overcome its artificiality – its denial of its cultural and historical ties with the Western part and its belief that the clock could be set to zero. Slowly, the initial enthusiasm waned. The proud monuments of the early years (genuinely fine buildings such as the Altmarkt in Dresden or on the Stalin Allee in East Berlin) gave way to a general impression of decay – symbolic of the gradual inner paralysis. 'Slowly the poison the whole bloodstream fills.' [20] In the 1980s the regime began efforts to re-appropriate the German past: the 500th anniversary of Luther's birth, or the legacy of Frederick the Great, for example. This was at one level a sign of growing self-confidence (which was also manifest in, for example, the assertive new television tower on the Alexanderplatz): but it was also the recognition that not all was new, after all. And in fact, underneath this more nuanced surface, the regime was becoming increasingly worried by its economic performance. The old formula of heavy industry and collectivisation was failing. The groundswell of consumer demand could be satisfied up to a point, but the comparisons were unflattering – the East German Trabi cut a poor figure beside a Mercedes. Increasingly the regime was becoming characterised by mistrust of its own people, a rising paranoia, and the spreading activities of the Stasi.

The end came surprisingly suddenly. In one sense, East Germany was just another of the dominoes of Eastern

Europe, knocked over one by one as change swept through the Soviet Union itself. But of course it was different: it was the main reason why the others had been forced to play the role of cordon sanitaire all along. As the Wall came down, it was not immediately clear whether unification would be the result. Famously, both Margaret Thatcher and François Mitterand were cool about the prospect; and it was far from clear whether it would be possible to get the Russian military out of East Germany. The Russian nightmare ever since 1945 had been of a strong, united Germany, and now this was what they were going to get.

Was there ever a chance of two genuinely democratic states coexisting? Surely not: Brandt's unforgettable line, on the day after the fall of the Wall, summed up a momentum towards unification that was irresistible: 'Es wächst zusammen, was zusammen gehört' – what belongs together is coming together. It was driven by East German longings for the West German good life, as well as by the deep seated cultural identity which the Westerners had to some extent forgotten and the Eastern ideology had tried to deny. Would it have been better to take the pace more slowly – to have avoided a one-to-one conversion of Ostmarks for Deutschmarks, which destroyed so much of East German industry? Yes, theoretically. But this is arguably to misjudge the exhilaration of the time, the determination to seize the moment, and the overwhelming sense that any monetary price was worth paying for reunification of a nation which had inflicted and suffered so much pain over the previous decades, which did after all have a shared identity, and which yearned to take its place amongst the nations again.

A generation after reunification, the Germans live in a new Germany. *Ossis* and *Wessis* still to a considerable extent lead separate lives, have different outlooks and have different economic prospects. The east has lost, and is still losing, too many of its young to the west. In 2013 the electoral map of Berlin, for example, looked uncannily like the map of the former divided city. It has all been more difficult, and taken longer, than expected in the heady days after the Wall came down. But the momentum of change – which is radically transforming cities such as Dresden and Leipzig – is now strong and irreversible. It may take another generation for the invisible walls to crumble. But it is striking that Germany now has both a President and a Chancellor from the East.

Germany is also part of a new Europe. The expansion of the European Union accelerated to the point where its extent now covers virtually the whole of the continent: Norway and Switzerland remain outside it by choice, but cannot avoid close relationships with it; the United Kingdom is a fractious member; but the rest of the south-east European countries that still remain outside of it will almost certainly join over the next decade or so. For all its many imperfections, the Union has delivered a stable political settlement in Europe for the first time ever. And for the first time in 1200 years, Germany's position amongst its neighbours is stable: if the post-war Federal Republic can be described as having been on a quest for a European Germany – rather than a German Europe – then this journey has surely reached its destination.

Germany has travelled a long way from Stunde Null. All in all, in fact, it has coped with extraordinary challenges since then: the ruins that had to be rebuilt; the trauma of dislocation for the easterners; the pain of division. All this could easily have reignited the old German sense of victimisation and nurtured new resentment and anger. It did not do so – at least not in the way feared by the generations of other Europeans who had fought them in the First and Second World Wars.

As it turned out, the risk was of something different and, at first blush, very surprising. The 68ers were angry not only with their parents but with America, which they saw as the exponent and exporter of fascism. The West German government was, they said, fascist: in fact, they provocatively equated it with the Third Reich. But some went further: an anti-Zionism, crystallised in some by the Arab-Israeli conflict, became anti-Semitism. That an attack should be carried out against the Jewish Community Centre in West Berlin – on the anniversary of Kristallnacht in 1969 of all dates – as part of a bombing and arson campaign against the icons of capitalism and imperialism, was almost too hard to believe. Yet it happened. It showed how close the belief systems of the extreme left and the extreme right could be – and how easy it could be to move from the one to the other.

Yet this proved to be evanescent. The challenge of the extreme left did not outlive some of its most vocal figures. At the other end of the political spectrum, after reunification there was an upsurge of anti-immigrant violence in some eastern cities, which raised fears again of a revival of pre-war Nazi behaviour patterns. This too proved evanescent. The broad fact is that the modern Germany is as peaceful and stable as any other major European country. The anger and the belligerence have gone. This is the most remarkable fact about the new Germany. The instinct for revenge was not just part of the stuff of Nazism; it is deeply ingrained in humanity everywhere. Yet – in sharp contrast to the mood after the First World War – it is as if the extreme and unique collapse has itself freed the country from that fundamental human reflex and enabled it to discover an unpredicted source of renewal and redemption.

Above all, the new Berlin tells the story of the new Germany. The Wall has gone, leaving little trace. Dramatic new architecture has transformed desolate areas along its former path. The old has been restored. The city has an edgy bohemian lifestyle and a cosmopolitan atmosphere that is reminiscent of its 1920s image. It remains an unfinished masterpiece. What the Nazis would have called degenerate art flourishes; at the same time, the Berlin Philharmonic is still arguably the best orchestra in the world. And not just Berlin. Siegfried has lost his status as national hero-figure; but Bayreuth remains the pilgrimage centre of Wagner-adepts and the *Ring Cycle* is as powerful a work of art as ever. Nazi parades have been replaced by football. For a while East Germany kept alive (in a new guise) the social corporatism of the Nazis; but all that is now gone.

The rich ancient heritage has begun to be restored and recovered. The old is resplendent again (sometimes having been completely rebuilt – above all in the iconic restoration of Dresden). In particular, a wealth of beauty and history is being rediscovered in eastern Germany: ancient castles and churches now beautifully restored; virtually untouched masterpieces such as Stralsund; the trails of Luther and of Bach; and the land of woods and lakes and canals. Nor is the legacy of the eastern lands completely lost. The Poles have carefully restored not only the Marienburg but also the ancient centres of Danzig (now Gdansk) and of Breslau (now Wroclaw). Even in Königsberg (now Kaliningrad), though much has been lost, the Russians have restored the cathedral and the tomb of its most famous citizen – Immanuel Kant (whose name the local university also carries).

This new Germany has taken its place at the centre of a new Europe, as its largest country and its dominant economic powerhouse. All roads lead increasingly to Berlin. In a sense, what the Germany of the Second Reich yearned for has been won by the Federal Republic – yet entirely peacefully and, indeed, distinctly reluctantly. But this very success has posed new questions. For the European Union has embarked on a new and completely unprecedented phase of integration, represented by the introduction of the eurozone – which we shall come back to as we explore its implications for the German role in the new Europe and for its identity in the 21st century.

The implications of this evolution are deeply unsettling to many Germans. Many take pride in their newly won peaceful prosperity. But many too agonise about this new Germany and its place in the world. They worry about its present: the unfinished business of the euro project and the risks it poses to their hard won stability and prosperity. They worry about the future: about the implications of globalisation, the rise of Asia, the sustainability of their economic and social model, the threat of climate change, the future of their culture and the general question of who they are becoming in the 21st century. They also agonise about the past: have they confronted it fully? Can it ever be left behind? Can Germany ever be normal?

So the next two chapters consider this new Germany and its identity: first, the long shadow of the past; then the future of this reluctant new leader of the new Europe.

9

Confronting the Ghosts
of Germany Past

JUST A KILOMETRE OR TWO outside the pretty town of
Weimar – home to Goethe and Schiller, where Germaine de
Stael fell in love with the culture of Germany and where the
Bauhaus had its beginnings – lie the beech woods of the Etter-
berg, where Goethe used to go riding for leisure with members
of the ducal household. There is a clearing in the midst of this
wooded upland which is nowadays just a flat gravel-covered
space with a handful of buildings in one corner. It is all that
is left of one of the more notorious concentration camps:
Buchenwald (which means, simply, Beechwood). During
the course of its eight-year existence under the Third Reich,
Buchenwald housed about a quarter of a million people. They
were systematically degraded and brutalised, and died – or
were killed – in their tens of thousands.

Famously, when the Americans liberated Weimar in April
1945, they compelled the worthy burghers to visit the camp,
and caught their reactions on film. What appears to begin as
something of an outing to the countryside soon turns into a
grim expedition: the sights and the stench reduce the women
to tears and the men remove their hats at the side of a mass
grave. On the following Sunday, Church Superintendent Kuda

told his parishioners in Weimar that in Buchenwald events had come to light about which they had known absolutely nothing, and he called on them to confess before God that they had played absolutely no part in this atrocity.

Plainly, at that point Germany had a long way to go in coming to terms with what had been done. Since then Germany has travelled far, on a journey which began by seeking to limit the crime and limit the number of those who were guilty, and ended with the discovery of a sort of spiritual atonement to parallel the political atonement the new Germany has found in the new Europe. It is a journey we should follow carefully, because it is both unique and at the same time universal. Can the pact with the devil be left behind? Yes, as the last chapter shows, in the sense that a new, restored, prosperous, peaceful and robustly democratic Germany grew from the very ashes of Nazi Germany. But in a deeper sense, there is still that gnawing question, which we shall come back to in the next chapter: who are we now, in a new century, but in the shadow of the last one? This is not just a German question: it is a question for all of Europe, indeed for all of us as human beings in a globalising era on a fragile planet. But Germans have had to approach it with the weight of this terrible past on their backs; as a result they have approached it with an intensity which is relevant to us all.

This dealing with the past – this *Vergangenheitsbewältigung* – has had two elements to it that are worth focusing on separately, even though they obviously overlap and interact: the need for recognition and the need to reflect – or, to put it differently, facing the facts, and then letting them confront us with all their implications, all that they tell us about human experience and capabilities. Both of these tasks have taken time; both have been undertaken more fully by Germany than by others; and the second can never be complete because each new generation has to undertake it.

At first, recognition was a matter mainly for the trials at Nuremberg. Amidst the ruins of this medieval city which had been a cross-roads of the Holy Roman Empire in its heyday, which seemed more than anywhere else to have embodied the essence of Germany's Gothic roots, in which Wagner had set his most German opera, and which had been the spiritual shrine of the Third Reich – the Allies tried those Nazi leaders they had got their hands on. In all, 22 of the most senior figures of the Third Reich establishment were prosecuted at the first trial which opened in November 1945; 12 were sentenced to death (one of them, Martin Bormann, in absentia); three were acquitted, the rest receiving long prison sentences. This had been meant to be the first of a series of Allied trials: in the event, the breakdown of relationships between the Soviet Union and the Western Allies meant that no more such Allied trials were held. It was the Americans who persisted; 12 more trials under US administration over a three year period from late 1946 saw the prosecution of doctors, judges, industrialists, Einsatzgruppen and military figures – 184 in all. Of these, 142 were convicted on at least one charge; 24 received death sentences, of which 12 were later commuted to life sentences.

There was little that was edifying about the testimony of those who had done terrible things and who were now being called to account. Strikingly, none had the consistency of world view to make an unabashed defence of what had been done. Did Hitler, as some have argued, have two main objectives, and as it became obvious that the one – the conquest in the east – was doomed, did he focus ever more strongly on the other – the liquidation of European Jewry? If so, then some might perhaps have been expected to take their stand on their nearly complete success in this frightful task. They did not do so. Famously, Göring blustered; too many others pleaded that they did not really know about the horrors, or that they were doing their duty by following orders.

But some of it was revealing, and chilling. There was, for example, the testimony of Rudolf Höss, camp commandant of Auschwitz. He was tried separately by the Poles, but his testimony was taken at Nuremberg, and it was factual, methodical, almost fussy in its precise detail. A court psychiatrist decided that he had low empathy skills – in itself, hardly an unusual trait. Twelve years after he was hung for his crimes, his autobiography, written whilst in prison awaiting execution, was published. It shows that same strange emotional distance from the substance of what was happening under his command. The chapter on his time as commandant at Auschwitz ends on a note of regret, but it is regret for something we all recognise:

heute bereue ich es schwer, daß ich mir nicht mehr Zeit für meine Familie nahm. Ich glaubte ja immer, ich müsse ständig im Dienst sein. Mit diesem übertriebenen Pflichtbewußtsein habe ich mir das Leben selbst immer schwerer gemacht als es an und für sich schon war.

(Today I deeply regret that I did not take enough time to spend with my family. I always believed I had to be constantly at work. With this exaggerated sense of duty I always made life more difficult than it already was.)

The inevitable reference to duty – and an absolutely normal complaint about work/life balance, which sounds, to say the least, completely bizarre in the circumstances.

The Nuremberg process had one profoundly important implication: it established a firm basis for the principle in international law that there are war crimes and that following orders is not an acceptable defence. This new principle of justice was a long way from the vengeance which lay behind the angry demand at the end of the First World War to hang the Kaiser. It marked an important step in the very gradual human development of a shared international system of values which both transcends raison d'état and requires the individual to answer for his or her own actions. But of itself it did little to help Germans more generally confront their past. Indeed, it ran the risk of making that more difficult: for one thing, it was a process run by the Allies – in other words, the victors. Moreover, it was selective, in that the war crimes of the Allies were not the subject of these trials (the Soviet judge sought to make it clear that what was on trial was not aggressive war in general but Nazi aggressive war in particular). Even if few said it, there were plenty of Germans for whom this made its justice more difficult to 'own'. What was more, too many of the bigwigs had got away, or seemed to have done so – Martin Bormann, for example, who had disappeared in the ruins of Berlin in May 1945. Where was he? There were known to be several people with a lot to answer for in South America. If Adolf Eichmann and Josef Mengele were leading new lives far away, what was the point of humiliating a cultured figure like Wilhelm Furtwängler? Finally, there was the risk that executing or gaoling the big figures would allow too many others to absolve themselves from any sense that they had questions to answer: the millions of members of the Nazi party; the soldiers who had transgressed any plausible understanding of a military code of ethics; or the ordinary citizens who had at the very least turned a blind eye to what was happening in their neighbourhoods.

Much more telling and uncomfortable for the Germans who remembered the Third Reich, and for their children who in 1968 would demand to know what they had been doing then, were the trials that came later on: the Eichmann trial in Jerusalem in 1961, and then the Auschwitz and Majdanek trials held in West German courts during the late 1960s and 1970s. Unlike the Nuremberg trials, these focused exclusively on the Holocaust, not on the more general crimes of the war and the way it had been waged. And they were not victors' trials. More effectively than Nuremberg, they drew the veil from what had happened. In the late 1940s most people were preoccupied with the daily struggle to survive: in more stable and prosperous times from the 1960s onwards, live television broadcasts of the Eichmann trial in Jerusalem had a vastly greater impact than the transcripts of Nuremberg would ever achieve. In West Germany the Auschwitz and Majdanek trials had the same effect. Trials continued to be held down into the 21st century – John Demjanjuk was convicted in 2011, but died before his appeal could be heard.

The trials also spawned a series of influential commentaries based on the court proceedings or on interviews with those convicted. Hannah Arendt – philosopher and former student of Heidegger – wrote a series of articles on the Eichmann trial for the New York Times, which focused on Eichmann's very ordinariness. This was no psychopath: this was, as she famously called it, the 'banality of evil'. Others have argued that she underplayed his virulent anti-Semitism; but she certainly exposed – and dissected – his claim both that he had followed the Kantian categorical imperative and that the *Führerprinzip* – or the leader principle – was the source of an overriding duty which denied him autonomy. As she had no trouble demonstrating, the Kantian imperative entails the autonomy of the individual and is completely incompatible with any Führerprinzip. Her judgement about the fundamental ordinariness of the man is surely correct. Like Höss, he is recognisable as a human being.

For the Germany journey of recognition, the establishment in 1958 of the *Zentralstelle der Landesjustizverwaltungen zur Aufklärung der NS-Verbrechen* – the Central Office of the State Judicial Authorities for the Investigation of Nazi Crimes – at Ludwigsburg was a milestone. Over the following decades this institute quietly worked away at assembling the data which underpinned a series of trials in the German courts, down into the 21st century. The same year also saw the first significant trial related to the Holocaust, before a German court in Ulm – of the Einsatzgruppe Tilsit. The Auschwitz trials which began in Frankfurt in 1963 were more important still. If the impact of the Nuremberg trials could be deflected by many because they were victors' justice, the Israeli trial of Eichmann could be blunted too, for those who wanted, as victims' justice. A judgement in a German court under the sovereign jurisdiction of the Federal Republic, on the other hand, could not be watered down psychologically: this surely had to be accepted – not just by the accused but by German society more broadly as uncontaminated justice, from the implications of which there could be no hiding.

Or could there? Over the next two decades trials were held in respect of the other death camps – Belzec, Treblinka, Sobibor and Majdanek. In all, thousands of people were tried for murders committed in these incredible places, and elsewhere. But over time the dramatic impact diminished: somehow the power to shock was blunted by the increasing familiarity with the awful facts – and perhaps also by the way the victims were depersonalised by the statistics and even by the repeated and nameless images of slaughter. Once more and more of the facts were in full view, they seemed somehow to become remote. The Frankfurt trials of 22 middle and lower level officials of the forced labour and death camp at Auschwitz were a media sensation, and the details of witness testimonies did much to bring home to the general public the specifics of horror in a way and to a degree which German society in the first decade or so after the war (in both West and East) had avoided confronting.

But the very judicial process itself made it difficult to secure reliable convictions. It was unclear what the legal status of crimes committed under orders was: in a totalitarian system those with executive authority could clearly be held guilty of murder; but what about those who did the killing if they were carrying out direct orders from a superior? Such people could only be prosecuted under German law as accomplices: hence the effort to focus on murders which could be shown to be direct, personally motivated and determined actions of the individuals on trial. Many were dissatisfied with the outcomes. There was a widespread sense that too many who were guilty were acquitted, or convicted but given too lenient sentences – or, on the other hand, that the real culprits were the so-called *Schreibtischtäter*, the administrators who ran the process from their desks and who were never brought to face their victims or to face justice.

Moreover, insofar as the media created the impression that those convicted were inhuman ogres, the risk was that they could be compartmentalised and distanced from the ordinary soldier of the Wehrmacht or the ordinary citizen. A sharp correction to this came in the form of Gitta Sereny's remarkable series of interviews – published in English under the title *Into That Darkness: From Mercy Killing to Mass Murder* and in German as *Am Abgrund: eine Gewissensforschung* – with one of the most notorious of the defendants at these trials: Franz Stangl, camp commandant at Sobibor and then at Treblinka. He was convicted and sentenced to life imprisonment in 1970.

Stangl had come from an unremarkable background in Austria and in normal times would have remained unremarkable for life. He was a policeman and was an early member of the Nazi party. After the Anschluss he found himself posted, first to a euthanasia centre, and then being promoted step by step as the system noticed his reliable efficiency and organisational skills, until he found himself in a position of responsibility for what was the heart of the extermination programme. It is as if he found himself at Treblinka through a process of serendipity, as if he laboured under the burden – and at times almost as if he would have got out of his position if he had had the courage to do so, which he explicitly recognised he did not have. He is perhaps the embodiment of that telling line from William Shakespeare's great study of evil in power, *Macbeth*: 'I am stepped into blood so far that to return were as tedious as to go o'er.' He, like Höss and like Eichmann, was no inhuman monster. The truth is worse than that. He had compartmentalised his life and had developed a thick carapace around his inner soul.

But Sereny showed that it was not impenetrable. In a revealing – and moving – exchange, she asks: 'Would it be true to say that you finally felt they weren't really human beings?' He replies:

When I was on a trip once, years later in Brazil, my train stopped next to a slaughterhouse. The cattle in the pens, hearing the noise of the train, trotted up to the fence and stared at the train. They were very close to my window, one crowding the other, looking at me through that fence. I thought then, 'look at this; this reminds me of Poland; that's how the people looked, trustingly, just before they went into the tins …'

'You said "tins"', Sereny interrupts. 'What did you mean?' But he goes on without hearing – or answering her.

'I couldn't eat tinned meat after that. Those big eyes … which looked at me … not knowing that in no time at all they'll be dead.'

He pauses. His face is drawn. At this moment to Sereny he looked old and drawn and real – it was his moment of truth. And then at the end Sereny records:

'I have never intentionally hurt anyone, myself,' he said, with a different, less incisive emphasis, and waited again, for a long time. He gripped the table with both hands, as if he was holding on to it. 'But I was there,' he said then in a curiously dry and tired tone of resignation. 'So yes, in reality I share the guilt.'

Somehow this was all the more honest for having been almost dragged out of him.

He died of a heart attack the next day.

Facing the facts was not, however, simply a matter of tracking down those directly guilty of crimes against humanity. It was also a wider confrontation. Whatever the deficiencies of the trials in bringing perpetrators to justice, they had certainly established a firm foundation of facts about the Holocaust. They begged an obvious question for all those who had been adult, responsible citizens of the Third Reich. What had others done or not done? As a stone thrown into a lake sends ripples outwards, so – particularly from the late 1960s onwards – the question began to be asked more and more insistently, and particularly by the next generation, those who became known as the 1968ers.

The decline of subservience which characterised those who were born from the 1940s onwards was, of course, a phenomenon of the whole of the Western world. The new, anti-establishment mood which came to the boil in 1968 had a variety of different kinds of underlying cause: the Vietnam war, the American civil rights movement, the tensions of mutual assured destruction, distrust of the faceless power of multinational corporate business, dissatisfaction at the crass materialism of post-war society, the loss of older metaphysical certainties, as well as a vocal left-wing idealism which defied the evidence of Soviet realities – to name but a few. Discussion of all this would take us well beyond the scope of this book. But in West Germany, the growing restiveness had an added, and peculiarly German twist: externally, the old Adenauerian staunchly pro-Western (pro-American) stance had lost its practical or moral imperative in the minds of many of the young. Internally, they wanted an answer to the question about the Third Reich: what were you doing and what did you know, Daddy (and Mummy), during those years?

Then came *The Holocaust*. This American TV miniseries about a fictional Jewish-German middle class family and its destruction was screened in Germany in 1979. With Hollywood panache and a star-studded cast, it brought home to West Germans, as nothing else had before, the human dimensions of what had been done. Perhaps half the population watched it: an unknown number of East Germans saw it too, illicitly on West German television. The word itself – holocaust – entered the vocabulary as the descriptor for the genocide of the Jews. There could be no more silence about it, no more gainsaying its centrality in the case for widespread German war guilt. A few extremists might continue to deny its reality, or to downplay its significance. But these met for the most part with outrage or ridicule; and in any event – for the avoidance of any possible doubt – the denial of the Holocaust was made a criminal offence. Over the following years the memorialisation of the Holocaust became a central feature of public life; and the *Mahnmale* – warning monuments and signs – spread all over West Germany (and later, after reunification, over Eastern Germany too, where the GDR had spent its whole official existence downplaying the fate of the Jews and trumpeting the sufferings and the deeds of anti-fascist resistance fighters).

So much so, indeed, that Auschwitz was on its way to becoming a cliché: and the very word holocaust, now that it had become a descriptor, was losing its power to shock. It had certainly lost its original religious connotations: few were conscious of its reference to the sacrificial burnt-offering which had been a central part of Israel's worship. But the public mood had nevertheless changed: from widespread avoidance to widespread confrontation with the facts – and thus to widespread recognition and a sense of shame and guilt.

This did not mean that everyone was happy freely to acknowledge their own sins of commission or of omission.

As Anna Rosmus[21] discovered as late as 1983 in the pretty Bavarian town of Passau, digging into the local past could stir discomfort and angry resentment – to the point where her notoriety eventually led her to emigrate to the United States. In fact, the vast majority of the (increasingly elderly) generation who had lived through it all as adults probably continued to tell themselves they could not have reasonably or safely acted in any other way than they did. In many cases, they will have denied and suppressed – even to themselves – a latent anti-Semitism which eased their tolerance of what they had known was happening in their neighbourhoods. But for the next generation, a sense not of personal objective guilt but of shame and of collective guilt remained. For the rest of their lives their consciousness would be conditioned by being the children of their parents and thus heirs to the history and the culture that had brought about the Third Reich.

In 1996 an American political scientist named Daniel Goldhagen published a book which caused huge anguish in Germany: *Hitler's Willing Executioners*. His thesis was in effect an extreme form of the Sonderweg: he argued that German culture had long been suffused with what he called an 'eliminationist anti-Semitism', which had become more virulent than ever by the end of the 19th century and which motivated widespread support for and active complicity in the Holocaust. This anti-Semitism was deep rooted; there was little to distinguish between Luther and Hitler. It was part of Germany's identity, as much as was human sacrifice in the Aztec culture of Mexico.

Goldhagen's thesis was triggered by another book which had been published earlier in the decade: Christopher Browning's *Ordinary Men*, an analysis of one particular reserve police battalion which had organised death marches and participated in massacres in Poland in 1942. Browning's theme was the potential for evil that lies in very ordinary people. Goldhagen's furious response was that this potential lurked specifically in the psyche of very ordinary German people, and that they were unique in their susceptibility to this 'eliminationist anti-Semitism'. Browning's thesis is in effect an instance of what might be called the *Lord of the Flies* view of human beings – after the famous novel by William Golding which takes the theme to its ultimate by portraying the capacity for evil even in children. Goldhagen argued instead for what might be called the bloodguilt of a whole culture, which perverted the identity of ordinary Germans over the centuries.

Few historians took this seriously; indeed, many professional historians around the world were incensed by it. It was not difficult to expose the inconsistencies in Goldhagen's arguments and use of material evidence. But what is striking is the reception the book received in Germany. Goldhagen addressed packed audiences when he went to Berlin on a promotional lecture tour. In 1997 he was awarded the Democracy Prize by the German Journal for German and International Politics – with Jürgen Habermas contributing one of the laudatory citations. Others noted that the debate about the book was conducted with an openness which showed Germany's readiness to confront its past – which itself, they argued, should be a source of quiet pride. Whatever the public made of the basic thesis, it is at least clear that German society had travelled a long way from the mood of the years after 1945. Confrontation with the facts of the Third Reich was now the order of the day.

So much so by then that there developed a noticeable propensity to see every aspect of pre-Nazi German life and culture as carrying the seeds of evil within it. It might well be that, as Adorno, Habermas and others had argued, the new history and identity of Germany had to begin again from Stunde Null. But the facts of Germany's real history were still there and still casting a shadow over the present. And not only the Third Reich. Well before Goldhagen, German historians had put the Second Reich in the dock: they had begun to re-examine the very sensitive question of German war aims in the run-up to and during the First World War.

Within a few years of the end of that war, it had become widely regarded, not just in Germany but in the West generally, as a terrible mistake in which all the European powers had played their parts. This view in turn underpinned the accepted verdict on the Versailles settlement after the Second World War – that it was unwise and unjust, and a significant contributor to the conditions which led to the rise of Nazism in Germany. But in 1961 Fritz Fischer published his *Griff nach der Weltmacht* – a title which means something like 'world power-grab' but which was translated into English rather lamely as 'Germany's Aims in the First World War'. This provocative work sought to demonstrate that Germany, so far from being one of the 'sleepwalkers'[22] who stumbled their way into catastrophe in 1914, had an aggressive expansionist strategy which it had begun systematically to implement from the very start of the war. This strategy had been laid out in the document which Chancellor Bethmann Hollweg prepared in September 1914, known as the September Programme. Later on, in *Krieg der Illusionen* – The War of Illusions – Fischer argued further that Kaiser Wilhelm had set Germany on a course to war as early as 1912 in a war council he convened with von Moltke and Tirpitz, the heads of the army and the navy, although without the presence of Bethmann Hollweg.

Fischer's revisionism was hotly contested amongst historians. Few denied that German strategic thinking became more aggressive and expansionist after the war had begun – witness not only the September programme but the views later on of Hindenburg and Ludendorff, who did indeed envisage the conquest and enforced Germanisation of whole swathes of Eastern Europe, and who thus foreshadowed much of the awfulness of the Third Reich. But many would contest the idea that there is any convincing evidence of clear strategic intent – either by the erratic and volatile Kaiser (whose council of war seemed to be inconsequential in its effects) or in governing circles generally – to precipitate a general European war in the months and years running up to the summer of 1914. This debate has livened up again with the onset of the 100th anniversary of those fateful times, in a spate of books and articles about the First World War.

All this shows how sensitive the past remains; the reason for the resonance Goldhagen achieved in Germany is precisely this sense of living with ghosts. Confrontation with those ghosts produced – and continues to produce – volumes of literature, both fictional and non-fictional, about almost every aspect of German life before and during the Third Reich, from at least the time of the Romantics onwards. Take, for example, the realm of music, in which, by the middle of the 19th century, Germans thought of their canon as supreme: modern musicologists have argued that this sense of supremacy was evidence of a hegemonism and of a sense of special destiny which underlay, or even defined, the German Sonderweg.

Goldhagen is thus only an extreme point on a spectrum of what became German responses to the past. Germans became increasingly determined to leave no stone unturned in the search for the sources of guilt – to ensure that no aspect of German life should be above arraignment.

This is, of course, not to say that confrontation has been without controversy, or that there has been automatic acceptance of any and all expressions of the nature of German guilt. The reaction to Goldhagen was intense, but it is doubtful whether the general public – any more than the professional historians – accepted his thesis. It was one thing to acknowledge that Germans had in fact done terrible things and that there had been pervasive and egregious moral failure on the part of a large majority of the people. It was quite another to accept that they had enthusiastically subscribed to a culturally determined eliminationist anti-Semitism.

And there was also the question of whether – or at what point – the new Germany had a right to consider itself 'normal'. Did facing up to the past mean accepting that it was completely unique? Did honest confrontation with the past mean accepting for the rest of time a collective and unique burden of guilt? The 1968ers – and their children in their turn – could certainly not be expected to shoulder a burden of individual guilt: at what point should they no longer be expected to feel ashamed? Lastly, did such confrontation rule out the ability to recognise at all that individual Germans in their millions had also been victims? Or did even asking the questions about the guilt of others amount to shirking or diminishing Germany's guilt?

It was only a matter of time before such questions would force their way to the surface. In fact, it had already begun to happen by the time Goldhagen's book appeared. A decade earlier German historians and intellectuals had become embroiled in the intense and often acrimonious so-called

Historikerstreit – historians' dispute. This had been triggered by the historian Ernst Nolte, who had argued that the race murder of Nazism was a reaction to the class murder of the Soviet gulags – that, faced with the horrors which resulted from the Russian revolution, the German turn towards fascism was explicable. Others joined in: Andreas Hillgruber, for instance, wrote passionately about the tragedy of the loss of the eastern lands and the sufferings of their German populations – his very passion reflecting his loss of his own *Heimat* in East Prussia.

The furious reaction of Habermas and others on the left was a graphic demonstration of just how neuralgic the whole question of the Holocaust had now become. Any suggestion that it was not uniquely terrible – let alone that it might have been, however distortedly, an intelligible reaction to events in Russia – could no more be tolerated than could, say, the publication of the banned *Mein Kampf*. The sensitivity of the debate was heightened all the more because this was a time when Helmut Kohl, as Chancellor, was beginning to take the risk of asserting a greater sense of pride in the German identity. As Kohl famously, if tactlessly, said, he was part of a generation lucky enough to have been born too late: Germany was now beginning to move out of the time when a sense of collective guilt could rely on personal guilt or shame to keep it vibrant.

In fact, the greater risk is surely not that of relativising or whitewashing the Holocaust in the German public mind. It is that a younger generation will feel less and less defined by Germany's past: they will have no compulsion to deny, diminish or relativise what happened because they will feel less and less any personal burden of guilt or shame. In the limit, the reaction will be the same as to other horrors of human history.

But not yet. The cultural creativity of the new Germany is still profoundly influenced, one way and another, by the trauma. That deep rooted German capacity to reflect on inner meanings, to muse on the mystery of things, is as evident now as it always was – in philosophical and religious debate, in art and literature and, yes, in the music, of post-war German culture. In all of these realms the impact of the Third Reich in general and of the Holocaust in particular is unmistakeable.

Philosophical debate in Germany in the post-war years has always been politically engaged, and broadly left leaning in its inspiration. The dominant figure is Habermas, whose perspective on the way human beings define themselves and relate to others – which he argued for against conventional Marxist theory on the one hand and against the postmodern deconstructionism represented by Jacques Derrida on the other – make him a crucial figure in the discussion of the modern German (and European) identity, as we shall see in the next chapter. For now, we need to note his role in opposing any elision of the significance of the Holocaust and his refusal to allow any construction of a new German identity on the basis of what had gone before. He was not alone: the foundational doctrine of the German Democratic Republic was – in sharp contrast with the approach of Adenauer – the building of a new, just society which would owe nothing to the corrupt, compromised, class-infected old German culture. The difference is, though, that for Habermas, Auschwitz was the caesura. The GDR never came to terms with its implications, because what it said about human nature could not plausibly be reduced to Marxist class analysis.

But even Habermas, in whose thought the influence at long distance of Kant is so clear, had no metaphysical framework within which to plumb the human mystery of what had taken place. Perhaps more than philosophical discussion, theological debate within an explicitly Christian metaphysical context might have been expected to be dominated by reflection on the nature of the evil which had been unleashed in the Third Reich – not to mention the evidence of Christian passivity, or even supine support for the regime.

Indeed, the impact of it all on German theological thinking and on the political engagement of the churches is evident from early on. The Swiss German Karl Barth, who is for many the presiding genius of 20th century Protestant theology, and who had been a formative influence on the confessing church in the Third Reich, wrote a forceful analysis of the condition of the German spirit in the wake of the disaster. Published in 1945 as *Zur Genesung des Deutschen Wesens* – On the Restoration of the German Character – its title deliberately played on lines from a poem by the mid-19th-century poet Emanuel Geibel which had become part of the rhetoric of the Third Reich:

Und es mag am deutschen Wesen
Einmal noch die Welt genesen.

(And the world may once again find restoration through the German character.)

Barth argued in his book that the vast majority of Germans had no idea just how much responsibility they had for the slavish way in which they had served their rulers from Bismarck to Hitler, and just how appalled the rest of the world was by the horrors of the Third Reich. In a striking passage which echoes, in subtler tones, the point behind AJP Taylor's diatribe quoted earlier in chapter three, Barth goes on:

Sie lieben es überaus, sich bald als die Vollstrecker, bald auch als die Opfer großer, schicksalsmäßiger geschichtlicher Notwendigkeiten zu verstehen, und es ist klar, daß es ihnen auch von da aus schwer fallen wird, endlich einmal recht nüchtern zu werden, sich zu einem verantwortlichen Denken, zu gesunden Einsichten und zu wirklich freien Entscheidungen aufzuraffen. Und man muß endlich mit dem religiösen Tiefsinn der Deutschen rechnen, der der Anerkennung eigener konkreter Schuld allzu gerne damit ausweicht, daß er auf die große Wahrheit hinweist, vor Gott seien schließlich alle Menschen und Völker gleich schuldig und gleich sehr der Vergebung ihrer Sünden bedürftig, aus der kühn der Schluß gezogen wird, daß eine besondere deutsche Buße offenbar nicht nötig und durchaus nicht angebracht sei.

(They love to see themselves sometimes as the perpetrators, and sometimes also as the victims of the historical necessities of destiny; and it is clear that therefore they will find it difficult to reach a more sober perspective, to bring themselves to think responsibly, healthily and insightfully, and to take free decisions. And we must finally reckon with that German religious pensiveness which all too easily avoids recognition of concrete personal guilt, by invoking the great truth that all people and nations are equally guilty before God and equally in need of forgiveness for their sins – from which they draw the bald conclusion that any special German repentance is obviously unnecessary and certainly not fitting.)

Soon afterwards the Protestant churches came together and issued what became known as the Stuttgart Confession. Its terms were clear enough – and very different from the words of Superintendent Kuda at Weimar the previous April:

Mit großem Schmerz sagen wir: Durch uns ist unendliches Leid über viele Völker und Länder gebracht worden ... wir klagen uns an, daß wir nicht mutiger bekannt, nicht treuer gebetet, nicht fröhlicher geglaubt und nicht brennender geliebt haben.

(With great pain we proclaim that endless suffering has been brought on many peoples and lands by us ... we accuse ourselves that we did not speak out more courageously, nor pray more faithfully, nor believe with more joy, nor show a more burning love.)

It is worth noting that these words, together with a preamble which speaks of the churches standing in a great community of suffering – and in a solidarity of guilt – with their people, were the outcome of some forceful debate. There were those who had wanted to steer clear of confessions of guilt which would be uncomfortable echoes of the trauma of Versailles. Nevertheless, the Stuttgart Confession was unambiguous in the end (albeit making no specific mention of the Jews or their annihilation), and called for a new start, cleansing the churches of influences alien to Christian belief so that they might become again the tools of God's grace and mercy.

This was the start of a journey: the churches were determined never again to allow themselves to be the pliant voice
of secular authority and the proponents of order and social
duty. Increasingly, their proclamations would be underpinned
by a socially engaged activism strongly influenced by a new
theological orientation which focused less on the traditional
mission to save individual souls and more on the outworking
of God's purposes as human history evolved. 'Behold, I make
all things new' (Revelation 21:5). This eschatological note
(to which the secular eschatology of the early GDR was an
intriguing parallel) became the dominant theme of post-war
German Protestant theology. This forward looking perspective was articulated in different ways particularly by Jürgen
Moltmann and Wolfhart Pannenberg – both of whom had
been young men in the war and had come to religious faith
through conversion experiences in the midst of the trauma
of defeat and disaster. The impact of Karl Barth is obvious in
both of them. So is that of Bonhoeffer's refusal to 'spiritual-
ise' or water down the implications of Christ's teachings as
reflected in the gospel record.

Moltmann's influential *Theologie der Hoffnung* – Theology
of Hope – took inspiration from left-oriented Hegelian and
Marxist sources, but called for a distinctively open Christian
engagement with human history. This he saw through the lens
of a religious hope which recognised, but was not in the end
overcome by, the pain and suffering of society. Pannenberg
saw in the death and resurrection of Christ the anticipation
of the full outworking of God's purposes in human history.
There were differences in perspective and emphasis between
the two writers, and differences in their sources of inspiration. But in both cases the broad implications for the German

Protestant churches' understanding of their role was clear: the church had a duty to be engaged in the realisation of a future which was God's future, and – by direct implication – a duty to work for justice and for reconciliation. This was a long way from the self-perceived role of the Prussian church in the Second Reich – let alone the fawning German Christian movement under the Third Reich.

Bonhoeffer would surely have approved. Indeed, the new voice of the churches in the new Germany has been very different from their 19th and early 20th century predecessors. The new voice constantly asserts that the lessons of history must never be forgotten – hardly a week goes by without sermons recalling the evil of the Holocaust and the sins of complicity in it – and that the social responsibility of the Christian must be active, inclusive and demanding. In the limit, it can become a voice which can sound politically engaged at the expense of any real spiritual dimension.[23] But the determination to learn the lessons of the Third Reich is unwavering. It is hard to imagine the Protestant churches ever again becoming – as the old Prussian church had been – the tool of authority or the voice of a self-satisfied elite many of whom wanted little more from it than a clear message about social duty and order.

But their influence in the wider community is weakening all the same, just as the influence of the Christian church is weakening in every other European country. Increasingly, the theologians – even more than the philosophers – have been addressing a limited audience. Their intellectual giants have been only dimly understood by church congregations, let alone by wider society. Theology has long ago ceased to be the primary framework for most people's reflection on the human condition.

It is arguable that Germany's post-war confrontation with the past has been more direct and more resonant in the realms of art and especially of literature than in the realm of theology (something which, however, would not at all have surprised those early Romantics of Germany's awakening some two centuries before).

The art of post-war Germany has been vibrant, and often jagged and acerbic, for the most part like that of post-war Western art generally. Much of it has no roots that could be described as identifiably Germanic (although of two prominent strands in modern German art – conceptualist and neo-expressionist – the latter certainly has at least part of its hinterland in the German expressionists of the early 20th century). But the ghosts of the Third Reich and the experience of war lurk nevertheless in some of Germany's best known modern artists: in, for example, Martin Kippenberger's 1986 photographic installation *Tankstelle Martin Bormann,* which he claimed was based on a real fuel station he had bought in Brazil and named after the famous supposed fugitive. Gerhard Richter, perhaps Germany's greatest – and certainly its most versatile – post-war artist, has produced landscapes with an atmosphere which has led some to see in him an echo of Caspar David Friedrich. He has also produced realist portraits of the families of Nazis, and memorialised the destruction of his home city of Dresden with a monumental version of the candle image he has used often as a kind of memento mori.

But the most conspicuous example of an artist whom the ghosts will not let go is surely Anselm Kiefer. Born just at the end of the war, Kiefer developed a distinctive style which often integrates the verbal with the visual. Many of his paintings make explicit, sometimes verbal, reference to themes from German history and culture – frequently as a direct or indirect comment on the recent past of Germany. His *Wege der Weltweisheit: die Hermannsschlacht* – Paths of World Wisdom: Hermann's Battle – is one of the starkest examples. The Germanic references are obvious: Hermann at the centre, set above a fire whose flames are spreading, and a series of recognisable figures from German history around this focus, against the background of a forest setting – and all this in a woodcut technique which stands in a German lineage extending all the way back to Dürer.

Kiefer was profoundly influenced by a poem which included a phrase that became part of the post-war German consciousness. 'Der Tod ist ein Meister aus Deutschland' – death is a master from Germany. Paul Celan was a Romanian Jew whose parents had been deported to their deaths. A gifted poet, he never found his peace, and committed suicide in 1970. His poem *Todesfuge* – Death Fugue – was one of very few attempts to express in poetry something which many felt was beyond words. Its haunting rhythms and vivid, allusive imagery – and that chilling refrain – came, for many, to sum up the horrors of the Holocaust:

Schwarze Milch der Frühe wir trinken sie abends
wir trinken sie mittags und morgens wir trinken sie nachts
wir trinken und trinken
wir schaufeln ein Grab in den Lüften da liegt man nicht eng
Ein Mann wohnt im Haus der spielt mit den Schlangen der schreibt
der schreibt wenn es dunkelt nach Deutschland dein goldenes Haar Margarete
er schreibt es und tritt vor das Haus und es blitzen die Sterne er pfeift seine Rüden herbei

er pfeift seine Juden hervor läßt schaufeln ein Grab in der
    Erde
er befielt uns spielt auf nun zum Tanz
[…]
Schwarze Milch der Frühe wir trinken dich nachts
wir trinken dich mittags der Tod ist ein Meister aus
    Deutschland
wir trinken dich abends und morgens wir trinken und
    trinken
der Tod ist ein Meister aus Deutschland sein Auge ist blau
er trifft dich mit bleierner Kugel er trifft dich genau
ein Mann wohnt im Haus dein goldenes Haar Margarete
er hetzt seine Rüden auf uns er schenkt uns ein Grab in der
    Luft
er spielt mit den Schlangen und träumet der Tod ist ein
    Meister aus Deutschland

dein goldenes Haar Margarete
dein aschenes Haar Sulamith

(Black milk of the early morning we drink it in the evening
we drink it morning noon and night
We drink and drink
we shovel a grave in the air where it is not too tight
A man lives in the house he plays with the snakes he writes
he writes as it darkens to Germany your golden hair
    Margarete
He writes and steps out of the house and the stars glisten he
    whistles his hounds up
he whistles up his Jews and makes them dig a grave in the
    earth

He orders us to strike up for the dance …

Black milk of the early morning we drink you at night
we drink you at midday death is a master from Germany
we drink you in the evening and in the morning we drink
    and we drink
death is a master from Germany his eye is blue
he shoots you with a lead bullet his aim is true
A man lives in the house your golden hair Margarete
He sets his hounds on us he grants us a grave in the air
he plays with the snakes and dreams death is a master from
    Germany

Your golden hair Margarete
Your ashen hair Sulamith)

Quoted almost too frequently, this vivid set of images risks losing its freshness. Yet, confronted for the first time, its power is obvious. The humanity of the master of death is unmistakable, as he writes to (yearns for?) the woman back at home, even whilst brutalising and murdering his Jewish captives. The images are laden with allusion: Sulamith was King Solomon's black-haired beauty; her hair is now ashen. Margarete's golden hair is the epitome of Aryan beauty; but her name also reminds us of Gretchen, seduced by Faust who has wagered with the devil. (And does her hair also recall the golden hair of Heine's sinister 'Die Loreley' who lures the boatman on the Rhine to his doom?) Do the glistening stars remind us of Kant's amazement at the mystery of the universe? Or of the Star of David? And then there is the galloping rhythm of that phrase which appears again and again in post-war German literary references (not to mention in graffiti in public places): *Der Tod ist ein Meister aus Deutschland...*

More than any other of Germany's major post-war artists, Kiefer was transfixed by this poem (which, incidentally, gave the lie to – or was the exception that proved the rule of – Theo Adorno's dictum that writing poetry after Auschwitz was barbaric). In a series of paintings he explored the complex resonances of the golden and the black hair – returning again and again to the use of images of ripened corn to convey the idea of the golden hair, and using straw – sometimes burnt – on canvases which became almost bas-reliefs.

But although Paul Celan wrote in German, he was not a German. Moreover, he was a Jew, a victim – not from the society that produced the perpetrators. The challenge to those who did come from that society – the children of the Third Reich – to reflect on that past could not be ignored. A generation of writers who were, to use Kohl's infelicitous phrase, lucky enough to be born too late – (but not necessarily too late to have served in the Waffen SS, as the greatest of them, Günter Grass, was later embarrassed to admit) – found themselves inevitably writing about the country where death indeed became the master. In fact, it became a preoccupation, almost an obsession, because its shadows were everywhere.

Heinrich Böll repeatedly returns to the theme of the destructive impact of the Nazi era on ordinary urban lives – perhaps most movingly in his 1972 novel *Gruppenbild mit Dame* – Group Portrait With a Lady – in which the anti-heroic figure of the simple, unsophisticated Leni is battered by the war years, yet retains her ability to cope in and beyond the war, and to find love even at the risk of provoking hostility and ridicule. Martin Walser's *Ein Springender Brunnen* – A Wellspring – was published a quarter of a century later, by which time the Holocaust had taken centre stage in the German consciousness of the war. It depicts the ordinary lives of a small town on the Bodensee in the Nazi time, and proclaims a normalcy which a Fontane might have recognised – but in a time which was far from normal. It was criticised for the absence of any focus on, or even reference to, the Holocaust; indeed, Walser was soon thereafter embroiled in controversy about whether any normalcy could be claimed for the Nazi period or by a Germany for ever tainted by it. Bernhard Schlink's hugely successful novel *Der Vorleser* – The Reader – also dates from the 1990s, but unlike the others, he makes his central theme the recovery of the horror, the acknowledgement of the guilt and the difficulty – perhaps the impossibility – of finding forgiveness or resolution other than through death. Schlink's story was the first German novel to top the New York Times bestseller list.

But the novel about the experience of the Third Reich which will most surely endure is Grass's *Die Blechtrommel* – The Tin Drum. Written in 1959 (and made into a celebrated film by Volker Schlöndorff in 1979), the story of Oskar Matzerath, the boy who refuses to grow up, is subtle and complex, part allegory, part polemic, part perverse Bildungsroman. It offers a quixotic critique of the German psyche not only of the Third Reich (particularly in the pathetic figure of his father, seen through the blatantly un-Aryan eyes of his son) but also of the post-war years of materialism, Americanisation and suppression of the past. Oskar's piercing shriek and his tin drum accompany him on a rumbustious journey from a dysfunctional pre-war Danzig family, through wartime experiences of performing for the troops as part of a dwarf group, through settling – like the millions of Easterners – in the West, in post-war Düsseldorf (the incarnation of the bland new Federal Republic success story?), to a career as a jazz drummer and performer, and finally to a mental asylum, having owned up to a murder he probably did not commit. This strange tale, a sort of nightmarish travesty of the Peter Pan motif, with echoes also of *Simplicissimus*, spoke uncomfortably and unmistakably to a society which was a risk of becoming too much at ease with its new prosperity and with its past. Many were outraged by the novel when it first appeared. Nothing else in post-war German literature was as powerful and disturbing as this eternal boy's shriek and his noisy, insistent drum.

And what about the music of post-war Germany? How did the 'most German of the arts' help the German spirit to deal with its past? At one level, the answer is: by providing an escape from it. The German *Schlager* – the populist hit music generated from within German culture – celebrated a traditional, often rural, life experience which was somehow timeless and untainted, either by urban attitudes or by the traumas of war. The last thing the Schlager were designed for was to challenge or unsettle: their role was much more the equivalent of American country and western – to connect an urban society with its roots in a simpler time, by idealising what had in any case largely vanished. Alternatively, this was a time of Americanisation – the time of jazz and of pop music. If the Schlager invented continuities that were not real, this trend denied any continuities at all. Neither was in any sense a vehicle for confrontation with the actual past.

Or is it too much to expect such confrontation in music? Was Schopenhauer in effect right in seeing music as being the art form which by its essence took the human spirit out of mere facticity? Hardly: even purely instrumental music can

engage powerfully with the facts of life – as Dmitri Shostakovich's relentless *Leningrad Symphony* had done. And words can
be given all the more power by being sung, as Germans had
demonstrated from Bach to Wagner – and as Benjamin Britten
showed in, for example, his haunting *War Requiem*, born of his
very personal and passionate pacifism. In both a Russian and
an English cultural milieu, music had given a deep resonance
to the experience of war. Where was the German equivalent?

The story of post-war German musical developments is
indeed revealing. In classical music, the mood of the time in
Germany, as elsewhere, was very different from half a century
earlier. The journey along the path blazed by Schönberg had
continued, in an atonal world where experiments in musical
patterns, electronic sound, extra-musical sounds and silences,
in freedom from traditional structures of key or rhythm, made
music more an intellectual than an aesthetic experience. No
composers of the post-war period were more absorbed by
these possibilities than Germans such as Karlheinz Stockhausen. And as ever in Germany, musical developments were
accompanied by philosophy; Theodor Adorno, who had been
so influential on Thomas Mann's work *Doktor Faustus*, was
an active campaigner for a music which forsook the tainted
paths of tonality and personal expression – anything that
smacked of the romanticism the Third Reich had harnessed to
its völkisch cause. Even Hindemith, with his quasi-tonal com-
positions, was accused by Adorno and others of representing
too much continuity with the past, despite the fact that he had
proved too much for the Reichsmusikkammer and had left
the country in 1938. Schönberg, the father of atonality who
had left Germany in 1933, was now the dominant influence on
the new generation of composers.

Discontinuity became something of an overriding objective – partly as a genuine manifestation of what might be called the Stunde Null mindset which, as we have seen, in different ways informed both the foundational ideology of the GDR and also post-war Protestant theology – but partly also as a more fundamental reassertion of music's spiritual independence. Hans Werner Henze, who is probably post-war Germany's greatest composer, wrote of his music as a 'political-ideological vacuum, a societal neutrum, a mystery, not open to rational explanation' – of music as being the only art which is incapable of judging or condemning. Thus the German propensity to philosophise about music lives on. So, in a seemingly uprooted new world, does Schopenhauer.

Yet Schopenhauer had of course seen the special power of music as being aesthetic, not intellectual. It is no surprise that it was not the works of Webern or Stockhausen, or even of Hindemith, which repeatedly filled concert halls and opera houses down the decades of rising prosperity in the post-war Federal Republic (or in the GDR). It was the old repertoire, sacred and secular, from Bach to Strauss. Schönberg is represented too: but it is his earlier works, before his rejection of tonality, that have enjoyed the widest resonance – his *Gurrelieder*, with their obvious Wagnerian and Mahlerian influence, or his *Verklärte Nacht* – Transfigured Night – in all its ethereal beauty. And of all the post-war composers, it was perhaps Henze who developed a tone which spoke more naturally to the German spirit. Henze's versatility is immense, incorporating tonality and atonality, jazz and Neapolitan textures, and it is – despite the comment quoted above – often very clearly engaged. His opera based on Kleist's play, *Der Prinz von Homburg*, is an open rejection of militarism and of the ethos of duty that infused it. He uses traditional harmonies for the prince's dreamworld and grating serial techniques for the military music of the waking, real world. There is no mistaking the message.

Perhaps not coincidentally Henze also produced a major work that directly engages with the experience of the Third Reich: his choral Symphony No 9. The reference to Beethoven and Schiller – both highly engaged political critics of their own time – is inescapable. The symphony, which is choral throughout, is a direct response to the brutal totalitarianism of the regime, based on the novel *Das Siebte Kreuz* – The Seventh Cross – by Anna Seghers, published in America in 1942. This tells an excruciating story of seven escapees from a concentration camp in pre-war Germany, of whom only one survives. Henze dedicated the symphony to 'the heroes and martyrs of German antifascism'. It is perhaps a worthy counterpart to the emotive and poignant war reflections of Shostakovich and of Britten.

In summary, this is the story of a society which was increasingly coming face to face with its past. The process of confrontation has been neither easy nor quick. There are undoubtedly many who have gone to their graves without being honest to themselves about their sins of omission and commission. But for all its imperfections, this atonement has been more thoroughgoing than in most other countries where human evil has been rampant within living memory. In particular, the contrast between this German purging and the failure to undertake any systematic confrontation with their own traumas by Japan or Russia is blatant.

Meanwhile, the time since reunification has seen further waves of Vergangenheitsbewältigung. The first was the increasingly insistent need to reflect on the German experience of victimhood. This had been difficult terrain from the start. Ambivalence and unease about the Allied bombing campaign was shared by many in Britain – as we have noted – but it was always going to be hard for Germans to take the high ground of moral outrage. And indeed, as WG Sebald noted there had been little literary or artistic reflection on this whole experience. The same was true of the appalling story of the expulsions from the East and of the behaviour of the Red Army in occupied German territory. Though the facts were well enough known, the focus on the Holocaust in West Germany went with a refusal to relativise, and therefore a reluctance to explore any sense in which Germans too had been victims; while in the East, the Red Army were officially the liberators and friends of the people, so that discussion of the widespread acts of rape and murder was taboo. On both sides before reunification, therefore, the voice of pain and anger was muted.

All this changed after reunification, partly because it was now possible to speak the truth about events in the East, and partly because the post-war generations with no sense of personal guilt felt less and less inhibited as time went by in exploring their reaction to what their country had suffered. Hence Jörg Friedrich's angry and detailed attack on the bombing campaign in his 2004 book *Der Brand* in which he accused the Allies of conducting a campaign of cultural *Vernichtung* – annihilation – of Germany. This was the very same word with which Hitler had threatened the Jews. Even more emotively, he described those who flew the bombers as Einsatzgruppen.

At a deeper level, there has arguably been relatively little reflection on the whole experience of an unprecedented degree of mass destruction – relatively little willingness to contemplate the spiritual and moral dimension of what occurred, or the effect the trauma had on the psyche of the individuals who lived through it and on that of German society as a whole. Why that is true was a question pondered by WG Sebald in *Luftkrieg und Literatur* – Air War and Literature – published in 1999 (in English under the title 'On the Natural History of Destruction'). The detailed and methodical description of the effects of the firestorm in Hamburg leave the reader feeling sick in the stomach. But his real theme is collective amnesia, and whether that itself was a mechanism of repression necessary for survival and for later success in the new Federal Republic.

Nevertheless, Friedrich's book was a bestseller – as was Grass's 2002 novella *Im Krebsgang* – Crabwalk – about the torpedoing of the 'Wilhelm Gustloff'. This may suggest that Sebald's collective amnesia is passing. And perhaps this has allowed the rekindling of a justified sense of victimhood; the passage of time has perhaps made it easier to acknowledge this without denying or in any way downplaying the crimes of the Third Reich. But what is striking above all is how little this has stirred the dragons of resentment, let alone any desire for retaliation or revenge – evidence, surely, of how far Germany has travelled on an extraordinary journey of atonement and renewal.

Absorption of the East has created yet another wave of Vergangenheitsbewältigung, as the reality and the secrets of the GDR have been exposed to the full light of day. Everyone knew how wide the gap between ideals – or ideology – and the real world had been. But now it became clear how paranoid the East German leadership had become – just how many Stasi files they had kept on their own people (and on others). Indeed, it became uncomfortably clear just how many people,

including several of the leading members of the protest movement and in the pre-unification government in the East, had
in fact been unofficial collaborators with the regime.

The literature and films of recent decades reflect the trauma
of separation. From the building of the Wall onwards the artificiality of the division has inspired mournful reflection on the
effects of cutting off part of a culture from its roots. Christa
Wolf's *Der Geteilte Himmel* – Divided Heaven – of 1963 is an
early and poignant example in which the heroine declines to
follow her lover to West Berlin and then is separated from
him for good by the Berlin Wall: she casts her lot with the new
society, knowing its imperfections but believing it to be the
better way. Later, in 1973, came the posthumously published
and incomplete *Franziska Linkerhand* by Brigitte Reimann,
whose writing career was cut short by cancer at the age of 39.
This is a long, complex story – with passages of great lyrical
beauty – of a young woman whose idealistic ambitions as an
architect come into conflict with the pragmatic objectives of
the real GDR and whose search for love is difficult and unresolved. A story of the failure of an ideal mirrored by failure in
human relationships, it was heavily censored at first; not until
1998 was it published in full. It is a sad and subtle marker of
the loss of faith.

All in all, the cultural life of the GDR retained an independence of spirit which was a long way from the strangu-
lating grip of the Third Reich; but it was slowly suffocating
nevertheless. In the end, for example, Wolf Biermann's biting
satire proved too much for the authorities and he was effectively expelled whilst on a concert tour in West Germany. The
growing gap between the ideal and the reality, the controlling
paranoia, the fear of failure, the gnawing pain of separation,

the abuse of those who did not conform, the yearning to be free and to travel – all this produced a growing trauma of waste, anger and guilt which needed expiation.

After reunification came films such as the mischievous *Goodbye Lenin* or the much more serious and sombre *Das Leben der Anderen* – The Life of Others – as well as novels such as Uwe Tellkamp's *Der Turm* – The Tower – which traces at great length the story of a family of intellectuals and their circle of friends in the Dresden of the GDR, before its reconstruction. It ends with the demonstrations of 1989 and with the sense of an uncertain new future. There were also the true stories that needed to be told. Anna Funder's lively *Stasiland* takes a human look at those who worked with and for the regime – at the ideals, the compromises and the calculations of self-interest which made up the mix of motives in these people's lives. And there were some famous confrontations with personal pasts: notably that of Christa Wolf, who in *City of Angels* describes her own dismay and shame on reading her Stasi file: she was painfully reminded of how she had been an informer and had forgotten – or suppressed – this as she became perhaps East Germany's best known dissident, after Biermann's expulsion.

Meanwhile, underlying all of these efforts at Vergangenheitsbewältigung – both the infinitely harder task of confronting the Nazi past and the lesser, but nonetheless real, need to confront the realities of the GDR – there has been the growing desire for normality: a normality which the adults who had lived through the Third Reich would never know, which their children the 68ers were denied as they pointed the finger at their parents; a normality which the *Ossies* did not easily find through reunification but a normality which the next generation in their turn began to see, not so much as their right, but as – just normal.

Yet Germany is not going to be allowed to be normal, if that means being a country with no weight of expectation on its collective shoulder – in the sense, therefore, that Austria has become normal. Germany remains afraid of its own gradually returning self-confidence. It continues to exude an angst focused on issues which concern the short, medium and longer term future of the new Germany in the new Europe.

There is, firstly, its leading role in the eurozone – to which it is existentially committed and which at the same time conjures up its perennial nightmare about the value of money. For five decades from 1949 the Deutschmark was a crucial symbol of value and stability in the minds of Germans (from the East as well as the West). Why? Because the searing experience of hyper-inflation in the early 1920s – and then again of currency collapse in the late 1940s – has never quite faded from the folk memory (a fact which has clearly been used by the Bundesbank to buttress its tough stance on monetary policy throughout the life of the Deutschmark and subsequently on the Board of the European Central Bank). It is this which underpins and explains so much about the German attitude to issues facing the eurozone. For Germans these are not just technical financial or budgetary issues, nor are they just reacting to stereotypes about Mediterranean work ethics; they are constantly unsettled by deeply buried memories (in the way that the Great Depression still lurks not far below the surface of American consciousness).

Secondly, Germany's commitment to a green economy appears more determined than that of any other major European country. Its reaction to the nuclear disaster at Fukushima in Japan in 2011 has been more decisive and instinctive (as well as controversial) than anywhere else – and, indeed, quite different from the responses in either Britain or France. The pervasive fear of nuclear catastrophe and unwillingness to take any risks with the nuclear genie, however remote, is surely animated in part at least by deep folk memories of catastrophe and collapse. For Germans, as for few others in Europe, it is an uncomfortable reminder of the ever-present possibility of 'ragnarok'.

Thirdly, Germans – like other European societies – worry about the longer term implications of demographic patterns and open borders. They look at their own below-replacement birth-rate and at the rising proportion of immigrants in the population and ask a mirror image of the question that was asked in earlier centuries. If in previous times the question was whether German identity could be found in language and culture in the absence of a political entity, now the question posed is: can German identity relate simply to a political entity with particular borders, where cultural and linguistic identity seem under existential threat? Has cultural identity given way to *Verfassungspatriotismus* – constitutional patriotism (has Fichte been replaced by Habermas)?[24] Or as Arnulf Baring put it,[25] with a tinge of bitterness: did Hitler cause the spiritual death of Germany even though he failed to bring about its physical death?

Such fears are not confined to Germany, of course. Nor are worries about the effects of secularisation on the values of society – and especially of the young. But the question of roots is more difficult for a society which has evolved through the trauma of Stunde Null and then of division. Old mechanisms of social integration were terminally vitiated by the experience of such entities at the Hitler Jugend (and uncomfortably similar organisations in East Germany). The moral authority of parents was called into question in the West Germany of the 1960s in a far more disorienting way than in other Western countries in that tumultuous decade. Meanwhile, the traditional expressions of culture have been weakened – partly because the 20th century everywhere is a demotic age in which all moral authority has weakened, and partly as a result of specific damage done to the standing of cultural authorities in Germany by their compromised pasts.

Meanwhile, the public voice of the Lutheran churches – as institutional guardians of a religious view of values and ethics – has responded to their own past by a determined political engagement, as we have seen. Yet they have at the same time hung on to an extraordinarily ponderous structure and style of worship which makes almost no concession to the moods and interests of a modern, urbanised generation. Pietism has largely disappeared as a manifestation of the inner life. As in any European country, all manner of alternatives are on offer in a sort of religious supermarket. But for significant numbers of people, it is probably the old musical staples which remain the most powerful means of reaching the soul at traditional religious moments in life – Bach's Christmas Oratorio, his St Matthew Passion, Brahms's German Requiem, for example. Music generally remains for many Germans what Schopenhauer said it was. This may or may not be enough for the interior life in a demystified age, but is surely not enough to underpin any broader sense of belonging.

All in all, the angst of modern Germany remains distinctive. It is in part an angst shared by many other Europeans. But it is in part particularly German. Now that a sense of past victimisation no longer serves as a catalyst for aggressiveness, does that mean a loss of any sense of purpose or destiny? And does that threaten a loss of identity? So the angst – the fear of the vacuum – remains. But it is also the angst of people who are following a venerable German tradition of agonised thought about the meaning of things. What they agonise about is gradually shifting from a focus on the past – from Vergangenheitsbewältigung – to the future, and to a set of issues which raise their heads more broadly in secularised, urbanised Europe. (And furthermore, although Asians are in a different space at present, there is no reason to believe that these questions will not raise their heads there too, as urban-isation and secularisation spread through our globalised world – as they will.) In this all-important sense, the newly resurgent, unified Germany of the 21st century is after all becoming normal.

There are, therefore, lessons in all this for others. Some are very specific: 20th century Germany is not the only example of a country whose relationship with neighbours is influ-enced by a sense of past victimisation: to take just one (very large and globally increasingly influential) country, China has some clear parallels with the fast changing and emerging new power that was the Second Reich. It has a distinct sense of having been victimised and patronised by the West and then brutalised by Japan during that terrible century and a half, up to that moment in 1949 when Mao announced on the steps of the Forbidden City that the people of China had at last stood up. And now, just as the Second Reich did in the 19th century, it is taking its rightful place on the world stage. Like 19th century Germany too, it is rediscovering a pride in its ancient culture, having gone through a period when all that was belittled. It would of course be simplistic in the extreme to push the parallel too far; but it is easy to recognise the challenges that a new international power in such a mood can pose – for itself and for others.

Or to take another particularly poignant example – this time of a small but determined and technologically gifted country: Israel has inherited an all too readily understandable sense of victimhood because of what happened in Europe and in the face of the sentiment that prevails in some Arab quarters that it should be wiped off the map. It faces the classic risk that aggressive defensiveness (combined with expansionary settlement policies) aggravates the very hostility it is responding to. Is there a faint echo of the East Prussian mentality in this – or of the attitude to France of the Second Reich? Again, it would be provocative nonsense to push the parallel too far. But one thing is for certain: Israel has yet to find peace with its neighbours.

Other lessons are more general. What Germany agonises about is not just the spiritual legacy of the Third Reich. It also relates to the universal impact of urbanisation and secularisation and to the universal human questions about values and identity. The country which is becoming the reluctant leader of the new Europe is grappling with questions that Europe as a whole is facing as it finds its new and diminished place in the modern world. Indeed, the world as a whole is facing these questions in a globalising 21st century. These are the questions which pose themselves for the future of the new Germany, but which are relevant to us all – and which we turn to in the next chapter.

10

The Reluctant Leader of the New Europe

AFTER THREE CENTURIES in which the German lands were the playing fields of European power politics and then a further century in which a unified, defensive/aggressive Germany sought to assert itself on the European stage with catastrophic consequences, there followed – from 1945 to 1989 – what can now be seen as a short interlude. A divided Germany was politically weak by the choice of Germans, as well as being in keeping with the desires – explicit or sotto voce – of their neighbours to the east and to the west. German energies were channelled into technical excellence. West Germany (together with Japan) was the capitalist world's star performer. East Germany was the communist world's laureate, and behaved towards the Soviet Union like a teacher's pet.

But now, in a new millennium and a generation after the fall of the Wall, the newly unified Federal Republic is becoming the reluctant leader of a new Europe, but at a time when there is a serious question – an existential question – about the very identity and the whole future of Europe. This question is one for all Europeans, but it weighs necessarily on the inevitable and reluctant leader of Europe.

Europe is now in long-term relative decline, both politically and economically. It is no longer the energetic, ambitious and aggressive continent it was when the Portuguese, the Spanish, the Dutch, the French and the British set out over the oceans to plunder, trade and colonise. It is no longer the continent whose technical brilliance the Chinese emperor Qianlong so notoriously spurned when Lord McCartney sought to open commercial dealings with China in 1793. It is no longer the continent where an aggressive Germany sought to settle and Germanise vast tracts of Slav land to the east and unleashed a campaign of unbelievable brutality in pursuit of that goal. And it is no longer the frontline of a Cold War between two superpowers with the capacity to destroy themselves and everyone else many times over. It has retreated from being the self-defined centre of the world to being what it had been before the 15th century – a corner of the Eurasian land mass. It remains fertile, populous and wealthy, but it is profoundly uncertain about its identity and its future.

France and Britain – alone of all those former great powers – still lay claim to the ability to project military might over long distances, and still preserve the legacy of their former global roles in the form of permanent seats with veto power in the Security Council of the United Nations. But neither has the strength or the mass to sustain a significant military campaign alone. And bruising experiences in the opening years of the 21st century have in both cases probably reduced the appetite as well as the ability to pursue major military adventures. Yet at no point in the decades after the war has Europe been able to develop any credible collective ability to project independent power. Looking forward, for reasons we shall come to, it is clear that it does not even want to do so.

Europe is also in relative decline as an economic force, not just as a locus of political power. Having led the world during the first industrial revolution of the 19th century, it then saw the centre of gravity shift away from it across the Atlantic from the beginning of the 20th century, and especially after the First World War. After the massive destruction of the Second World War, the United States was firmly ensconced as the overwhelmingly dominant economic power. At least this meant that (Western) Europe could position itself as part of a transatlantic relationship with shared interests, a common commitment to democracy, and – up to a point – a common economic approach. And the economy grew rapidly for a while as it recovered from devastation, bringing the people of Europe a degree of widespread prosperity they had never known before.

But this proved to be only an interlude. For since the epochal year of 1989, the rise of Asia has driven a new and historic shift of the centre of global economic gravity, this time to the east. The re-emergence of China as a great power, and the modernisation and urbanisation of so many countries in Asia – and increasingly in other continents which had in a previous era been dominated by imperial powers from Europe – has contrasted sharply with a sustained sluggishness in the old economies of Western Europe. Even if all had gone well for the Europeans there would have been a decline in their share of the world's income; and they would have had to become used to dealing with new actors on the world stage. But in fact the European performance has been weakened – partly by extreme stress within the eurozone, of which more shortly, and partly because the global financial and economic crisis which was unleashed in 2008 caught them in a weaker position than many of the emerging countries with which they are now in ever more intense competition. So the crisis has, if anything, accelerated the historic shift towards the East. Europe is left struggling to find a secure foothold in a global marketplace which is becoming more and more interwoven – and where its ever more sophisticated Asian competitors are conscious that their time has come. China and the United States may be wary of each other; but both recognise what is happening and know that Europe has lost much of its significance.

Loss of market share was of course inevitable. It has been the fate of all the early developers, including both the United States and Japan. It is the result of a historic reversion to the norm: before the 19th century a country's share of global output was roughly in proportion to its share of world population. Then as now, China had the largest population in the world; hence around 1820 China had the largest economy. That changed with the onset of the industrial revolution, which for the first time in human history enabled some economies to produce consistently above subsistence level, thus creating a gap between the two ratios. So the Europeans first, then the Americans and then later the Japanese, were enabled to achieve enormous increases in world market share. At their peak, these developed countries represented less than a fifth of the world's population and yet created around three quarters of world output. But the gap is now closing again, as not only China but country after country in Asia and elsewhere in the emerging world start to catch up with the standards of living which Europeans have come to take for granted. By 2020, on present trends, China may well be the world's largest economy again. This great convergence, with all that it implies, is the most important fact about the first half of the 21st century.

Europe's response to the new reality – to its diminished position on the world stage, to the new economic competition and to the challenges this poses for its own evolution – has been underwhelming. It has been hobbled, firstly, by the complexity of a Union which now has 28 member states and will have well over 30 within the next 20 years or so. Yet its governance was basically designed for a community of less than half that size, with far less disparity of wealth and development than is now the case. Its cumbersome and dysfunctional structure cries out for reform; but the process of building consensus for change is painfully slow. In fact, radical change in the interests of efficiency and flexibility in the face of the global challenge may be effectively impossible in the absence of a major crisis. There is, secondly, widespread though inchoate disaffection amongst its citizens; all too often they want to be assured of a predictable continuity which is not in fact available. At the same time they feel very distant from the corridors of power. This public mood has been exacerbated, thirdly, by the absence of any strong and clear leadership based on a real democratic mandate at the Union level, ready to set out the right blend of vision and home truths about Europe's place in this changing world. The result has been a dramatic increase in the anti-European vote in elections to the European Parliament – most spectacularly in Britain and France.

Underlying all of this malaise is a fundamental uncertainty about identity. This identity crisis in Europe has been exacerbated by the rise of Asia. Admiration for – and nervousness about – the extraordinary achievements of the modern Asia has brought Europe's own uncertainties about its place in the world into sharp relief. Europeans are unsettled by the fear that the Asians will challenge and eventually overtake them. No longer is Asia just a limitless supply of hardworking cheap labour. Europeans fear that Asian technical brilliance may overwhelm them in the very areas of strength they have prided themselves on.

All this risks nurturing a sense of inferiority and uncertainty about who the Europeans really are. Many are beguiled by, for example, Singaporean and Chinese intellectuals who argue that their societies are more socially integrated, less individualist, more long-term in their orientation – and yes, more patriotic – than the selfish, short-termist societies of the Western democracies. Almost every European business with any significant international strategy intones a mantra that says 'go east'. Many of their leaderships secretly – or indeed openly – agree with this Asian critique of their own societies. And more generally, many Europeans accept much of its force even if they may not enjoy being bracketed with America as 'Western democracies'. There is widespread respect, in short, for this Asian special path – which might be termed a Sonderweg – rather as the Second Reich, the newcomer on the stage in the 19th century, relished its own claim to be following a Sonderweg.

Not that this Asian special path is any less materialistic for that – judging by the shape of emerging middle-class demand throughout the region. From McDonalds to Johnnie Walker, to Mercedes and Jaguar, to pop music and to branded fashion accessories, their appetite for the paraphernalia of Western life seems limitless. And as for the cultural authenticity and creativity that societies with such long and rich traditions might have been expected to project, the truth is rather that there has been a wholesale proliferation of kitsch and glitz. In particular, what has been done to the ancient cities of Asia in the name of modern development is in many cases tragic. Future generations will surely curse all the destruction – the loss of the old Beijing, for example, and comparable losses in so many of the big cities of the new Asia. So we could well ask of the Asian Sonderweg: how real is it? How durable, how deeply rooted in the cultural identity of their societies? And indeed, it is perfectly clear that the leadership in more and more Asian societies is becoming well aware of the spiritual vacuum being created in the hell-for-leather rush towards modernisation.

Yet whilst some of the 21st century's most important new challengers lay claim to their own new special path, the Europeans agonise. After two decades of the new Europe, what exactly is its identity in the 21st century? For if that question cannot be answered, how will Europe ever rise to the Asian challenge? What does it have to offer in this new, globalised world? Does Europe mean 28 different cultures, and therefore 28 different identities, each striving to make its own way in the global competition? Or is there some level at which there are fundamental commonalities, shared by 28 different member states, which give them a common vision of their place in the world? Is there, in other words, a European identity? Is there a European special way?

It is tempting to avoid the question because of the historical resonances of the Sonderweg. But we cannot: it is a question about identity which cannot be avoided. And if the question is faced, it is easy to assume the answer is no. There are surely just too many differences – of language above all, but also, and indeed partly as a result, in whole ways of life. No one could mistake a southern Italian town for a north German one, for example. The language, the appearance, the atmosphere, the style of living is so fundamentally different. This variety is thrown into relief all the more clearly by the sharp contrast with the broad and bland similarity between American cities from one end of the country to the other – the physical manifestation of the famous American melting pot.

On the other hand, it could be argued that there is indeed a European identity and that this very variety is itself a crucial element in that identity – that it is precisely that rich, colourful kaleidoscope, from the west coast of Ireland to the islands of Greece and from Malta to northern Scandinavia and everything in between, which makes Europe what it is: a variety which is not just geographic, but a rich social and cultural variety as well.

Is this real? Can it really be the basis of an identity?

Well perhaps, if the variety is about what might be called social 'colour'. But if so, we have seen this identity come under real stress in recent years with the growth of internal migration from east to west within the Union. Identity on the basis of variety appears to require at least a measure of equality of wealth; and enlargement over the last 20 years has introduced huge inequality into the Union. But there is a still more testing problem: what if the variety that matters is of a much deeper kind? What if it is a variety, not just of local colour, but of radically differing world views – of different meta-narratives about individuals, about the nature of society and about the nature and the role of the state? Wouldn't that get in the way of the formation of a common or shared identity? Wouldn't it undermine any claim that there is a special European way?

And isn't that precisely what does characterise Europe? Just amongst the three largest members of the Union there are obvious differences of world view whose origins lie firmly embedded in their history and significantly affect their behaviour to this day. Famously, the British are deeply imbued with an individualism and a sceptical empiricism inherited from Locke and Hume. Equally, the French are rooted in a rationalism with a propensity for elitist social engineering, born of a tradition which goes back to Descartes, to the *philosophes*, to the French Revolution and to Napoleon. And Germany? Was it not always the land of metaphysics and Romanticism – das Land der Dichter und Denker (the land of poets and thinkers) – where even the music, that 'most German of the arts', had its very own philosopher in Schopenhauer to explain its spiritual significance in coping with the blind will of the cosmos?

One thing is certain: the very idea of a common identity and a European special way stirs uneasiness in all three countries. The British dislike grand schemes and have a longstanding fear of continental entanglements. The French dislike integrationist ambitions unless reflecting their own world view and built on the premiss of French leadership. (In Paris, on the Rondpoint Champs Élysées, there is a statue of Charles de Gaulle which perfectly sums up that view: it bears a quotation of his which reads 'Il y a un pacte, vingt fois séculaire, entre la grandeur de la France et la liberté du monde' – 'There is a two thousand year old pact between the greatness of France and the liberty of the world.') As for Germany, whose size and centrality had always been such a risk to itself and to others, and which finds that it is the centre of a new Europe, it winces at the very idea of leadership. Etched very sharply in the new German psyche is a revulsion against anything that could look remotely like a resurgence of the Führerprinzip.

So does all this mean that there is – at this profound level

– no common identity? Does it mean that in the case of the three largest European countries (quite apart from the others) there are such fundamental differences of world view, and therefore of identity, that the formation of a coherent and meaningful European identity has no chance of success? The answer surely has to be: no. Those differences cannot be all there is to be said about the existence of a European identity. For the converse is absurd; plainly, the concept of Europe is more than just a geographical designation, and the Europeans have things in common which are not in the end overwhelmed by these differences, important though they undoubtedly are. Even the British know deep down they are different from the Americans, and in general Europeans have become more conscious of those transatlantic differences over the last five decades, after those first heady years of cultural Americanisation after the war. Furthermore, no one could be under any illusion about the differences between the cultures of Europe and the cultures of Asia.

In any case, Europeans are bound together by the facts of geography and of history, both longer term and more recent. The facts of geography have resulted in common interests; and the facts of both geography and history have led Europe to embark on common projects which have created new history and a new common future filled with both potential and risks.

The common interests are clear and extend well beyond the peace and unity which Europe has so clearly achieved (and which modern Europeans perhaps take too much for granted). Europe's relationship with its huge neighbour to the east has always been fractious; the Cold War may have come to an end, but Russia's determination to define a sphere of influence into which neither the European Union nor NATO shall spread has become much more obvious in recent years – most clearly in the case of the Ukraine. The relationship is further complicated by energy politics: Europe is short of energy and strategically dependent on supplies from Russia, whilst Russia is now developing massive new markets in China and may thus become less dependent on Europe as a source of revenue.

Moreover, even though the energy equation may vary significantly amongst European countries, the challenge of creating a green economy does not: all face the challenge and it is clear that it would be absurd for each to tackle this task independently. Finally, Europe's immediate neighbourhoods to the south and south-east are a continuous source of demographic pressure and of insecurity, whose impact is increasingly felt throughout the continent. All of this and more binds the Europeans together in a common destiny. To (only slightly) paraphrase the English poet and preacher John Donne, no country is an island, entire of itself ...[26]

And what of the common values of Europe? At one level, these values are indeed common to the Western democracies – values shared with America – and all too often taken for granted by those who have never had to live without them and never had to fight for them. But at another level there are important and obvious differences too – differences in social attitudes, differences in policies. The difference between Europe and America in the degree of geographical and social mobility; in the extent of religious conviction and of religious observance; in assumptions about the right of privacy; or on the right way to provide health care in society; or in the law on such matters as capital punishment or gun control – these are all reminders that the centre of gravity of American attitudes is very different from that of Europe. (They are also a reminder to the British, who are more apt than other Europeans to overlook these differences, that they in fact have more in common with their continental neighbours and less with their transatlantic friends than they usually recognise.)

The common projects to build the new Europe began in the early 1950s. It has been a difficult, slow journey, with several false starts and wrong turns. It is just possible that some form of United States of Europe might have emerged during the early years, when a European Defence Community and a European Political Community were in the air. Famously, Churchill trialled such a concept in a speech he made as early as 1946 – though he never envisaged British participation. The truth is that this vision was doomed, even if the British were happy to cheer from the sidelines. But it is easy to forget how far the idea did in fact progress. The treaty to establish a European Defence Community was signed in 1952 by the same six countries which had already formed the Coal and Steel Community and which later became the founders of the European Economic Community. The planned European Political Community would have established a directly elected lower house and an upper house indirectly elected by national parliaments.

But the project was killed off when the French parliament refused to ratify the EDC treaty. Instead, the journey progressed from an economic starting point, from a coal and steel community through a common market and the European Economic Community to what is now the European Union, through a series of treaties which have continually increased the degree of integration. But what is the essence of the project? What is its destination? These questions expose the divergences and the fractured identity of Europe. At one end of the spectrum are the British, who would have the Union be a customs union and a single market but very little more than that. At the other end are those who see growing political and economic integration on the basis of an increasingly harmonised socio-economic model – with the eurozone at its core – as both inevitable and desirable. To be clear, even the former position involves a strong Union, because full blooded implementation of a single market requires a lot more integrative leadership and management of the European Union as a whole than many British Euro-sceptics would want. But the difference between the two ends of the spectrum is nevertheless a wide one: is Europe little more than a trade bloc, or is it indeed a project of increasing political cohesion which will converge in the limit towards a United States of Europe?

The truth is that neither of these alternative ends of the spectrum is an adequate description, either of the Union as it is actually evolving or of the expectations (however inchoate) of the broad majority of the Union's citizens. Whatever the emerging European identity is, neither captures it. For the reality is clearly something in between – something sui generis: an evolving set of arrangements for governance and management which seeks to recognise both a wider commonality and specific identities. There is nothing quite like it anywhere in the world today. It is of course hard to define, and begs a whole series of questions about how it should actually work. What kinds of relationships between member states or regions does this entail? What should the balance be between centralising, regionalising and localising tendencies? How can the democratic process work to express the public will effectively at all levels – Union, member state, region, local? And can this emerging Europe ever win the real loyalty of its people?

The identity crisis has become acute. The aspiration to achieve 'ever closer union amongst the peoples of Europe' which was presumed by the signatories of the Treaty of Lisbon in 2008 is now openly challenged in many parts of Europe. Few believe that this Union is one in which 'decisions are taken as openly as possible and as closely as possible to the citizen' – to quote the words in the Treaty which directly follow the statement of that aspiration. And few have much confidence in the emergence of a European identity with any real hold on the loyalty of its people.

Identity is always a composite. It can have many elements: geography, history, culture, language, common interests and the way societies govern themselves. No single element is necessary to it (the Jews throughout most of their history had no geographic identity, for example, and the Swiss have no language in common). And no single element is sufficient for it (language alone does not entail a common identity amongst English or Spanish speakers). Sometimes these sources of identity – notably history – can be problematic; but they cannot be avoided, as Germany knows so well. And they can shift over time, as the Austrians have shown. Crucially, too, identities based on these various elements can overlap and are not exclusive. Communities can define themselves in different ways for different purposes. In some cases this is a comfortable mix: in many cases, however, it is a source of potential or actual tension (religious or ideological affiliations have often been seen as a challenge to geographic loyalties in Europe – as shown above all by Jewish experience down the centuries, but also by Catholic experience under Bismarck in the 19th century, in a different way by Marxist internationalism in the 20th century, and now increasingly in many Muslim communities too).

For better or worse, it is striking how familiar this complexity is to the German psyche. It has historical resonances from the long standing and complex balances within the Holy Roman Empire. Germany is a land where over a long history people have seen themselves as involved in layered identities: the all important Heimat, the region, and at the same time the German Kultur which was defined by their language. Heimat has a resonance that is hard to replicate exactly in British experience. Often it became a focus of identity especially when people had left their home town or village behind – either during the urbanisation which accompanied the industrial revolution or in the very different circumstances of expulsion at the end of the Second World War. In the modern Germany it is a fading force; but it has left its sediment in the literature and in the Schlager. Then there are the regions, with their distinctive identities and proud histories – Freistaat Bayern, the reconstituted Freistaat Sachsen, Hansestadt Hamburg, and so on. The Third Reich sought to suppress all separate identities in its levelling state; so, later, did the highly centralised GDR. But the new Germany clearly shows that the ancient strong regionalism of the German lands is still a vibrant source of identity which carries real political significance.

The struggles of postwar Germany, both with the past and with reunification, have drawn attention to the undoubted fact of a German identity, however complex and however problematic this was in the 20th century, both before Stunde Null and thereafter. Germany may well remain mistrustful of itself in a leadership role: and it is clearly more used to living with layered and overlapping identities than some other member states of the Union. But that is not the same as having no identity of its own. As we have noted, not even Adenauer's Westpolitik amounted to a denial of German identity. And certainly now, two generations and half a century later, Germany's sense of identity is stronger than it has ever been since the demise of the Third Reich.

One well known index of 'national brands' has for several years now ranked Germany in second place only to the United States.[27] Various factors have played their part in this seemingly surprising result: the success of the economy and the image of German technical excellence, admiration in countries such as China for German engineering, the stature in Europe and beyond of Angela Merkel, the success of the 2006 World Cup and the vibrancy of the new European crossroads that is Berlin – to name but a few. Many Germans feel a continuing ambivalence about this identity; but it is an indisputable fact, nevertheless. Famously, Habermas argued that the only acceptable identity or loyalty for the modern Germany was Verfassungspatriotismus. And he argued that the US and Switzerland were good examples of such a basis for national identity formed, not on the basis of history or ethnicity, but on the basis of shared values embodied in a democratic constitution. But he has not apparently won the day: the German identity is plainly more than that.

This longstanding German experience of layered and overlapping identities is remarkably well attuned to the realities of the new Europe, which needs to enfold and embrace the various specific identities without demoting or cancelling them. What is more, it is this Germany, with its much greater readiness than either the impatiently pragmatic British or the Cartesian French to see identity in terms of a wider reality, which is now inevitably playing the central role in the gradual emergence of the distinctive phenomenon which is the European Union.

This was inevitable, from the moment of reunification. Even whilst the absorption of the East and the inevitable spiritual and cultural stock-taking was still under way, the new Germany – so far from basking in the satisfaction at last of its own longstanding and deep yearning for reunification – was in the process of taking another fundamentally significant step into the unknown. For it was not only a new Germany that had emerged from the extraordinary events of 1989: it was a whole new Europe that was being born. Enlargement to the east would change the European project just as much as the reunification of Germany would. The implications were profound, as the new Union sought to drive the modernisation and integration of those societies into the new Europe.

The main vehicles of this integration have been two flagship projects: the single market and the single currency (as well as substantially enhanced regional development assistance, in recognition of the challenges faced by economically weak new member states emerging from 40 years behind the Iron Curtain). The single market with its four basic freedoms of movement – of goods, services, capital and labour – should, to the extent that it is fully implemented, allow anyone to sell goods or services from anywhere to anywhere in the Union; it is clearly at the heart of the raison d'être of the whole project. The common currency, on the other hand, was notoriously more controversial: there were those who believed it was equally clearly implied by the European project and that all new members had to commit to adhesion when ready. But there were others – above all the British – who saw it as an integrative step too far. In the event, the more ambitious view carried the day: the British secured their opt-out from the euro, but Europe embarked on both projects in parallel.

Yet the two projects have very different implications for the degree of policy and executive integration needed for sustainability and success. The single market is a matter of degree: it is a work in progress and its advantage is that each extension of it – from goods to services and into the world of online business – adds value. But its disadvantage is due to the same fact: there is nothing to force the pace of implementation. It requires painstaking work to remove barriers to the four freedoms in sector after sector, often against entrenched interests protecting their traditional patches. The result has been slow progress in a project which is crucial to the long term ability of the Union to create jobs and to compete in the new global arena.

In sharp contrast, the common currency is all or nothing. For countries that are members of the eurozone, the remorseless logic of currency and debt markets forces an integrated approach to fiscal and monetary decision-making which cannot avoid material dilution of national sovereignty.

The drive for a single currency gathered momentum well before enlargement, at a time when the Cold War division of Europe seemed still to be permanent. The first concrete step was taken in the 1980s with the establishment of an exchange rate mechanism which was seen as the preparation for a single currency. It was always contentious – for Britain because in its mind the central focus of the European project was always the creation of a single market for commerce and nothing more than that – and for Germany because it meant the surrender of the Deutschmark whose strength and stability was revered as the source of all they had been able to achieve since the 1940s.

British scepticism about the project was both philosophical (based on a deep-seated antipathy to integration) and pragmatic (many argued that a common currency should come at the end of a process of market integration anyway, not at the start). The German dilemma was more complex. All the instincts of the post-war German establishment have been integrationist: after the terrors of the Third Reich the way to atonement lay through the European project. But at the prospect of giving up their beloved Deutschmark, deep in their subconscious the demon of hyper-inflation twitched. Only one prize was big enough to warrant this sacrifice: reunification. And that was in effect the deal which Kohl sponsored: the euro for reunification. The four powers came together in agreement at last on reunification and on the integration of Berlin into the Federal Republic, and Germany swung its weight fully behind the euro project. The Treaty of Maastricht in 1992 established the European Union and committed it to the common currency.

It was this project of the common currency above all which ensured that Germany would find itself in the position of leader in the new Europe. Had European integration developed around the structure of the stillborn European Defence Community, Germany would certainly not have found itself in this role. The single market has not had consistent leadership by the institutions of the Union (although amongst the leading member states the British have been its most instinctive champions) – which is part of the reason for the slow progress it has made. But the eurozone has been unambiguously dominated by the country which is by far its strongest member; and its guardian institution, the European Central Bank, has inherited all the rigour and the credibility of the

Bundesbank. Germany was strengthened by the eurozone, France was weakened, and the British excluded themselves from it. So Germany has embarked on a project which is at one level an economic and monetary framework but at another level has existential implications for the German self-aware-ness in the 21st century. Its consequences will be as profound and enduring as those of reunification or of the establishment of the new Federal Republic in 1949.

These consequences have not yet been fully worked out. As principal paymaster, Germany has found itself increasingly in the leading role of the eurozone, which has in turn meant an increasingly dominant role in the European Union as a whole. The shift of the centre of gravity in Europe is clear for all to see. It is a shift which is difficult for France and challenging for Britain: France has been used to the political domination of the European project ever since the start, but is now losing this position; Britain would be widely welcomed – not just by a Germany which is distinctly uncomfortable with leadership – as a force for the reform and openness that everyone knows is needed, but has been too ambivalent about its commitment to take this role on effectively.

The introduction of the euro was a technical success; but within the first few years the weakness of the crude mecha-nism designed to ensure fiscal responsibility by the members of the zone – the so-called stability pact – was exposed when not only France but Germany itself ignored its constraints. It was hardly a surprise that other, weaker members did so too. The imbalances and stresses that built up in the system were then brutally exposed by the financial and economic crisis from 2008 onward. As a result, the struggle to stabilise and strengthen the zone has been the major preoccupation of member governments since then – involving painful adjustments by the weaker economies, hugely expensive financial bail-outs by the stronger ones (above all Germany), and intensive efforts to put in place robust fiscal oversight measures and a comprehensive banking union backed by the monetary firepower of the European Central Bank – for whose credibility this was the most serious test yet.

The euro has become the source of profound German (and other European) angst since the huge strains placed on it in the worst financial and economic crisis since the Great Depression. Germany itself benefitted from the euro: the powerful German industrial machine has been able to trade internationally in a currency much lower in value than an independent Deutschmark would have been. But too many members of the zone increasingly suffered from the opposite problem, and the stresses became more and more obvious as the crisis unfolded. In Germany the result has been widespread low-level resentment at having to play the role of paymaster, as well as dismay at the accusations in some of the Mediterranean countries that Germany has reverted to type and shown itself to be a patronising bully (with the caricature extending inevitably to swastikas and the toothbrush moustache). Many have foretold and/or hoped for the demise of the euro – both in Germany and elsewhere.

Yet the fact is that the impetus for it was never just a matter of the technical pros and cons of monetary union. It was always, particularly in the minds of its German protagonists, an essential step on a journey which was never just towards monetary integration but towards ever broader and deeper integration and away for ever from the continent's blood-stained past. In the minds of the French too the eurozone is the core of the new Europe – even if there are obvious differences between the two countries about what this commitment means for policy and governance.

Every crisis in the eurozone has seen the members, led increasingly openly by Germany, grope towards a new degree of integration to make the zone more and more of a stable economic whole, subject to coherent fiscal and financial policy. Many have seen this as drift rather than the pursuit of a clear strategy – with each stage being cobbled together like the crew of a leaking ship doing repairs in rough seas. Yet this is to misjudge what is afoot. There is no turning back from this journey. From a technical point of view the increasing integration of the eurozone is a one way street; but even more fundamentally, it would be existentially impossible for Germany to withdraw from a project whose collapse would unravel the whole tissue of European integration which has been woven since 1949. And what is true for Germany is true at least for the founding members of the original European project – the signatories of the original Treaty of Rome – and in all probability for all the other members of the eurozone too. There is an inevitable price to pay for this: painful adjustments in weaker economies and financial support from the stronger ones – both of which are of course deeply unpopular. But they will be paid because there is neither a practical nor an existential alternative. And the strongest country will be the reluctant leader on this journey – a journey which will change Germany for ever.

Germany's leadership is exactly that – reluctant, not sought after, let alone seized on. It is the leadership of a country firmly embedded in this new European union of nations, playing a role thrust on it largely by economics, not by any sense of destiny. This reluctant leadership is a million miles from the sort of dominance the Second and Third Reichs sought in the Europe of the decades leading up to 1945. It is reluctant partly because ordinary Germans resent being the paymaster; and at a deeper level because the German psyche remains deeply sensitive about anything which stirs memories of leadership as exercised by the Third Reich. The reluctance has sometimes been almost tangible, to the point where the foreign minister of Poland – of all countries – was moved to urge publicly that Germany should accept its position and responsibilities, taking the leadership which Europe needed. How times have changed.

It is also for now a leadership limited to the political economy. In no sense has Germany shown any readiness to play any strategic role in the world of foreign affairs of the kind both the British and the French have taken for granted. The Bundeswehr has played a somewhat low key role in NATO actions outside of core Europe (including in Afghanistan). But notoriously, Germany abstained from the UN Security Council resolution authorising air attacks on Libya in 2011 – just one sign of what might be termed a distinct reluctance even to follow – let alone lead – in foreign affairs. And in the case of the Ukraine, there has been no sign of any German appetite to take an aggressive stance towards Russia (in a region where both uncomfortable historical resonances and current energy dependency make for an extremely sensitive and careful approach to any German engagement).

Nevertheless, the fact is that German leadership is becoming more and more evident in the governance of Europe and above all in its macroeconomic management. The implications of this journey for the Union and for all the key European states are of course profound. The Union faces the challenge of keeping the plates spinning as the eurozone stabilises and consolidates itself and as efforts continue to drive implementation of the single market forward. Amongst the main member states, France faces deeply unsettling implications; whilst for Britain it is also forcing an uncomfortable clarity of choice which it has managed to fudge for half a century.

For Germany, on the other hand, the implications are easier to accept, although no less profound. They appear on the face of it to put in play the very identity of Germany – at just the point in history when it has reached a stable geographic identity and is at peace with its neighbours (so completely so, indeed, that conflict with them is now unthinkable). But the whole lesson of German history over a thousand years is that its identity is tied only loosely to its polity. Furthermore, the whole experience of Stunde Null and its aftermath has left a deep aversion to any nationally assertive understanding of identity. So the prospect of gradual coalescence into a wider framework is much less psychologically daunting than it is for France. In fact, at one level, it may even be something of a relief. Germans will find this journey much easier than the British would or the French will have to.

So what will the structure of the new Europe end up being like? Over the last six decades the project has evolved not according to a clear blueprint but in a general direction on which there has not always been complete consensus, and with a considerable measure of improvisation. The future will see more of the same. Somehow, the evolution of the Union is like the construction of one of those great cathedrals of medieval Europe: those who laid the foundation stones knew they would not live to see the completed building, and also knew that the design would evolve as the generations went by. Some of those cathedrals collapsed because they were just too ambitious. Some remained incomplete for hundreds of years (famously, Cologne). Others were never completed at all. Many of them came close to bankrupting the cities which undertook their construction. Yet many also became structures which were perhaps beyond even the boldest imaginations of those who started laying their foundations.

This reminds us of something about the European project. The Europeans have already been at it for 60 years or so: it has evolved over the years; and plainly there is a long way to go. We will not see its completion or its final form in our lifetimes.

The metaphor also makes one more point: too many of those cathedrals are now virtually empty – except perhaps for crowds of Asian tourists. This reminds us again of the identity question facing Europeans. For one thing, geographical identity is in question in several countries these days. What does the United Kingdom consist of? And what does it mean to be British? Such questions have been pushed to the centre of politics in the 21st century in several other member states too (Spain and Belgium, for example). Germany may not have these issues: but identity is not just about place. It is about history too – with which of course Germany has a more complicated relationship. But with or without such geographical and historical complexities, it is very clear that Europe faces a significant challenge to its foundational assumption of ever closer union. The much discussed democratic deficit has assumed serious proportions in virtually all member states. The political and intellectual elites watch the growth of various forms of rightwing nationalism with dismay.

So will this work? Will Europe be able to become a flexible, cohesive and strong economic and cultural competitor and counterpart to those new Asian giants? The answer is not clear. Might the cathedral fall down? Might it bankrupt its builders?

The broad German answer is clearly that building this cathedral is worth the risk and the struggle. And the crises and challenges of recent years have not changed this German answer. The German answer to the identity question is that Europeans do have a common way, hard though it may be to define, and even if they only know it by contrast with other cultures; they have important values in common which make them different from others; and as such have much to offer the world. Germans would further argue that Europe has an urgent need – which it can meet much better together than separately – to ensure that it has an economy with enough scale and competitiveness to enable European mind and management to be successful in the global marketplace. So yes, it is worth the struggle.

Will the reluctant German leadership in this struggle last? There are those who argue that it will not: that German demographics will slowly weaken the economy as the burden of the elderly rises in a society which is not replacing itself; or that energy dependencies are a continuous threat to a country which has taken a political – and surely irreversible – decision to close down all its nuclear power generation; or that its economy is too dependent on cars and capital goods for long term sustainability, even if at present this is exactly what the world seems to want; or that Germany might grow weary of supporting the weaker members of the eurozone (and perhaps even demand its beloved Deutschmark back);[28] or more generally that German politics might lose the stability that has been its most conspicuous feature for the last 60 years and that the country might turn in on itself again. And so on.

Indeed, Germany faces some new risks. Its demographics are such that Germany could end up being the third or fourth largest country in Europe within a generation (with both Britain and France as well as – depending on the answer to another historic question confronting Europe – Turkey overtaking it). But this will not of itself undermine the economic strength which is the secret of Germany's position. It will make no difference to the Chinese perspective on Europe, which is less interested in the Union as a whole and more in what individual countries have to offer, and which clearly sees Germany as its key strategic partner for the foreseeable future. So there are indeed risks (not least what the fallout would be from any weakening or upheaval in the Chinese economy, now that it has become so important to Europe in general and to Germany in particular). But the central forecast must surely be for continued German pre-eminence in an increasingly integrated Europe.

Some have speculated that the result of all this will make the European Union look like the Holy Roman Empire redivivus. The complex interplay of powers at the Union level would be reminiscent of the patterns of interaction amongst the electors, the imperial cities and the church in pre-Reformation times (though who would the equivalent of the Emperor be?). And perhaps the increasingly integrated eurozone with Germany at its heart will come to be seen as the equivalent of the Habsburg dominance of the later centuries of the Empire.

The parallel has limited value, however. Apart from any other limitations in such a parallel between two polities which are best seen as sui generis, the suggestion clearly under-states the extent to which the Union will continue to impact the political life of its individual members. The story of the Empire was one of gradual fragmentation of central author-ity (although it is important not to exaggerate this trend or to overlook the continued functioning throughout the 18th century of the imperial legal system). But this is not likely to be the fate of the Union in general and certainly not of the eurozone in particular.

What the Union will indeed have in common with the Holy Roman Empire is that Union members will continue to have separate objectives and their own relationships and influence internationally. Thus in particular both Britain and France will continue to pursue their own foreign policies and reserve the right to project independent military power (even if with diminishing confidence and effectiveness). More generally, individual member states will continue actively to market themselves – at least as commercial counterparts for the fast growing emerging economies of the world – often drawing on older connexions as they do so (as in the case of Spain in Latin America). To borrow marketing terminology, there is no sign whatever of the European Union brand replacing or outshin-ing these individual country brands. Germany in particular will continue to build its very strong brand around the world.

All of this cannot but remind the historian of the inde-pendent behaviour of the 18th century members of the Holy Roman Empire – and especially of the Prussia of Frederick the Great. But even this analogy is of limited relevance, because of one fundamental difference from the Holy Roman Empire as it evolved in its last century. By then, the growing sense of a common German identity from Luther's time onwards was being translated increasingly into a demand for political identity. By contrast, there is no sign at all now of a common European identity emerging to the point where the Union as a whole could plausibly become the dominant European identity on the world stage. In the 21st century Europeans may have a sense of shared cultural history and values. But those values are a long way from translating into anything like a Fichtean 'national' identity at the European level. There is no sense in which existing European structures or the emerging framework for the eurozone are either enhancing or – alternatively – holding back some stronger European identity yearning to express itself.

This absence of a strong, primary European identity has been the source of much perplexity and worry amongst the intelligentsia of Europe. Habermas and many others have lamented the weakness of transnational discussion and debate in the public space in Europe. Irritatingly for many, national identities have proven remarkably robust; what is more, there is arguably more of a transatlantic public sphere than a European one (or, in plain English, there has been a ready appetite for all things American). Some are realistic enough to recognise the inevitability of this, as well as to question whether a strong and primary European identity is even the right objective in an increasingly globalised world.

The truth is that it is difficult to see how this objective could ever be realised, given that the one reasonably secure basis for a shared European identity in a secularised and increasingly multicultural age – the Enlightenment – is by definition non-proprietary. In the modern era a European identity clearly cannot be based on religion, notwithstanding its Christian history: all of its societies are becoming more and more secularised and most of them are also becoming pluralities of religious belief. If there is a parallel to the religious awareness of the modern Europe, it is not the uniformity of Christendom or the later *cujus regio ejus religio* of the post-Reformation Holy Roman Empire: it is rather the late Roman Empire, of which Edward Gibbon quipped that for the people all religions were equally true, for the philosophers all were equally false, and for the government all were equally useful.[29]

As for a language based identity, it is hard to see how this could come about at the European level either. If there is any candidate for a language as a basis for a European identity it is of course English as the lingua franca – more and more not just of the world of business and politics but also of learning and research. Certainly it is not German. But can identity be based on a lingua franca? Probably not: it is easy to see how a lingua franca can become the language of Zivilisation, but it is much harder to see it becoming the language of Kultur. In any case, English is now the lingua franca of the world, not just of Europe.

What Europe does have are core values which come from the Enlightenment, which in turn owes much to Renaissance Christian humanism – a point repeatedly emphasised by one of Europe's most distinguished thinkers, the Catholic theologian and cleric Joseph Ratzinger, who became Pope Benedict XVI, the first German pope for almost 1000 years. But Europe's commitment to rationalism, democracy and human rights is by definition something it would regard as universal: Europe would not even want these values to be a distinctive characteristic of a European, as opposed to any other, identity. Another thinker in the Catholic tradition, Hans Küng, has followed through some of the implications of this with his efforts to establish a global ethic on the basis of what is common about the moral and social insights of the religions of the world.

To put the point differently, it is probably inevitable that a European identity will be based on a constitutional patriotism of the kind Habermas and others have argued for – whilst other more complex identities based on history, culture and language will continue to define national, regional and local loyalties. For Germans this is a complexity with which they have been familiar for a long time.

This is not to say that for Germany and for Germans the question of identity has been or will be trouble free. The country has the second largest number of immigrants in the developed world, after the United States. Immigrants represent about the same proportion of the population as in France and Britain, but a lower proportion of immigrants in Germany has taken citizenship than in either of the other two. This results – at least in part – from a German citizenship law which makes this more difficult, in particular by not permitting German citizens normally to hold other citizenships (unlike both the British and the French). This restrictiveness, which impacts especially Germany's large and well established Turkish community, sits oddly with that German readiness to live with multiplex, layered identities. At its root, of course, is that deep-seated and long-standing sense that the German identity is embedded in the history, culture and language of a people with a continuous lineage – an identity which took this form at least partly in the absence for so long of any geographically defined unity. This remains a neuralgic issue: occasional neo-Nazi attacks on, and murders of, immigrants have produced justifiable outrage. The outrage is particularly sensitive, partly because such episodes stir the fear of demons from the Third Reich – even though it is plainly the case that other countries in Europe have suffered quite as much from this scourge – but partly also for deeper reasons. In other words, the plasticity of the German identity has its limits. It is better at accepting complex layers of geographical and cultural identity than it is at accepting newcomers to the German Kultur – something which the French and the British, for all their differences, both seem to find easier to do.

Meanwhile, the wider world is changing around Europe, with the rapid acceleration of internet connectivity and with the continued shift of the the world's economic centre of gravity from west to east and from north to south. Germany will increasingly engage with that wider world on the basis of that layered identity – as European, as German, and in all sorts of regional, local and other identities.

For Germany the trader, this means opportunity. In medieval times the German lands were criss-crossed by trade. Cities such as Leipzig, Nuremberg and Augsburg were great centres of trade, and grew rich on the proceeds. The Hanseatic League around the Baltic was led by the German cities of Hamburg and Lübeck. Later on, as the ocean trade routes opened up, the German lands lost out to countries with Atlantic coast lines. Yet the evidence of insatiable German curiosity about the wider world is there for all to see in the travels and work of such people as Winckelmann, Schliemann and Alexander von Humboldt. The Second Reich felt hemmed not only in Europe but also through the domination of the high seas by Britain. But all that has of course gone; in the 21st century the readiness of the Germans to go anywhere on business (or on holiday) no longer knows any restraints, perceived or actual. So their international exposure has soared. It is not for nothing that German trade fairs (like its exports) remain important out of all proportion to Germany's share of world output. This is another of those continuities of German experience – in this case going back, not just to before the Second Reich, but to medieval times.

This also means that Germany's identity not just in Europe but also in the wider world is as relevant as ever. For – important as commerce is, and as good at it as Germany is – there is another and deeper level at which we need to ask what the German culture will mean in this brave new world which is no longer unipolar or bipolar but multipolar, and in this new Europe with its layered and overlapping identities. Although German technical brilliance, with its deep cultural roots, will continue to be a dominant feature of the German identity for the foreseeable future, this identity remains that of a Kultur, not just of a Zivilisation. It has certainly changed radically since Stunde Null; Germany is no longer Germania. The last thing it wants to do is to sacralise its past. Furthermore, its identity is no longer primarily defined (possibly even for itself, and certainly for the rest of the world) by its language. But the continuities with the past remain. This is not just Verfassungspatriotismus.

In fact, there are three distinctive features of the German identity which will surely have enduring resonance and relevance to human experience universally. All three have grown out of the experience of the German Kultur as it has evolved through the glories and the tragedies of recent centuries.

Classical music is the first. More transportable than literature, more distinctive than its visual arts, Germany's musical legacy remains prominent throughout the world. Everywhere in the new powers of Asia, from concert tours by international orchestras to piped music in shopping malls, the evidence of the universal appeal of German music to the human spirit is clear. There is perhaps no longer the same sense that music is the most German of arts, or that the German canon is dominant, in the way 19th century German musicologists wanted to believe. And after Strauss, it can hardly be argued that German composition has dominated recent output of classical music – let alone the newer worlds of jazz and of popular music. But the world will never tire of the extraordinary German classical canon either: this is not a legacy that will ever be exhausted. From the perfection of Bach to the versatility of Mozart, to the passion of Beethoven and the lyricism of Schubert, to the autumnal beauty of Brahms and the grandeur of Wagner, and into the 20th century edginess of the early Strauss and of Schönberg – German music will go on filling concert halls, opera houses and the air waves for ever. It is also a vehicle for universalising German word and thought patterns: from Bach's settings of Lutheran Gospel texts through Beethoven's use of Schiller's 'Ode to Joy' to Schubert's settings of Goethe's poetry and to Wagner's glorious love music in *Tristan und Isolde*; music gives the language a universal resonance it will never lose.

The second is all that German philosophy. Human beings everywhere and always will wrestle with questions about meaning and values. A more and more interconnected world will have ever more sources to draw on as it does so. An Asia which has rushed towards modernisation and which has prized technical education above all things is increasingly recognising that it runs the risk of creating a hollow materialistic life with little sense of shared obligation. The more people wrestle with the deep questions this poses, the more they will explore the different human responses – those of their own cultural histories, of course, but also those of the Europeans who created the first modern societies. As they do that, they will find the German tradition to be distinct, profound, alive – and enduring in its relevance. The questions Kant sought to address will continue to be at the heart of philosophical debate; and the legacy of German thought from Hegel to Heidegger will continue to exercise minds from every culture. (And there will surely come a time when the world will be sufficiently distant in time from the traumatic experience of societies run on Marxist ideological bases, to be able to arrive at a balanced assessment of that other great German thinker whose impact on the 20th century was so profound.) Moreover, contemporary German thinkers continue to have a major influence, particularly on the debate about identity, as we have already noted: Habermas, but also – from their own different perspectives – theologians such as Pope Benedict and Hans Küng.

Then thirdly, and arising directly out of the experience of Stunde Null, there is the knowledge of evil and the promise of Vergangenheitsbewältigung. This is not – or should not be – just the story of a particular redemption after a unique moral catastrophe. The Third Reich was indeed horrific. But the need to deal with and overcome the past is a human universal, both at the level of whole peoples as well as at the level of individuals. No country has done this more honestly than Germany. It is a painful process, but there is no alternative way to atonement. And there are clear lessons for others. The list is long, but certainly includes Japan and Russia, to name but two examples where the absence of open and unreserved German-style Vergangenheitsbewältigung continues to poison relations with neighbouring countries, not to mention preventing the psychological development of their own societies. (And perhaps there are other countries which need to be more honest about their own pasts. It could certainly be argued, for example, that Britain has never properly come to terms with the attitudes and failures that produced its Irish debacle and which still undermine its national identity today.) The German record over the last 60 years has certainly not been complete or trouble free: no fully honest process of acceptance and atonement ever can be. It is nonetheless a precious gift to the world.

And finally, there is Faust …

11

Transfiguration and Apotheosis?

IF THERE IS ONE PIECE of German literature which, more
than any other, has become part of the patrimony of the human
race, it is surely Goethe's *Faust*. This very German story, rooted
as it is in German history and myth, has become a theme for
us all. We have seen the rampage through life of the Faust
who wanted experience and satisfaction and was prepared to
bargain with the devil to get it. We have seen the evil, and
we have seen the suffering it brings (of which Gretchen is the
symbol). We have seen the ambiguity of his moment of self-
discovery. But what about his mysterious transfiguration and
apotheosis in the closing scene of this extraordinary work, at
the end of his long spiritual journey?

To see this drama as a form of allegory of the German experience would be to distort and indeed trivialise its purpose,
which has a universal resonance for the human condition. The
last thing Goethe had in mind was Germania. And yet, highly
ambiguous though it is, it can nevertheless be seen – not as
any form of intended allegory – but as a sort of metaphor for
the German story, past, present and future. This is because, in
the final analysis, Faust is a universal figure and the German
story is of universal significance.

The climax – Faust's apotheosis – is one in which he is

rescued at the last minute from the demons, not because of any good he has done, but because Mephistopheles seems to have failed to deliver that one moment of perfect satisfaction which was the basis of the bargain. As the angels transport Faust to heaven, the old god who was there at the beginning is now absent; instead of condemnation and judgement Faust finds gentle forgiveness and renewal, when the spirit of Gretchen, whom he had crushed, proclaims his salvation:

> Vom edlen Geisterchor umgeben,
> Wird sich der Neue kaum gewahr,
> Er ahnet kaum das frische Leben,
> So gleicht er schon der heil'gen Schar.
> Sieh, wie er jedem Erdenbande,
> Der alten Hülle sich entrafft
> Und aus ätherischem Gewande
> Hervortritt erste Jugendkraft!
> Vergönne mir, ihn zu belehren!
> Noch blendet ihn der neue Tag.

(Surrounded by the noble choir of spirits, the new one hardly becomes aware of himself. He hardly senses the fresh life, as he already resembles the heavenly hosts. Look, how he escapes from his earthly bonds and the old veil, and how the first strength of youth steps out from his ethereal garments. Grant me that I may teach him: the new day still blinds him.)

Then there are those last mysterious lines which have spawned endless analysis and reflection amongst scholars:

Alles Vergängliche
Ist nur ein Gleichnis;
Das Unzulängliche,
Hier wird's Ereignis.
Das Unbeschreibliche,
Hier ist's getan;
Das Ewig-Weibliche
Zieht uns hinan.

(Everything transient is but a metaphor; the unattainable is realised here; the indescribable is accomplished here: the eternal feminine draws us on.)

For Goethe, the tempestuous male identity is torn by all its striving and aggression: Faust is the archetype of the relentlessly driven male, torn from his roots by his own insatiable and pitiless ambition. As he at one point cries out, in one of the most quoted lines in all German literature: 'Zwei Seelen wohnen, ach!, in meiner Brust' – 'Alas! two souls live in my breast'. Salvation from this fractured identity, from all this restless tension and temptation, could only come through the wholeness, the harmony, the acceptance and the mystery which for Goethe was represented by the feminine. Those final lines offer a vision of a sort of transfiguration in which all aggressiveness falls away, and Faust is introduced into a wider reality which offers peace to his spirit for the first time.

There is something in this which speaks not only to the story of Germany as it now is in the 21st century, but to all human society. To suggest that the new Germany has reached a perfect equilibrium is of course nonsense. But it is clear that the country has been on a journey which is in a sense a discovery of the truth behind Goethe's great parable of the human condition. Germany from the 19th century onwards succumbed to that tortured Faustian assertiveness: it was certainly a society with very male characteristics. The Germany of the Third Reich was its terrible outcome. But the new Germany is changed and, as if still blinded by the day, can often find it difficult to appreciate how radical that change is. If it has reached a degree of maturity, of wholeness, then this is in part because it has emerged from the terrible trauma imbued with more balance, with more of the characteristics which Goethe saw as essentially feminine.

The theme is plainly universal, which is why the story of the German journey is of such relevance to all human societies in this globalising world of ours. Of course the parable can only be imperfect – not least because Goethe's *Faust* ends with this mysterious consummation. Germany's story, on the other hand, is neither complete nor perfect – because nothing in reality ever is – but it is remarkable nonetheless, and it is of universal human significance. And it continues.

Notes

1. It is worth noting that 'nation' in this context does not refer to a political unity in the modern sense, but rather to a shared cultural and linguistic identity. No official constitution, no clearly defined borders and no standing army united the territory of the Holy Roman Empire of the German Nation.
2. See for example Johannes Fried, *Canossa. Entlarvung einer Legende. Eine Streitschrift* (Berlin: Akademie Verlag, 2012).
3. There is a certain irony in the fact that Frederick, just before becoming king, wrote his Enlightenment-inspired *Anti-Machiavel* (1740), condemning the ruthless use of power that Niccolò Machiavelli justified in his famous treatise *The Prince* (1513). Frederick went on to display a ruthlessness which Machiavelli would have admired.
4. The phrase is from Christopher Clark, *Iron Kingdom: The Rise and Downfall of Prussia, 1600–1947* (London: Allen Lane, 2006).
5. See, for example, Niall Ferguson, *The Pity of War: 1914–1918* (London: Penguin, 2012) pp 395–397.
6. See in particular the hugely influential study by David Blackbourn and Geoff Eley, *The Peculiarities of German History: Bourgeois Society and Politics in Nineteenth-Century Germany* (Oxford, New York: Oxford UP, 1984).

7. In conversation with Dr Anneliese Poppinga in 1962
8. It is worth noting that the adjective *'fremde'* – foreign – is picked out and emphasised in Schiller's own text.
9. A significant illustration of this is the fact that the Weimar Republic was proclaimed in Weimar's National Theatre in 1919, a symbolic venue which was intended to demonstrate the importance of *Kultur* to the new German constitutional identity.
10. The 1611 Authorised Version of the Bible is based extensively on William Tyndale's translation which is more or less contemporaneous with Luther's.
11. One of the key characters in Thomas Mann's *Zauberberg*, Settembrini, exclaims: 'Bier, Tabak und Musik … Da haben wir Ihr Vaterland!' – Beer, tobacco and music … there you have your fatherland!
12. Famous examples of 19th century thinkers and artists who discovered or rediscovered a lively Catholic faith include Friedrich Schlegel and his wife Dorothea (daughter of Moses Mendelssohn), Clemens Brentano, Joseph von Eichendorff and Franz Liszt.
13. According to Martin Schmidt this is the most important principle of Pietism (see his article on Pietism in the encyclopedia *Religion in Geschichte und Gegenwart.*)
14. The Belt refers to a strait between the Danish island of Funen and the Jutland Peninsular. It was understood as marking roughly the northernmost limit of the German lands.
15. Kant used this phrase to refer to the real essence of the external world which is not directly accessible to the senses and thus cannot be directly known.

16. The sword alone is seven metres high; on the blade are the words 'Deutsche Einigkeit meine Stärke – meine Stärke Deutschlands Macht' (German unity is my strength – my strength is Germany's power).
17. The words of a gentle 94 year old Briton with a long and distinguished career as a professional musician behind him.
18. A story told to the author during a visit to the Lutheran church in Kaliningrad in 2013.
19. See, for example, Max Hastings, *All Hell Let Loose: The World at War 1939–1945* (London: HarperPress, 2011) pp 89–90 on the relative performance of British and German fighter aircraft production.
20. William Empson's famous phrase from his 1940 poem 'Missing Dates'.
21. The story of Anna Rosmus is told in Ian Buruma, Wages of Guilt (London: Cape, 1994). A fictionalised version of her experience was made into a highly acclaimed film in 1990 under the title *Das Schreckliche Mädchen* – the nasty girl.
22. Cf. the title of Christopher Clark's influential book on the actions of the various European powers in the run-up to the First World War: *The Sleepwalkers: How Europe Went to War in 1914* (London: Penguin, 2013).
23. A few weeks after the tragedy at Fukushima, the author listened to a sermon in Berlin devoted largely to the dangers of nuclear power – on Easter Sunday morning.
24. Habermas popularised – though he did not originate – this concept, which envisages political identity being based on shared values (the commitment to liberal democracy), rather than on shared history or ethnicity.

25. In a conversation with the author.
26. 'No man is an island entire of itself; every man is a piece of the continent, a part of the main ...' From John Donne's Meditation XVII in: *Devotions on Emergent Occasions* (1624).
27. See the Anholt Nations Brand index.
28. A central demand of the party Alternative für Deutschland, which came close – out of nowhere – to achieving the 5% vote required for Bundestag representation in the 2013 election.
29. Edward Gibbon, *The History of the Decline and Fall of the Roman Empire*, Volume I, chapter II.

Selected Bibliography

What follows is not a comprehensive list of books on the vast subject of the German phenomenon – how could it be? But it is a list of books I have enjoyed reading, as an amateur without any claim to be an academic specialist, on my journey of exploration of a country and a culture that has given so much in so many ways to the human spirit.

Applegate, Celia and Potter Pamela (eds), *Music and German National Identity* (Chicago: Univ. of Chicago Press, 2002).

Amann, Wilhelm, *Heinrich von Kleist* (Berlin: Suhrkamp, 2011).

Baring, Arnulf, *Es lebe die Republik, es lebe Deutschland!* (Stuttgart: Dt. Verlags-Anstalt, 1999).

Barraclough, Geoffrey, *The Origins of Modern Germany* (Oxford: Blackwell, 1946).

Barth, Karl, *Zur Genesung des deutschen Wesens: ein Freundeswort von draußen* (Stuttgart: Mittelbach, 1945).

Beevor, Anthony, *Berlin: The Downfall 1945* (London: Viking, 2002).

Beiser, Frederick, *German Idealism: The Struggle Against Subjectivism 1781–1801* (Cambridge Mass.: Harvard UP, 2002).

Beiser, Frederick, *Hegel* (London/New York: Routledge, 2005).

Bessel, Richard, *Germany 1945: From War to Peace* (New York: Simon & Schuster, 2009).

Bielenberg, Christabel, *The Past is Myself* (London: Chatto & Windus, 1968).

David Blackbourn and Geoff Eley, *The Peculiarities of German History: Bourgeois Society and Politics in Nineteenth-Century Germany* (Oxford, New York: Oxford UP, 1984).

Blanning, Tim, *The Pursuit of Glory: Europe 1648–1815* (London: Allen Lane, 2007).

Blanning, Tim, *The Romantic Revolution* (London: Phoenix, 2012).

Bismarck, Ruth-Alice von and Kabitz, Ulrich (ed), *Brautbriefe Zelle 92, 1943–1945* (München: Beck, 1992).

Boer, Wolfgang de, *Hölderlins Deutung des Daseins* (Frankfurt: Athenäum, 1961).

Bonhoeffer, Dietrich, *Nachfolge* (Gütersloh: Gütersloher Verlagshaus, 2002). (Originally published in 1937.)

Brady, Thomas, *German Histories in the Age of Reformations, 1400–1650* (Cambridge: Cambridge UP, 2009).

Brecht, Martin, *Martin Luther* (Stuttgart: Calwer Verlag, 1987).

Browning, Christopher, *Ordinary Men: Reserve Police Battalion 101 and the Final Solution in Poland* (New York: Harper Collins, 1992).

Bruhns, Wibke, *Meines Vaters Land: Geschichte einer deutschen Familie* (München: Econ, 2004).

Buruma, Ian, *Wages of Guilt* (London: Cape, 1994).

Clark, Christopher, *Kaiser Wilhelm II: A Life in Power* (Harlow: Longman, 2000).

Clark, Christopher, *Iron Kingdom: The Rise and Downfall of Prussia, 1600–1947* (London: Allen Lane, 2006).

Clark, Christopher, *The Sleepwalkers: How Europe Went to War in 1914* (London: Penguin, 2013).

Crankshaw, Edward, *Bismarck* (London: Macmillan, 1981).

Decker, Kerstin, *Heinrich Heine: Narr des Glücks* (Berlin: Propyläen, 2005).

Ferguson, Niall, *The Pity of War: 1914–1918* (London: Penguin, 2012).

Fergusson, Adam, *When Money Dies: The Nightmare of the Weimar Inflation* (London: Kimber, 1975).

Fischer, Fritz, *Griff nach der Weltmacht: die Kriegszielpolitik des Kaiserlichen Deutschland, 1914–1918* (Düsseldorf: Droste, 1961).

Fischer, Fritz, *Krieg der Illusionen: die deutsche Politik von 1911 bis 1914* (Düsseldorf: Droste, 1969).

Fraser, David, *Frederick the Great* (London: Allen Lane, 2000).

Frevert, Ute, *Gefühlspolitik: Friedrich II. als Herr über die Herzen?* (Göttingen: Wallstein, 2012).

Fried, Johannes, *Canossa. Entlarvung einer Legende. Eine Streitschrift* (Berlin: Akademie Verlag, 2012).

Friedrich, Jörg, *Der Brand: Deutschland im Bombenkrieg 1940–1945* (München: Propyläen, 2003).

Fulbrook, Mary, *Anatomy of a Dictatorship: Inside the GDR 1949–1989* (Oxford: Oxford UP, 1995).

Fulbrook, Mary, *German National Identity after the Holocaust* (Cambridge: Polity Press, 1999).

Goodrick-Clarke, Nicholas, *The Occult Roots of Nazism* (London: Tauris Parke, 2004).

Garton Ash, Timothy, *We The People: the Revolution of '89* (Cambridge: Granta, 1990).

Goldhagen, Daniel, *Hitler's Willing Executioners: Ordinary Germans and the* Holocaust (London: Little Brown, 1996).

Gutman, Robert William, *Richard Wagner: The Man, his Mind and his Music* (London: Secker & Warburg, 1968).

Guyer, Paul (ed), *Kant and Modern Philosophy* (Cambridge: Cambridge UP, 2006).

Hädecke, Wolfgang, *Theodor Fontane* (München: Hanser, 1998).

Habermas, Jürgen, *Ach, Europa* (Frankfurt: Suhkamp, 2008).

Haffner, Sebastian, *Anmerkungen zu Hitler* (München: Kindler, 1978).

Hastings, Max, *Armageddon: The Battle for Germany 1944–1945* (London: Macmillan, 2004).

Hastings, Max, *All Hell Let Loose: The World at War 1939–1945* (London: HarperPress, 2011)

Kershaw, Ian, *Hitler* (London: Penguin, 2009).

Kershaw, Ian, *The End: Hitler's Germany 1944–1945* (London: Penguin, 2011).

Koch, H.W., *A History of Prussia* (London: Longman, 1978).

Köhler, Joachim, *Wagners Hitler: Der Prophet und sein Vollstrecker* (München: Blessing, 1997).

Kundnani, Hans, *Utopia or Auschwitz: Germany's 1968 Generation and the Holocaust* (New York: Columbia UP, 2009).

Levi, Erik, *Mozart and the Nazis: How the Third Reich Abused a Cultural Icon* (New Haven: Yale UP, 2010).

Liulevicius, Vejas G., *The German Myth of the East* (Oxford: Oxford UP, 2009).

Lukacs, George, *Goethe and his Age* (London: Merlin, 1968).

MacCullough, Diarmaid, *Reformation: Europe's House Divided 1490–1700* (London: Penguin, 2003).

MacMillan, Margaret, *Peacemakers: the Paris Peace Conference of 1919 and its Attempt to End War* (London: John Murray, 2001).

MacMillan, Margaret, *The War that Ended Peace* (London: Profile, 2013).

MacDonald Ross, George and McWalter, Tony (eds) *Kant and his Influence* (London: Continuum, 2005).

MacDonogh, Giles, *After the Reich: From the Liberation of Vienna to the Berlin Airlift* (London: John Murray, 2007).

Mann, Golo, *Deutsche Geschichte des 19. und 20. Jahrhunderts* (Frankfurt: Fischer, 1958).

Marius, Richard, *Martin Luther: The Christian Between God and Death* (Cambridge, Mass: Belknap, 1999).

Markert, Dorothee, *Lebenslänglich besser: Unser verdrängtes pietistisches Erbe* (Norderstedt: Books on Demand, 2010).

Metaxas, Eric, *Bonhoeffer: Pastor, Martyr, Prophet, Spy* (Nashville: Thomas Nelson, 2010).

Mitford, Nancy, *Frederick the Great* (London: Hamilton, 1970).

Moltmann, Jürgen, *Der Gekreuzigte Gott: das Kreuz Christi als Grund und Kritik der christlichen Theologie* (Gütersloh: Gütersloher Verlagshaus, 2002).

Mommsen, Hans, *Alternative zu Hitler: Studien zur Geschichte des Deutschen Widerstandes* (München: Beck, 2000).

Münkler, Herfried, *Die Deutschen und ihre Mythen* (Berlin: Rowohlt, 2009).

Niven, Bill (ed), *Germans as Victims* (Basingstoke: Palgrave Macmillan, 2006).

Pakula, Hannah, *An Uncommon Woman: the Empress Frederick* (London: Weidenfeld & Nicolson, 1996).

Paret, Peter, *Clausewitz and the State: The Man, his Theories and his Times* (Oxford: Clarendon Press, 1976).

Pettegree, Andrew (ed), *The Reformation World* (London: Routledge, 2000).

Pinkard, Terry, *Hegel's Dialectic: The Explanation of Possibility* (Philadelphia: Temple University Press, 1988).

Radkau, Joachim, *Max Weber: Die Leidenschaft des Denkens.* (München: Hanser, 2013).

Reed, TJ, *Mehr Licht in Deutschland: Eine kleine Geschichte der Aufklärung* (München: Beck, 2009).

Reed, TJ, *Thomas Mann: The Uses of Tradition* (Oxford: Oxford UP, 1974).

Richardson, John, *Heidegger* (New York: Routledge, 2012).

Röhl, John, *Wilhelm II: the Kaiser's Personal Monarchy, 1888–1900* (Cambridge: Cambridge UP, 2004)

Safranski, Rüdiger, *Romantik: Eine deutsche Affäre* (Frankfurt: Fischer, 2009).

Schieder, Theodor, *Friedrich der Große: ein Königtum der Widersprüche* (München: Propyläen, 2002).

Schlaffer, Heinz, *Die kurze Geschichte der deutschen Literatur* (München/Wien: Hanser, 2003).

Schlink, Bernhard, *Vergangenheitsschuld* (Zürich: Diogenes, 2007).

Sebald, WG, *Luftkrieg und Literatur* (München/Wien: Hanser, 1999).

Sereny, Gitta, *Into That Darkness: From Mercy Killing to Mass Murder* (London: Deutsch, 1974).

Sereny, Gitta, *The German Trauma: Experiences and Reflections, 1938–2001* (London: Allen Lane, 2000).

Shirer, WL, The Rise and Fall of the Third Reich (New York: Simon & Schuster, 1960).

Simms, Brendan, Europe: The Struggle for Supremacy, 1453 to the Present (London: Allen Lane, 2013).

Spender, Stephen, European Witness (London: Hamish Hamilton, 1946).

Stahlberg, Alexander, Die Verdammte Pflicht: Erinnerungen 1932 bis 1945 (Berlin: Ullstein, 1987).

Steinberg, Jonathan, Bismarck: A Life (Oxford: Oxford UP, 2011).

Stern, Fritz, The Politics of Cultural Despair: a Study in the Rise of the Germanic Ideology (Berkeley: University of California Press, 1961).

Tanner, Michael, Wagner (London: HarperCollins, 1996).

Taylor, AJP, The Course of German History (London: Hamish Hamilton, 1945).

Taylor, AJP, The Struggle for Mastery in Europe 1848–1918 (Oxford: Clarendon Press, 1954).

Toews, John E., Hegelianism: the Path Towards Dialectical Humanism (Cambridge: Cambridge UP, 1980).

Urban, William, The Teutonic Knights: A Military History (London: Greenhill, 2003).

Vassiltchikov, Marie, The Berlin Diaries 1940–1945 (London: Chatto & Windus, 1985).

Vierhaus, Rudolf, Deutschland im Zeitalter des Absolutismus (1648–1763) (Göttingen: Vandenhoeck & Ruprecht, 1985).

Wallmann, Johannes, Der Pietismus (Göttingen: Vandenhoeck & Ruprecht, 2005).

Watanabe-O'Kelly, Helen, Beauty or Beast? The Woman Warrior in the German Imagination from the Renaissance to the Present (Oxford: Oxford UP, 2010).

Watson, Alan, *The Germans: Who Are They Now?* (London: Mandarin, 1994).

Watson, Peter, *The German Genius: Europe's Third Renaissance, the Second Scientific Revolution and the Twentieth Century* (New York: Harper, 2010).

Wedgwood, CV, *The Thirty Years War* (London: Jonathan Cape, 1938).

Weitz, Eric D, *Weimar Germany: Promise and Tragedy* (Princeton: Princeton UP, 2007).

Wilson, Peter, *Europe's Tragedy: A History of the Thirty Years War* (London: Allen Lane, 2009).

Whaley, Joachim, *Germany and the Holy Roman Empire* (Oxford: Oxford UP, 2012).

Winok, Michel, *Madame de Stael* (Paris: Fayard, 2010).

Young, Julian, *Schopenhauer* (New York: Routledge, 2005).

Young, Julian, *Friedrich Nietzsche: A Philosophical Biography* (Cambridge: Cambridge UP, 2010).

Index